Biblical Literalism:
A Gentile Heresy

ALSO BY JOHN SHELBY SPONG

Honest Prayer

Dialogue in Search of Jewish-Christian Understanding
(with Rabbi Jack Daniel Spiro)

Christpower (compiled and edited by Lucy Newton Boswell)

Life Approaches Death: A Dialogue in Medical Ethics
(with Dr. Daniel Gregory)

The Living Commandments

The Easter Moment

Into the Whirlwind: The Future of the Church

Beyond Moralism (with the Venerable Denise Haines)

*Survival and Consciousness: An Interdisciplinary Inquiry into
the Possibility of Life Beyond Biological Death* (editor)

Living in Sin? A Bishop Rethinks Human Sexuality

*Rescuing the Bible from Fundamentalism:
A Bishop Rethinks the Meaning of Scripture*

*Born of a Woman: A Bishop Rethinks the Virgin Birth
and the Role of Women in a Male-Dominated Church*

This Hebrew Lord: A Bishop's Search for the Authentic Jesus

Resurrection: Myth or Reality? A Bishop Rethinks the Meaning of Easter

Liberating the Gospels: Reading the Bible with Jewish Eyes

Why Christianity Must Change or Die: A Bishop Speaks to Believers in Exile

The Bishop's Voice: Selected Essays (1979–1999)
(compiled and edited by Christine Mary Spong)

Here I Stand: My Struggle for a Christianity of Integrity, Love and Equality

*A New Christianity for a New World: Why Traditional Faith
Is Dying and How a New Faith Is Being Born*

*The Sins of Scripture: Exposing the Bible's Texts
of Hate to Reveal the God of Love*

Jesus for the Non-Religious: Recovering the Divine at the Heart of the Human

*Eternal Life: A New Vision—Beyond Religion,
Beyond Theism, Beyond Heaven and Hell*

Re-Claiming the Bible for a Non-Religious World

The Fourth Gospel: Tales of a Jewish Mystic

Biblical Literalism: A Gentile Heresy

A JOURNEY INTO A NEW CHRISTIANITY
THROUGH THE DOORWAY OF MATTHEW'S GOSPEL

John Shelby Spong

HarperOne
An Imprint of HarperCollinsPublishers

HarperCollins books may be purchased for educational, business,
or sales promotional use. For information please e-mail the Special Markets
Department at SPsales@harpercollins.com.

HarperCollins website: http://www.harpercollins.com

FIRST HARPERCOLLINS PAPERBACK EDITION PUBLISHED IN 2017

Designed by Terry McGrath

Library of Congress Cataloging-in-Publication Data is available upon request.

ISBN 978-0-06-236231-5

17 18 19 20 21 LSC(H) 10 9 8 7 6 5 4 3 2 1

FOR
Christine,
My Wife,
Whose love
Expands my life endlessly
and almost miraculously;

AND FOR
Our Five Children,
Ellen
Katharine
Jaquelin
Brian
Rachel

AND

IN MEMORIAM
John Elbridge Hines (1910–1997)
John Arthur Thomas Robinson (1919–1983)
Michael Douglas Goulder (1927–2010)
My Three Greatest and Most Appreciated Mentors

Contents

Contents

PART IX: PASSOVER AND PASSION:
THE CLIMAX

PART X: MATTHEW'S EASTER STORY:
A NEW PERSPECTIVE

Preface

I DID NOT THINK I WOULD EVER WRITE another book. The time, the study, the sheer discipline and the rigor of writing just did not seem to fit into my life at this stage. When this book comes out in 2016, I will be eighty-five years old. Did I still have either the desire or the will to complete such an arduous task? Does the Christian world want or need another "Spong book"? After all, my autobiography came out in the year 2000 under the title *Here I Stand: My Struggle for a Christianity of Integrity, Love and Equality*.* Normally, one is supposed to die in the last chapter of one's autobiography or, at the very least, to move along with sufficient haste that an editor's note must be added to the text explaining that the author had passed from the stage of history in that critical interval between the time the book was completed and the time it was published. Somehow, I failed to cooperate with that tradition!

Indeed I went on to experience the years of my retirement as the most creative and growing years of my life. Among other things, I was named the William Belden Noble Lecturer at Harvard Univer-

---

*See bibliography for details.

sity. While delivering these lectures at Harvard (published under the title *A New Christianity for a New World**), I also taught two classes at the Harvard Divinity School, where I had the pleasure of meeting the most engaging theological students I have ever encountered. I formed stimulating friendships with a number of the theological faculty, including Peter Gomes, Harvey Cox, Diana Eck and Dorothy Austin. I also got to know and to interact with members of the university faculty and with those at the Kennedy School of Government, where the former senator from Wyoming, Alan Simpson, was teaching.

Following that, I taught for a semester at the University of the Pacific in Stockton, California, and formed a lasting friendship with Professor Lawrence Meredith and his wife, Pat. Larry had earlier headed up the department of religion at this university. I also served on the faculty of the Graduate Theological Union in Berkeley, California, and the Pacific School of Religion, also in Berkeley, on seven different occasions as part of their summer school. These experiences gave me new insights into West Coast Christianity and introduced me to some rather remarkable and very diverse students and faculty. Over a period of two years I taught three different courses in the Theological School of Drew University, a Methodist institution possessing the most international student body that I have ever engaged. In that capacity I was privileged to get to know three different and very gifted deans. The first was Maxine Beach, one of the earliest women clergy to head a denominational seminary; the second was Jeffrey Kuan, an Old Testament Scholar from Malaysia and the first Asian to head a Methodist seminary in America; the third was a young His-

---

*See bibliography for details.

panic scholar named Javier Viera, whose vision for contemporary theological education is exciting and demanding. The Theological School at Drew University became a major asset to my life. Not only did it regularly affirm my gifts, but it also made available to me its magnificent theological library. The dean of the libraries at Drew was Dr. Andrew Scrimgeour, who time after time aided my research and, in the process, became a close personal friend.

Perhaps the highest honor of my life also came during those retirement years, when my portrait was commissioned to be painted by Morehouse College in Atlanta, to hang in its "Hall of Honor" at the Martin Luther King Jr. International Chapel, among those who had contributed deeply to the Civil Rights struggle in the United States during the years of the twentieth century. The dean of the chapel, Dr. Lawrence Carter, said in the unveiling ceremony: "You have done for gay and lesbian people what Martin Luther King Jr. did for people of color." I hang today just beneath Justice Thurgood Marshall.

During the years of my retirement I also wrote and Harper-Collins published five new books, each of which expanded my life and my intellectual scope enormously. I lectured extensively on these books all over the world, including appearances at some five hundred universities, colleges and theological seminaries in the United States, the United Kingdom, Australia, New Zealand, South Africa, Finland, Sweden, Germany, Denmark, Spain and Thailand.

When my books began to be translated into German, French, Italian, Spanish, Korean, Arabic and the languages of Scandinavia, my work and ideas reached an expanded world audience. I was able to develop European lecture tours and to have articles published in prominent journals in Latin America.

In my retirement I have also developed a career as a weekly

columnist on the Internet, working ultimately for a company that my wife Christine and I earlier helped to found entitled Progressive Christianity Inc. I have now written that column for sixteen years, and through its question-and-answer feature, I have been able to develop a dialogue with people around the world.

One other great privilege of my retirement years was that I was made a "fellow" of the Jesus Seminar, that remarkable biblical and early Christianity think tank founded by Dr. Robert Funk, a brilliant scholar, who once served as the executive secretary of the Society of Biblical Literature. In this seminar some 250 scripture scholars, of all religious traditions, meet regularly to explore contemporary biblical issues and to do so in a very public way. It was the intention of the Jesus Seminar not to allow its findings to remain hidden inside the ivy-covered walls of academia, but through the use of public media to reach the working clergy and, perhaps more importantly, the thinking laypeople who occupy the pews of our churches on Sunday mornings.

Above all I continued in retirement my lifelong habit of serious study in the early-morning hours of each day. My appetite for exploring the Bible outside the boxes of traditional religion was whetted anew by the five years from 2006–2010, a period that I devoted to the study of the Fourth Gospel, which resulted in the publication of a book entitled *The Fourth Gospel: Tales of a Jewish Mystic*.* It was, I thought, the most creative piece of writing in my career. The responses I received from audiences around the nation convinced me that a case can be made for the continued power of the Bible among educated people, if biblical scholars are

---

*See bibliography for details.

courageous enough to break out of the straitjackets of their threadbare and time-warped approaches to traditional religion.

In 2014, at the Chautauqua Institution in western New York, more than ten thousand people attended my five days of lectures on John's Gospel, and about twenty-five percent of that audience was Jewish! When this book on the Fourth Gospel was complete, I felt, once again, that my writing career was over. Just to continue the habit of a lifetime, however, I began to engage the gospel of Matthew, reading continuously and exclusively on this subject for more than four years. This study was so enriching and so "eye-popping" that it led eventually to the publication of this present volume. I have now begun a time of intense study of the gospel of Luke, but I am doing it for the joy of the study alone. I do not believe that I have sufficient longevity left in what William Shakespeare called "this mortal coil" to produce yet another book at age ninety! No one other than my mother would probably want to read it anyway! So this book on Matthew will (probably) be my final book.

In addition to my wonderful wife, whom I love beyond measure, and who has been my primary editor on this volume, and to our five now adult children, I have dedicated this book "in memoriam" to the three people whom I acknowledge as "the three greatest mentors" of my life. I want to say just a word about each of them in this preface. Time moves so rapidly that brilliant, magnificent and heroic people are quickly forgotten. This is the inevitable fate of all of us, but let me roll back the curtain of time for just a moment and pay a final tribute to these three heroes of mine.

The first is John Elbridge Hines, a native of Seneca, South Carolina. His distinguished career as an Episcopal priest carried him from St. Louis County in Missouri to Hannibal, Missouri,

to Augusta, Georgia, to Houston, Texas, where in 1945 at age
thirty-five he was elected bishop in the Diocese of Texas. He served
that diocese until 1963, when the entire Episcopal Church elected
him to be its presiding bishop. He was in that post from 1964 to
1973. John Hines thus served and steered his church during those
tension-filled years in America, marked by racial desegregation,
urban riots and the Vietnam War protests. In the process he taught
me to value honesty, integrity and courage as the primary qualities
of leadership. He did not know how to compromise when truth
was at stake. He called his church and, through it, all of American Christianity into a new level of engagement with the world
that was startling, controversial, demanding and life-giving. I have
been in John Hines' presence when threats on his life were so regular from fellow members of his own Episcopal Church that he was
forced to wear a bulletproof vest, even on one occasion while presiding over a national General Convention of that church. When
he retired in 1973 under great pressure from the reactionary elements in his church, I had just been elected to the Executive Council, the national governing board of the Episcopal Church, where
I could begin to press the same issues that he represented. With
his consent and cooperation I was invited to study his life with an
eye toward being his biographer. The book was published in 1995
under the title *Granite on Fire*, but I was not the author. I had been
elected bishop in 1976 and the time to write that book was simply
not available to me. I turned over my massive notes and reams
of taped interviews to Kenneth Kesselus, a priest in Texas, who
ably wrote the book using much of my research. He did a splen-
did job. I talked to John Hines by telephone once a week for most
of the years of his retirement. In many ways he was like a father

to me. He addressed my Diocesan Convention in Newark every year of my episcopacy until aging made travel difficult. He died in 1997, while the General Convention of our church was actually in session in Philadelphia. In the last speech that I would make in that national assembly, I was asked to pay tribute to him. I was so touched by having been given that honor that I decided not to speak again in that body. John Hines showed me that the church, as an institution, can affect our society in dramatic ways if its leadership is informed, filled with integrity, and willing to pay the price that effective leadership always requires, namely the willingness to absorb the abuse of those people who are terrified by change. I loved this man dearly and to this day his portrait sits on my desk so that looking at him I can always recall his example.

The second of my three great mentors was also a bishop, but this time in the Church of England. His name was John A. T. Robinson, the bishop of Woolwich, an area south of London inside the diocese of Southwark. John Robinson was a New Testament scholar and lecturer at Cambridge University when he was appointed bishop of Woolwich by the diocesan bishop, Mervyn Stockwood, one of the Church of England's more notable "characters." John Robinson broke upon the national scene in England when he defended the right of D. H. Lawrence to publish the unexpurgated version of his book *Lady Chatterley's Lover* in the face of efforts brought in the name of public morality to suppress it. This novel was about the adulterous relationship of a gamekeeper with a titled English lady for whom the gamekeeper worked. John Robinson served notice in this episode that he was not going to be one of those typical Anglican bishops who could be colored "gray," as so many of that church's bishops tended to be.

A few years later John, having been confined to his bed by his
doctor for several months to treat a deteriorating spinal condition, decided to use his time to write a book. It came out in 1963
under the title *Honest to God*.* This book had the quality of a
hot journalistic piece of writing. It was not a long tome, only 130
pages in length, and originally published in paperback, not hard-
cover, but this book touched a nerve and opened the floodgate on
religious debate. It made available to the lay public the theological thinking that was commonplace in Christian academic centers. Because of that book people in the pews, London cabbies
and those members of English society who had their "pint" in
the pubs of England at the end of every day suddenly began to
discuss and to debate theology.

What John Robinson did in that book was simple. He took
the work of three of the twentieth century's most seminal theological thinkers—Rudolf Bultmann, Paul Tillich and Dietrich
Bonhoeffer—and he made their ideas something the average
person could understand and appreciate. Bultmann had talked
about "de-mythologizing" the New Testament; Tillich had rede-
fined God not as "a being," but as "Being Itself"; and Bonhoeffer had spoken of developing a Christianity without religion, or
"religionless Christianity." The leaders of institutional Christianity had steadfastly refused to introduce laypeople to any of these
concepts, feeling that the average person's "Sunday School faith"
could not stand the shock. Ironically, it turned out to be the
clergy and the bishops who could not stand the shock. Laypeople
devoured this book, breaking on the church scene, as it did, with
volcanic power. It was translated into almost every language of

---

*See bibliography for details.

the world and it sold more copies than any religious book since *Pilgrim's Progress.*

My first book, *Honest Prayer,** published in 1972, was inspired by John Robinson's *Honest to God.* I met John for the first time in 1973. It was a brief meeting in a public gathering. I had the chance to give him a copy of my book and to thank him for what he had meant to me. I thought that would be the end of my relationship with him.

Five years later, however, I had been elected a bishop and found myself in attendance with him at the Lambeth Conference of the world's Anglican bishops that convened in 1978. There we not only met again, but we bonded in a friendship. Neither of us enjoyed the endless discussions among the bishops at this conference, which often sounded like last Sunday's sermon being preached under the guise of debate, and so John and I would vacate the assembly and walk together in the woods of the county of Kent in England until we found a country pub. On these occasions we would discuss the New Testament. They were rich conversations. After that, we corresponded regularly. The Church of England did to John Robinson what religious institutions normally do to their most creative bishops. He was marginalized as "too controversial" ever to be given his own diocese. Rather than remain for his whole career in the secondary role of an assisting bishop, he resigned his position as the bishop of Woolwich and returned to teaching the New Testament at Cambridge University. Even there, however, he was marginalized, for the university declined to restore to him the title of "lecturer," which he had held before becoming a bishop. He rather was forced to serve in positions of secondary importance, while

---

*See bibliography for details.

he continued to write. He died prematurely of cancer in Yorkshire in 1983, just a few months before he was scheduled to visit me in New Jersey, where he had agreed to lead my clergy conference. My wife and I have on two occasions made a pilgrimage to his grave in Arncliffe, Yorkshire, and we regularly visited his wife, Ruth, when we were in the United Kingdom, until her death.

John Robinson broke open the theological ground onto which I was to walk in subsequent years. In many ways I felt it was my vocation to pick up the gauntlet that he had laid down. I, too, was a bishop challenging the church theologically. Our paths had curious connections. When I wrote a book on sexual issues, published in 1988 under the title *Living in Sin? A Bishop Rethinks Human Sexuality,** I became as controversial in that dispute as he had become in his testimony regarding the publication of *Lady Chatterley's Lover.* When I wrote *A New Christianity for a New World* in 2001, I felt I was moving the work that he had started to a new place, and I said so in the preface. In my role as a theological gadfly in the House of Bishops, I had become his heir. In the worldwide Anglican Communion, I, like him, forced church leaders all over the world to react to new possibilities.

In 2011 an annual lectureship was established in the United Kingdom at a conference center in Hawarden, Wales, previously called St. Deiniol's, but now called Gladstone's Library. It was built originally to house the books and papers of William Gladstone, prime minister of Great Britain on a number of occasions during the nineteenth century, rotating regularly in the office of prime minister, it seemed at every election, with Benjamin Disraeli. That lectureship is called "The John A. T. Robinson–John Shelby Spong

---

*See bibliography for details.

Lectureship on Contemporary Theology." I was and am delighted to be linked in this way with my mentor.

The last of my trio of honored mentors was a professor of New Testament at the University of Birmingham, also in the U.K. His name was Michael Douglas Goulder. I will speak of him in more detail in the course of this book, so I will be very brief here. It was Michael Goulder who opened the door for me to linking the order of the gospel of Matthew to the liturgical calendar of the synagogue. That step, more than anything else, enabled me to escape the effects of biblical literalism without losing my great love for the Bible. I am not a disillusioned ex-fundamentalist. I am a transformed Christian. Michael was never as close a friend as the other two, but he probably influenced my life the most. He died in 2010. He remains one of the three great mentors of my life. In this preface I have the privilege of saluting all three just this one more time.

There are a few other people I need to acknowledge. Not to do so would violate both my love for them and my appreciation of them. At the top of the list is Christine, my wife, about whom I never seem able to say enough. She organizes and sustains my career, making me twice as effective as I could ever be without her, and the love that we share is transformative. She is also the best editor with whom I have ever worked. Next to her come my three daughters: Ellen, Katharine and Jaquelin. All three of them are rather incredible women whose careers in banking, law and science still amaze me. I treasure every opportunity I have to spend time with them. I also have great affection for their life partners: Gus Epps, Jack Catlett and Virgil Speriosu.

To this threesome I acquired through my marriage to Christine a wonderful stepson, Brian, and stepdaughter, Rachel. Brian is a tower of strength forging a life in northern Vermont as an executive for a telephone company and developing the lifestyle of a Vermont farmer. Rachel is an M.D. practicing in Delaware, after having had a number of other careers. Those included nine years as an officer in the United States Marine Corps piloting the Cobra helicopter, with three tours of duty in the second Iraq war. Both of these unique people are helped and supported by their spouses, Julieann Barney and Scott Carter.

Beyond this there are six grandchildren: Shelby, Jay, John, Lydia, Katherine and Colin, all of whom enrich our lives greatly. Finally, there are the menageries of creatures—dogs Jersey Rose, Brown Dog, Gretchen, Clyde, General, Lucca, and Emma, followed by cats, horses, chickens, turkeys, lambs (named Cain and Mabel), pigs and bees. There is additionally a single cow also named Mabel and her new calf, Ellie Mae. All of these creatures are now, by adoption and grace, part of our family.

The person who typed this manuscript, turning it from handwritten legal pads into a Word file, was Rhian Jeong, a graduate of the Church Divinity School of the Pacific in Berkeley, California, who is now the public relations and communications officer for the dean of Drew University's Theological School. I appreciate her work.

Finally, Christine and I are sustained by two congregations in which our lives are regularly nurtured. So to St. Paul's Church in Richmond, Virginia, and its rector Wallace Adams-Riley, and to St. Peter's Church in Morristown, New Jersey, and its rector Janet Broderick, and our many friends in both churches we express our deep gratitude.

JSS, Morris Plains, New Jersey
March 2016

PART I

How the Gospels Came to Be Written: The Liturgical Year of the Synagogue as the Organizing Principle

CHAPTER 1

Stating the Problem, Setting the Stage

I WILL TRY IN THIS VOLUME to reclaim the Jewish past that can illumine our gospel narratives in a way that is almost unimaginable. I will seek to demonstrate that the presence of an anti-Jewish bias over the centuries has kept the Christian church locked inside an anti-Semitic, Gentile exile. Part of my task in this book will be to pull back the layers of a long-standing Gentile ignorance of all things Jewish that has marked our traditional approach to the New Testament. In the process I will reveal that biblical fundamentalism is, in fact, a product of that ignorance. I will also seek to show just how deeply Jewish the Christian gospels are and just how much they reflect the Jewish scriptures, Jewish history and Jewish patterns of worship. To read the gospels properly, I now believe, requires a knowledge of Jewish culture, Jewish symbols, Jewish icons and the tradition of Jewish storytelling. It requires an understanding of what the Jews called "midrash."

Only those people who were completely unaware of these things could ever have come to think that the gospels were meant to be read literally. It was this same Gentile ignorance, I will argue, that created in the minds of Christians over the centuries the necessity of defending the literalness of such events in the life of Jesus as the virgin birth, the miracles, the details of the passion narrative, the understanding of resurrection as physical resuscitation and the cosmic ascension as an act that actually took place in both time and space. In this book I will show how these stories would have been understood by both the Jewish authors of the various gospels and by the Jewish audiences for which these gospels were originally written. I hope it will be a work that will radically reorient my readers to look at the gospels with a brand-new set of eyes.

Before I can begin that task, however, I must seek to explain how it was that Christianity, born in a Jewish world, developed into the primary source of the anti-Semitism that has plagued our world and that remains today as the darkest blemish on the Christian soul.

I have a second and equally compelling reason for writing this book. Since I regard biblical literalism as a Gentile heresy, I feel a burning necessity to expose fundamentalism for what I believe it is. Unless biblical literalism is challenged overtly in the Christian church itself, it will, in my opinion, kill the Christian faith. It is not just a benign nuisance that afflicts Christianity at its edges; it is a mentality that renders the Christian faith unbelievable to an increasing number of the citizens of our world. The irony of the task that I undertake in this book is that many literalistic Christians will see this book as an attack on Christianity itself. Not knowing any other way to read the Bible except to claim literal truth for it, they will suggest that I have abandoned "every tenet of traditional Christian thought." I have heard that charge more than once. So distorted will this point of view be that they will be unable to see either how deeply Christian I am or how deeply Christian this book is. So let me begin with a brief autobiographical statement.

I have lived my life professionally and personally between two polarities that seem to tear at the deepest part of my soul. The first reality is that I am a convinced and committed Christian. The second is that I despair daily about the state of institutional Christianity, including its denominational seminaries. Is it possible for both of these things to be true? Read carefully and I think you will discover that it is.

I walk the Christ path by a deliberate and conscious choice. I have lived my entire life inside the Christian church. The church for me has been like a second home. I cannot remember a time in my life that I did not want to be a priest. Indeed I still treasure that vocation. I had the pleasure, indeed the privilege, of serving in that role for twenty-one years. Then, after being elected a bishop by the clergy and laypeople of the diocese of Newark, I had the even greater privilege of serving in that capacity for twenty-four years. The Christian church and its faith are not tangential to who I am; they are at the heart of who I am.

Being a priest opened doors that allowed me to enter deeply into the lives of many people. I have rejoiced with new parents at the birth of a child, and then celebrated that event publically in that child's baptism. I have worked with young adolescents struggling with their identity issues as they lived through that period of life when they ceased to be children but had not yet become adults. I have been with these teenagers when they were trying to deal with all their conflicting emotions and clanging hormones. Then I have celebrated their maturity publicly in the act of confirmation, the church's liturgical "puberty rite." I have sat with passionate lovers as they contemplated forging a life together. Then I have celebrated publicly their union in the liturgical event we call "holy matrimony."

I have also walked with families through valleys of excruciating pain. I think of an eleven-year-old girl who died of Hodgkin's disease; a two-year-old baby who died after ingesting a poisonous substance in a house that was not "childproof"; a mother and father who lost their only two children, both daughters, in separate, strange, unrelated and unpredictable accidents before either of these young women reached the age of twenty-six. I have tried then to make sense of these events in a liturgy called "the burial of the dead." I have walked as a friend and confidant with a young doctor, barely into his forties, married and with small children, who would soon die of a virulent form of leukemia that he understood completely and that he knew full well would be both mortal and quick. I have accompanied couples at different ages, who once had pledged their love to each other "till death us do part," as they now endured the pain and the embarrassment of public hearings in a domestic relations court prior to their being granted a divorce. I have sat with elderly people in their twilight years as they journeyed through stages of an illness that both they and I knew would soon bring their lives to an end.

Throughout these highs and lows of human experience, I have loved my priestly vocation, and I cannot imagine any other profession in which I could have found a more fulfilling, expanding or affirming life. If I had the chance to live my life a second time, I would not change my journey in any appreciable way. I identify myself quite self-consciously with a man named Melchizedek, who was described in the book of Psalms as "a priest forever" (Ps. 110:4).

Yet I also live in despair when I see the state of the Christian church today. The Bible, a text that the Christian church claims to hold dear, is frequently an embarrassment in the way it is used and understood. The Bible reflects a worldview of an ancient, premodern time and holds as truth many things that no one believes today. I watch members of the church continuing to quote these literal texts as if they should still be authoritative. The Bible on almost every page depicts God as a supernatural, miracle-working deity who lives just beyond the sky of a three-tiered universe. I see the centuries of Christian history as a time when the literal words of the Bible have been used in such a way as to guarantee the development of killing prejudices. I see a biblically based anti-Semitism that has resulted in the beating, robbing, relocating, ghettoizing, torturing and killing of Jews from the time of "the church fathers" in the second century to the Holocaust in the twentieth century. I weep at the evil and the pain that we Christians have done to Jewish people in the name of God.

I watch representatives of a militant Islam beheading or burning alive their prisoners in televised murders in order to protest what they believe the Christian world has done to the followers of Muhammad throughout Western history. There were first the crusades of the eleventh, twelfth and thirteenth centuries, led by the Vatican, in which the murder of "infidels"—that is, Muslims—was made a virtue. Later, in the twentieth and twenty-first centuries, Muslim nations were once again deeply violated by the industrializing "Christian" world's thirst for oil. The nations of the West have placed the Islamic citizens of the Middle East into a state of constant turmoil, war and devastation.

I have seen how in our history, people of color have been enslaved by "Bible-quoting" Christians. When slavery was finally threatened with being relegated to the dustbins of history in America, it was that section of this country known as "the Bible Belt" that rose to defend the enslavement of black people in the bloodiest war of American history. When slavery finally died as a legal option on the battlefields of Gettysburg, Antietam and Appomattox, the Christians of the Bible Belt, once again quoting their scriptures for justification, instituted laws of segregation with the full support of the federal government. When those segregation laws finally began to fall in the 1950s and 1960s, I watched the Bible being quoted to justify the use of lead pipes, police dogs, fire hoses and even the bombing of black churches in which little girls in their Easter finery were killed—all in an attempt to preserve "white supremacy." I notice that even today the political party in America that most claims to represent what is called "the Christian vote" is still working to impede the political process for black people, to make voting so difficult as to prevent them from casting their ballot.

I have watched women being denigrated, reduced to second-class citizenship, and denied education and access to the professions, while this life-destroying, prejudiced behavior was being justified time after time with quotations from the Bible.

I have watched a killing homophobia being promoted by the Christian churches of the world, both Catholic and Protestant, based on literal texts from an ancient Bible. I have heard Pope Benedict XVI refer to gay and lesbian people as "deviant." I have listened to the Reverend Pat Robertson, a television evangelist, interpret all sorts of natural disasters as God's punishment for our culture's toleration of homosexual people. I have listened to the

Reverend Jerry Falwell, another of America's well-known evangelical personalities, blame the disaster of September 11, 2001, when
terrorists struck the World Trade Center in New York and the
Pentagon in Washington, on the leaders of this nation for allowing legal abortions, encouraging feminism, giving public support
to homosexual people and tolerating such organizations as the
American Civil Liberties Union, because it was a known supporter
of the rights of minorities. It is so often embarrassing to continue
to identify oneself as a Christian and to see how the Christian
church's holy book is used in the service of prejudice, hatred and
oppression.

There is one other great challenge with which I struggle in order
to pursue my continued loyalty to the Christian faith. This challenge is not new. Indeed it has been part of the life of our world for
almost five hundred years. In those years succeeding generations
have watched the incredible explosion of new knowledge and new
understandings of how our world operates. Our discoveries have
ranged from a startling sense of the enormity of the universe, to a
new non-interventionist understanding of the weather and to new
knowledge of the meaning of sickness that does not include divine
punishment. A literal understanding of the Bible has been used as
the weapon of choice in opposition to almost every one of these
new discoveries. Galileo was condemned at a heresy trial in the
seventeenth century for his challenge to the idea that the planet
earth was the center of a three-tiered universe. The biblical text
quoted to seal Galileo's fate was from the book of Joshua, a passage that described God as stopping the sun on its path around the
earth so that Joshua could have more daylight in which to kill more
of his enemies (Josh. 10:12–14). Later the work of Charles Darwin
was attacked and ridiculed by Christians on the basis of the literal

accuracy of the seven-day creation story in the book of Genesis (chapter 1) and on the biblical calculation made by Irish Bishop James Ussher that the world was created in 4004 BCE. There are artifacts that clearly refute his dating, such as a 27,000-year-old sculpture in a cave in the south of France that I have seen and which I know to be authentic, but which literalists dismiss as a forgery, since it does not fit into their biblical worldview. I have watched as local school boards, in the service of "biblical truth," seek to impose "creation science" or "intelligent design" on the science departments of local high schools as a way of providing equal treatment for what they absurdly suggest are "equally valid" theories.

When Louis Pasteur discovered germs, and when later generations discovered and learned to treat viruses, coronary occlusions, tumors, and leukemia, I watched as various Christian groups, quoting the Bible, opposed these breakthroughs in medical science because "they removed God from the arena of sickness and health."

I recall reading the charges made by the Reverend Dr. Timothy Dwight, a Congregationalist clergyman and the president of Yale University from 1795 to 1817, who railed against vaccinations because if God had intended to punish people by sending sickness upon the wicked, then those vaccinations were standing between God and the divine ability to punish sinners.

So this is my dilemma. At one and the same time, I have found the Bible and my study of it to be a deep resource to my life and my faith, but I have also been deeply embarrassed by the way the Bible has been used over the centuries to justify one dehumanizing attitude after another. I cannot apparently have it both ways. I must either reject the Bible to live in a modern world or I must reject the modern world in order to cling to the Bible. That is a choice I cannot and will not make. So I am driven to find a different way to read the Bible that allows me simultaneously to be both a person of faith and a person thankful for and dedicated to the century in which I am privileged to live. For anyone to call the Bible the "Word of God" or to treat the words of the Bible as if they were words spoken by the mouth of God is to me not just irresponsible, it is also to be illiterate. To read from this book in a Sunday worship service and then to end that reading with some version of the phrase "this is the Word of the Lord" is, to me, little more than the perpetuation of religious ignorance and religious prejudice. To watch a church procession in which someone holds the Bible, or the book of the gospel readings, high above his or her head, as if to offer this book to the people as an object of worship, is repulsive to me. Yet I love this book. My life has been fed by this book, and I do not want to see it abandoned in an increasingly secular society. This is what drives me to search for an alternative way to read and to study the Bible. That is what compels me to go so deeply into this book that I can free it from the peril of literalism that has been imposed on it by well-meaning but uninformed "believers." I feel called to free the Bible from those who read it literally, no matter how much they say that they are associated with either God or Jesus.

Can biblical ignorance be attacked and laid bare by one who is not an enemy of the Christian faith, but a committed practitioner of that faith? Can one who defines himself as a disciple of Jesus open people's minds to see that biblical idolatry is not a virtue? Can I help to bring to the general public the kind of biblical knowledge that renders biblical fundamentalism inoperative, indeed that reveals it to be both ignorant and unlearned, and still present myself as a Christian, a believer and one who by conviction continues to walk the Christ path? That is my goal in this book, and I shall pursue that goal with passion.

In the process I will disturb many. That is not my desire, but I believe it is inevitable. The Bible has been misunderstood for so long by so many that overturning what most churchgoers have been taught to believe as "gospel truth" will inevitably destabilize their religious convictions. That will naturally bring distress and anger. I also expect that I will irritate many in academia who will suggest that all the things I say have been known for hundreds of years! They will conclude, therefore, that I am guilty of some unequivocal need for sensationalism. I only ask these people, who have lived their lives behind the ivy-covered walls of academia, to step out of their intellectual ghetto for just a minute, where they can see clearly that very few people seem to have heard the news that those academicians say is hundreds of years old. They will also see that people are today walking away from Christianity in droves because it seems so out of touch with the world in which they live. More importantly, these academic Christians need to face the fact that their work has never been successful in helping to define "popular" Christianity. That rather was the accomplishment of the biblical literalists. So in this book I will begin with a brief story of the Bible in general, which, if successfully conveyed, will inevitably destroy the unthinking assumptions of fundamentalism. I will not stop there, however. Then I will develop a very different way of reading the text of the Bible itself. When I get to this second phase of this book, I will lean on one gospel as my guide. I will do that for two reasons. First, to do more than one gospel would make this book so long that no one would read it. Second, the principle I seek to show can be established and developed by using one gospel alone. Matthew is the gospel I have chosen, because it was the one that the early church placed first in the New Testament and it lends itself to a non-literal reading better than any other. I have loved my study in preparing to write this book. I hope my readers will love the results. More than that, I hope they will discover a way to worship God with their minds. I hope they will find themselves able to live inside the Christian story without denying the tenets of the world in which they are also citizens. I hope they will no longer have to twist their minds into a first-century pretzel in order to walk the Christ path.

So let the story begin.

CHAPTER 2

Setting Jesus into the Context of History

W E BEGIN OUR ANALYSIS of the Jesus story with some statements that contemporary men and women clearly no longer believe, no matter what the Bible says. Stars do not announce a human birth. Wise men do not follow a star that moves so slowly through the sky that these magi can keep up with it. Angels do not break through the midnight sky to sing to hillside shepherds. Virgins do not conceive. The skies do not open at the time of a baptism to allow the Holy Spirit to drop from heaven on the one being baptized, nor does a voice from behind a cloud in that sky proclaim that the one being baptized is really God's child. A multitude of people cannot be fed by the miraculous expansion of a lad's lunch of five loaves and two fish. No one can walk on water. A four-days dead and buried Lazarus cannot be called out of his grave to resume his life in this world. A man born blind cannot receive his sight. Water cannot be miraculously changed into wine. A man crucified and buried on Friday cannot be miraculously resuscitated and able to emerge from his grave on Sunday. No one returns to God's dwelling place by rising into the sky of a three-tiered universe.

I have not in this brief and limited set of statements covered all the unbelievable episodes in the literalized understanding of the gospel narratives, but these will serve as illustrations of what might be said about many other parts of the biblical story. The gospels, I am suggesting, were not meant to be read literally, and they become nonsensical and unbelievable if one seeks to do so. The gospels are not biographies of a man named Jesus of Nazareth. They do not contain tape recordings of the things that he actually said. They are not historical chronicles of the things he actually did. No one who knows anything about the gospels, such as when they were written, how they were written or the context of history in which they were written, could possibly believe these narratives to be literally and entirely true. What are they then? It will be the task of this book to discover that.

I start with some basic background material. Since the New Testament is above all else a witness to the life, the message and the meaning of a person who is called Jesus of Nazareth, perhaps it is appropriate to begin by setting his life into the context of history. To determine the dates during which Jesus lived, we draw on data available to us from two sources. First, there is the Christian written tradition, which sometimes, almost unconsciously, provides us with clues. These clues are then expanded by what we can discover from secular sources. The two together serve to corroborate each other better than we might imagine, building for us in the process something that can be termed at least a "high probability" that the life of Jesus is based on history, not fantasy, even if many of the details that surround his life are surely mythological.

We have two narratives in the Bible that purport to describe events surrounding the birth of Jesus. Neither of these narratives, however, was written earlier than the ninth decade, and so they in and of themselves cannot be relied on with much confidence for accuracy. Both of them, however, do assert, as an internal dating guide, that Jesus was born during the reign of a king who was known in Judean history as Herod the Great. If that fact can be determined to be accurate, as it seems to be, then we can go to secular records, where we discover that King Herod died in the year 4 BCE. This means that if Jesus was born when Herod was king, he had to have been born in or before the year 4 BCE. There is further biblical corroboration of this date. The way the land of the Jews was governed by the Romans, as reflected in the adult narratives of Jesus, is consistent with the changes in government that Rome made following Herod's death. The Roman leaders at that time divided Herod's former realm on the eastern edge of the Mediterranean Sea into three parts, placing one of Herod's three sons over each of the new jurisdictions. After a few years, however, the jurisdiction that included Jerusalem, having proved far more volatile than the others, was placed under direct Roman control. Herod's son was removed and replaced by an appointed prefect or procurator from Rome. That is the pattern that the gospels portray when they chronicle the Jesus story. These are the data that make us fully confident in dating the birth of Jesus in or just slightly before the year 4 BCE.

On the other end of Jesus' life, the gospel narratives are very clear that the crucifixion of Jesus occurred under the administration of the Roman prefect-procurator Pontius Pilate. Once again, armed with that gospel assertion, we can go to secular records, and there we discover that Pilate began his reign in Judea in the year 26 CE and ended it when he was recalled by Rome in 36 CE. So if the gospels are accurate in maintaining that the crucifixion took place under the reign of Pontius Pilate, it had to have occurred during the time span of his rule. We also know from Roman history some of the tensions and political problems endured by Pilate that caused him to be terminated by Rome in 36 CE. These events appear to have happened well after the crucifixion of Jesus, so the evidence points to the earlier years of his administration as the time of the crucifixion, with the years 28–32 CE being the best historical guess by those who have devoted the most study to this issue. I choose the midpoint of the time span and seek to fix our date of the cruci-fixion in or near the year 30 CE. I cannot be certain that this is the exact year, but I can be certain that it is close, indeed close enough to adopt it with some confidence, as the best bet for dating the end of Jesus' earthly life. So I set down our first time marker: The life of the man Jesus can be fairly accurately dated as having been lived between 4 BCE and 30 CE, which means that when he died he was around age thirty-four. With these dates fixed in our minds, we begin to build the case for dating the books that now constitute the New Testament.

If the crucifixion took place around the year 30, how long was it before the writing of the first book of the New Testament occurred? Scholars now believe that the earliest written part of the New Testa-ment was Paul's first epistle to the Thessalonians; and the consensus gained from internal evidence and from some autobiographical notes that Paul included in other epistles, especially Galatians, enables us to set the date of I Thessalonians in or near the year 51 CE.

The first conclusion we can draw from this dating process is, therefore, that we do not possess a single scriptural document written any less than twenty-one years after the crucifixion that purports to tell us anything about the historical life of Jesus of Nazareth! We then have to face the fact that, at the very least, there is absolute silence for twenty-one years. This means that a whole generation stands between the Jesus of history and the first mention of his name or of any detail of his life that appears in any document that we possess today!

Paul wrote, according to the best scholarship available, between the years 51 CE and 64 CE, or some twenty-one to thirty-four years after the crucifixion. So we look at Paul and ask what it is that one can learn about Jesus from his writings. The answer is very little, as we shall quickly discover. Paul's mode of communication was epistles—that is, letter writing. His letters were addressed to particular congregations, sometimes written in response to letters received from them, which obviously have not been preserved. Clearly, however, because Paul's responses dealt with problems and circumstances in the various churches, we assume that these were the things about which they wrote in their letters to the one who was their founder. Because this is the mode of correspondence, it does not lend itself to the inclusion of many biographical details about Jesus. That fact limits our ability to learn much about Jesus from Paul's epistles.

There is one other issue that we need to face if we wish to be historically accurate. We need to gauge the level of authenticity of the fourteen epistles that have at some time or other in Christian history been attributed to Paul. The best scholarship we have available to us today suggests that Paul is the author of no more than seven of them. In the generally accepted order of their time of writing, the seven are: I Thessalonians, Galatians, I and II Corinthians, Romans, Philemon and Philippians. So if we are going to seek the earliest data about Jesus in the New Testament, these are the books to which we must turn. Three of the others that have traditionally claimed Pauline authorship, namely II Thessalonians, Colossians and Ephesians, appear, from internal references, to have been written about a decade after Paul's death, and perhaps by one of Paul's disciples or associates. If that is so, then these three epistles might still reflect some of Paul's thinking, but they are certainly not Pauline. Three others, which also claim Pauline authorship, I and II Timothy and Titus, appear to have been written about a generation or more after Paul's death. These epistles reveal a structure in the life of the church that did not develop until well after Paul's death and which he would not have recognized.

Finally, the epistle to the Hebrews, which was attributed to Paul by the King James translation in 1611, in the face of absolutely no evidence to support that assertion, is today universally dismissed as Pauline.

The fact that these Pauline claims were originally made for this list of clearly non-Pauline epistles reflects the struggle among the early followers of Jesus over which writings could provide authoritative answers to their questions. To assert that a particular epistle was the work of the apostle Paul gave that writing a status that it would not have had without that claim, and if the claim was successfully established, it guaranteed the epistle's place in the canon of scripture and thus among the authoritative books used by the church. No scholar today, however, believes that Paul was the author of all the epistles that bear his name.

Once we have clarified the authentic Pauline epistles we can gather from them the earliest written data we possess about the life of Jesus. An examination of this earliest written material, however, reveals rather quickly that it is a very limited source for actual data about the life of the Jesus of history.

On ten separate occasions in the authentic Pauline material, this apostle makes a reference to the term "crucified." Most of these uses are clearly in reference to Jesus. To the Galatians Paul writes: "O foolish Galatians! Who has bewitched you, before whose eyes Jesus Christ was publicly portrayed as crucified?" (Gal. 3:1). To the Corinthians, he writes: "We preach Christ crucified, a stumbling block to Jews and folly to Gentiles" (I Cor. 1:23); and again: "For I decided to know nothing among you except Jesus Christ and him crucified" (I Cor. 2:2). Because the crucifixion of Jesus, as a fact of history, is clearly attested by Paul, this becomes the first piece of data on which we can begin to build. The next thing we notice is that while the crucifixion of Jesus appears to be assumed by Paul, he provides us with almost no details about that event. The details he does supply appear to come to us from only one of his epistles, I Corinthians, written around the year 54 CE.* Twice in this single epistle Paul does something he never does anywhere else. He asserts that he is passing on a tradition that he has "received," although from whom he is not clear.

In the first of these two "received" references we are told about the inauguration of the Christian Eucharist (I Cor. 11:23–26). There Paul says: "On the night that he [Jesus] was betrayed, he took bread." We note first that the word translated "betrayed" (*paredideto*) really means "handed over." Those two renditions,

---

*Dating I and II Corinthians is not easy, for they seem to be a combination of at least four separate letters, but to unravel that would involve more detail than I want to go into in this volume, for the matter is not germane to my thesis. I do want to say, however, that the dating used here is close, but still debated.

"betrayed" and "handed over," are not quite the same, but with that caveat filed for our consideration, we note that this is the only mention of what came to be called "the betrayal of Jesus" prior to the time the gospels were written. Note also that Paul gives no hint that this "handing over" was associated with one of the twelve, nor does he suggest anywhere that the meal at which this bread was broken and said to be symbolic of Jesus' body was the Passover meal. Those two details begin to look like later developments in the narrative.

The second of these "received" messages from Paul deals with the final events in Jesus' life (I Cor. 15:1–8). The details given here are also "bare bones" at best. About the crucifixion Paul gives no details whatsoever. All he says is found in this one line: "He died for our sins in accordance with the scriptures" (I Cor. 15:3). Note all the things that are missing here, things which make up the very familiar later tradition. There is no mention of a trial, either before the high priest and the Jewish Sanhedrin or before Pilate, the Roman governor. There is no reference to Barabbas or to the thieves who were later said to have been crucified on each side of Jesus. There are no words that claim to have come from Jesus while on the cross. There is no account of Peter's denial, or of the abandonment of Jesus by the twelve.

When Paul finally comes to the place where he will describe the "Easter experience," once again his words are very few. Quite simply, he says: "He was raised on the third day in accordance with the scriptures" (I Cor. 15:4). Paul then proceeds to provide a list of those who can bear "witness" to the reality of this "Easter experience," those to whom he claims the raised Christ "appeared." He gives us, however, not a single detail that relates any of these "appearances" to his list of witnesses. The list itself, however, is revelatory and needs to be looked at closely. We will do that as this book unfolds, but for now let me just state the names of those on the list. It includes Cephas (that is, Peter), the twelve, five hundred brethren at once, James, the apostles and finally Paul himself (I Cor. 15:5–8).

This list leaves us begging for answers to obvious questions. Without dealing yet with any of these questions, we have to face the fact that this is the total extent of the knowledge about the life of Jesus that was available in writing to the followers of Jesus until we get to the eighth decade, when the first gospel, the one we call Mark, makes its appearance.

When Mark writes, approximately forty-two years, or two full generations, have passed since the crucifixion. This is one of the reasons we know that we are not dealing with eyewitness accounts in the gospels. Although this fact is seldom embraced by traditional Christian understandings, it is nonetheless quite true.

We now need to embrace the fact that it was not until Mark wrote that many of the most familiar aspects of the Jesus story are heard for the first time. Mark provides us, for example, with the first mention in Christian history of the figure we call John the Baptist. Mark is the first to relate the story of Jesus' baptism and the account of his temptation in the wilderness. He is the first to suggest that the betrayal was by the hand of one of "the twelve." He is the first New Testament writer to associate miracles with the memory of Jesus. He is the first to assert that Jesus taught in parables. Even here, however, he appears to be unaware of the most familiar and best loved parables of the New Testament, for they will not appear for about two more decades, and only in Luke. Mark is also the first person to give us a narrative of the events of the crucifixion, from the Last Supper to the burial. He is the first to mention Judas Iscariot, the thieves crucified on each side of

Jesus, the women at the tomb and the role of Joseph of Arimathea in the story of the burial. The Christian story did not drop from heaven fully written. It grew and developed year by year over a period of forty-two to seventy years. That is not what most Christians have been taught to think, but it is factual. Christianity has always been an evolving story. It was never, even in the New Testament, a finished story.

A little more than a decade after Mark was written, Matthew composed his gospel. It was, in effect, an expansion of Mark, a text with which Matthew was obviously familiar. About ninety percent of Mark was incorporated directly into Matthew's gospel. Some major things, however, which had not been part of the Christian tradition before, entered the Christian story with the arrival of Matthew. Among Matthew's additions was the narrative of Jesus' miraculous or virgin birth (Matt. 1, 2). We need to be aware of the fact that the virgin birth, which was exalted to its current prominence in the Apostles' and Nicene Creeds of the third and fourth centuries, was not part of primitive Christianity at all. It is a ninth-decade addition found first in Matthew's gospel. We will look at this powerful story in detail later, and especially at the way that Matthew introduces it. Suffice it now to say that the virgin birth narrative and the reasons for its inclusions are not what most people think. Matthew seeks to ground every aspect of his birth-of-Jesus story in the Hebrew scriptures, and those familiar with the Jewish sacred story can find references in his virgin birth account to the books of Genesis, Numbers, Isaiah, II Samuel, Jeremiah, Hosea, and many others in the Hebrew Bible.

Matthew is also the first to add content to the story of Jesus' temptations in the wilderness (Matt. 4:1–11). Matthew is the only writer to suggest that Jesus ever preached the Sermon on the Mount (Matt. 5–7). Matthew is the first to record that Jesus taught the disciples what came to be called the Lord's Prayer (Matt. 6:9–13). He introduces a number of parables that have never been heard of before, perhaps the best known of which is called the parable of the judgment, in which on the final day at the end of the world the king separates the sheep from the goats, inviting the sheep into the kingdom and dispatching the goats to "outer darkness" (Matt. 25:31–46).

In the story of the resurrection, Matthew also adds crucial new material to the tradition. He is the first gospel writer to describe a narrative of a resurrection appearance, and thus the first to suggest that the resurrection was "physical." Matthew's final unique contribution to the developing resurrection story is that he is the first to suggest that the raised Christ actually spoke words to the disciples that were remembered.

About a decade after Matthew, Luke composed his gospel.* He too used Mark as a primary source. He also may have used Matthew—a minority position, but one of which I am increasingly convinced. Other scholars postulate a second, now lost, source of the sayings of Jesus that they believe both Matthew and Luke incorporated into their texts along with Mark. They call this presumed lost source "Q." I find myself unimpressed with this supposition, but this debate is not critical to my thesis and I do not want to divert attention from that thesis by spending much time on it. The Q hypothesis has been the standard assumption of most New Testament scholars since the middle years of the nineteenth century. It is certainly still the majority opinion today. It is, however, more

---

*Dating Luke is more debated than dating any of the other gospels. The range is from the 80s to about 140. I believe the proper range is between 88 and 93, but that is a fluid conclusion.

strongly held in the United States than it is in the United Kingdom, where it appears to be weakening. The Q hypothesis refers to the fact that there is material common to both Matthew and Luke that they did not get from Mark. So a source available to both of them has been proposed. If Luke had access to Matthew, however, that would also account for the material common to them both. That would also mean that Q was really Matthew expanding on Mark, which content Luke then also included. This is still a minority position today, but I am increasingly skeptical of the Q hypothesis. Many reasons for the skepticism will become obvious as this study develops. Let me move on here to analyze those things that Luke specifically adds to the developing Christian tradition.

Luke has more of Jesus' teaching packed into his gospel than any other evangelist. The journey setting in which Jesus is going from Galilee to Jerusalem near the end of his life is significantly longer in Luke than it is in either Mark or Matthew. Luke is the source of the best-known parables in the Christian story, which means that these parables did not enter the Christian tradition until the late ninth or perhaps the early tenth decade. Luke is the gospel writer who did the most to encourage people to think of the resurrection of Jesus as a physical, bodily resuscitation. Luke is also the first to give us any version of what we now call "the ascension," as well as the story of the first "Pentecost" or the "birth of the church."

When the Fourth Gospel enters the Christian story, which most scholars date between 95 and 100 CE, its author also adds a number of new ideas to the growing story. John alone suggests that Jesus is somehow a pre-existent being (John 8:56–58). He attributes clairvoyance to Jesus (John 1:46–48). He presents us with a Jesus who is in a one-to-one relationship with God (John 1:10b and 14:9–10). All of these are late-first-century additions to the tradition. Another interesting feature of the Fourth Gospel is that the virgin birth story has disappeared. It is replaced by a hymn to the eternal *Logos* or "Word" of God, suggesting that Jesus is the "enfleshment of the Word." On two occasions the Fourth Gospel refers to Jesus quite simply as "the son of Joseph" (John 1:45 and John 6:42). Parables have also disappeared from John's gospel, and miracles have been turned into "signs." Jesus in John shows no anxiety in anticipation of the crucifixion and utters no cry of despair from the cross. Finally, John suggests that the second coming of Jesus occurred when the risen Christ breathed on his disciples during the evening of the first Easter day.

Most people have never read the New Testament chronologically. When they do, they see at once that Christianity is clearly evolving. Here is a quick review of what the major New Testament authors contributed, and when. The reality of the crucifixion and an undefined transcending of the barrier of death are the primary themes established in the epistles of Paul, who wrote between the years 51 and 64. Miracles, John the Baptist, Judas Iscariot, the transfiguration and the narrative of the passion enter the tradition in the eighth decade with Mark. The virgin birth, the Sermon on the Mount and narratives giving details about Jesus' resurrection first enter the story with Matthew in the ninth decade.

The most familiar parables, the resurrection as resuscitation, the story of the ascension, and the Pentecost experience of receiving the Holy Spirit are gifts to the Christian narrative received from Luke, and they enter the tradition in the late ninth decade or early tenth decade. The ideas suggesting that Jesus was pre-existent, that he was of one substance with God, are introduced by John in the late tenth decade.

Once we recognize how the story grows, it is hard to literalize any part of it, but that was the fate the gospels were to face. So powerful was this literalizing force that even the writings of Paul were caught up in it. I suspect that Paul would be the most surprised of all people to learn that words from his epistles have been called the "Word of God" and quoted as authoritative texts in major church disputes.

Having laid out this case for the developing, non-fixed story of Christianity between 51 and 100 in those parts of the New Testament that are still available to us, we must now ask: How much did the story change between 30 and 51, a time for which we have no written sources to check? Is there any way we can get into those lost years? If so, can we search in that period of our history for the original essence of our faith story and can we reclaim it? Does it offer us a clue as to what Christian future might be? I think we can and I think it does. We begin this probe in the next chapter.

CHAPTER 3

The Oral Phase: Entering the Tunnel of Silence

WE HAVE TRACED THE DEVELOPMENT of the Christian story from Paul to John. We have seen how the story developed and when various aspects of that story were added. That, in and of itself, should be enough to establish the fact that the various elements of the Christian story did not drop out of the sky fully written, but rather evolved in history. We looked at the fact that though Paul broke the silence about Jesus, he added very little to the development of the Jesus story. If we had nothing but Paul, we would have no account of Jesus' birth, his baptism, his temptations, his transfiguration, or the details of Holy Week. Paul appears to have known nothing of the Palm Sunday procession, the role played by Judas, the details of the crucifixion, the burial by Joseph of Arimathea, the women coming to the tomb on the first day of the week, or any narrative of the resurrected Jesus. Paul also seems to be unaware

that miracles were associated with the memory of Jesus, or even
that Jesus taught in parables.

Most people are not aware of just how scanty Paul's material
about Jesus really is, because for centuries Christians have been
taught to homogenize the New Testament into a single continuous
story with little or no idea of just when it was that these familiar
narratives entered the text. Paul's lack of information means that
for all practical purposes, the silent period about Jesus is not just
from 30–51, but from 30–72, in which year finally the first gospel
was written.

So our question now becomes, Can we find a trustworthy doorway through which we can enter to explore those silent years? I
believe that we can; and when we do, I believe that we will discover some radical and revolutionary things about primitive
Christianity. Perhaps we will even discover the central core of the
Christian experience, uncorrupted by the doctrinal excesses into
which Christianity moved once it became an established religion.
Perhaps even more uniquely, here we will find the Jesus experience
that lies behind the evolving stories of the gospels. Perhaps we will
touch that originating power of Christianity, something that can
still engage the post-Christian, secular world that we now inhabit.
We turn our attention, therefore, to those years bounded on one
side by the crucifixion and on the other by the beginning of the
gospel-writing tradition.

I begin with the literal historical data that I believe we can discover about Jesus in the gospels themselves. First, Jesus was a Jew!
His name was Yeshuah. It is of interest to me that Luke, the most
cosmopolitan of the gospel writers, the one who reflects a tradition in which dispersed Jews were joined by a growing number of
Gentile proselytes, wrote the gospel that concentrates on the fact

that Jesus was made to fulfill the ritual acts required of all Jewish male children. Jesus was, according to Luke, "circumcised on the eighth day" (Luke 2:21), "presented in the Temple" on the fortieth day (Luke 2:22b) and Luke alone has the childhood story of Jesus being taken up to the Temple in Jerusalem when he was twelve years of age (Luke 2:41–52), which looks like a puberty rite, perhaps a pre–bar mitzvah experience, since neither bar mitzvah nor bat mitzvah traditions had at that time become ritual practices of the Jews.

When the later story of Jesus is being related in all four of the gospels, the presence of the synagogue in the life of both Jesus and his disciples is regularly attested. Interestingly, Paul never uses the word "synagogue" in any of his writings, but the book of Acts employs the word in its singular or plural form twenty-two times. Almost all of these usages are about the place in which Paul did his missionary preaching. Paul, according to Acts, always started his visits to the cities of Asia Minor and Greece in the synagogues of those cities. Thirty-nine times in the four gospels, Jesus is related directly to the synagogue in which he was teaching, healing, or simply attending worship. This means that the tradition on which the gospel writers drew was of Jesus regularly participating in synagogue worship. In the course of doing that he would have listened to long readings from the Torah, as well as regular readings from the prophets. These writings were for him, as they were for all Jews, the sacred scriptures. One could not attend the synagogue in that era without being exposed to these scriptures, for the reading of the scriptures was the primary event when Jews gathered for worship on the Sabbath.

What we Christians today call the Old Testament was in fact Jesus' Bible. What we call the book of Psalms was Jesus' hymnal.

So significant a part of Jesus' life was his participation in synagogue worship that Luke's gospel called his regular synagogue attendance something he did "as was his custom" (Luke 4:16).

If, as the gospels reflect, the community's memories of Jesus were associated deeply with the synagogue, is it not reasonable to assume that his disciples would have continued this pattern of life after the crucifixion? People do not seem to realize that the disciples of Jesus, and thus the first Christians, were—like Jesus—Jews. As Jews they were presumably active participants in the worship life of the synagogue. Would not the synagogue then have been the actual setting where the teachings of Jesus and the stories about Jesus would have been recalled and passed on? Is the synagogue not the obvious place where the oral tradition would have begun and where it would have continued? The fracture between the synagogue and the church did not occur officially until around the year 88 CE. This means that Paul died a Jew, and the missionary goal of his life was not to destroy Judaism, but to open Judaism to Gentile inclusion. Synagogue worship was at the heart of Paul's life, and when his converts gathered on the first day of the week to "break bread" in the name of the Lord, it was not designed as a step toward founding a new religious movement so much as it was in the service of adding a new dimension to their life in the synagogue.

If the separation of the church from the synagogue happened as late as the year 88 CE, as is now commonly understood, then certainly the earliest gospels of Mark and Matthew were created while the Christian movement was still part of the synagogue congregation. The gospel of Luke, while it was probably written after the split in 88 CE, clearly leans on the work of Mark and possibly on Matthew as well and thus still reflects the same synagogue pattern found in both of these earlier gospels. John is thus the only gospel that, at least in its final form, was written after the fracture that caused the followers of Jesus to be expelled from the synagogue. The pain of that fracture is everywhere present when one reads the pages of the Fourth Gospel. Even that pain, however, still bears witness to the original situation: that the Jesus movement was, during Jesus' life, grounded in the synagogue and after his death was still grounded in the participation of his followers in the life of the synagogue. That being so, then we should find echoes of synagogue life in the writings of at least the three synoptic gospels: Mark, Matthew and Luke. If we can establish as a fact that the story of Jesus was first recalled and passed on in the synagogue, then we can enter each of these gospels in search of clues that will reveal or point toward their synagogue origins.

Before these clues can be identified, however, one must have some understanding of what synagogue life and synagogue worship were like. One will never see the influence of synagogue life in the gospels without that understanding. Fortunately, for our purposes, Luke, writing in the book of Acts, describes one of Paul's visits to a synagogue. The book of Acts is dated no earlier than the tenth decade of the Common Era, which would place it some 65–70 years after the life of Jesus had been brought to a conclusion. Given the fact, however, that all liturgies change very slowly, tenth-decade synagogue life should still be quite similar to synagogue worship during the life of the Jesus of history. The former dean of the seminary I attended, when asked how rapidly the liturgy of the church should change, replied, "It should move at the rate of about one word per century."* Given that pace of liturgical

*The Very Reverend Richard Reed, dean of Virginia Theological Seminary in Alexandria, VA, from 1983–1994.

change, I think we are safe in assuming that what the book of Acts describes would be very close to the pattern of worship in the synagogue in Jesus' lifetime. I turn, therefore, to that episode in Acts (13:13–52) and look at the best insight we have into what worship was like in the first century in Galilee and Judea.

The context is that Paul and his group had come to worship in the synagogue in Antioch of Pisidia, located in what we today call Turkey or Asia Minor. As the service began, Paul was obviously seated in the body of the worshippers. The liturgy is described in detail: "After the reading of the law and the prophets, the rulers of the synagogue sent a message to Paul and his entourage saying: 'Brethren, if you have any word of exhortation for the people, say it.'" Then we are told that Paul stood up and, motioning to the people with his hand, began to relate the story of Jesus to the story of the people of Israel.

Let me go back now and examine, as best we can, the meaning behind the words we just read. "After the reading of the law" is a reference to the Sabbath Torah tradition. The most important part of the synagogue worship was a reading from the books of Moses, as they were called—the first five books in the Bible: Genesis, Exodus, Leviticus, Numbers, and Deuteronomy. These five books were the "holy of holies" in the Jewish scriptures. In traditional synagogue practice, the Torah was read in its entirety at public worship throughout the Sabbaths of a single year. Getting through the Torah in that time frame meant that each Sabbath Torah reading might last thirty to forty minutes.

This reading of the Torah progressed from beginning to end, starting on the first Sabbath of the new year with the book of Genesis and ending on the last Sabbath of the year with the completion of the book of Deuteronomy. It was read from sacred scrolls, which were kept in the tabernacle and were solemnly and ceremoniously brought out for reading. A given Sabbath's scroll would be opened to the place where the previous Sabbath's reading had concluded. One did not skip around in a scroll!

There was some question as to when the Jewish year actually began. The Torah itself, however, is determinative: It describes the Jewish New Year, Rosh Hashanah, as coming on the first day of Tishri, the seventh month of the year (Lev. 23:24). If Tishri is the seventh month, then the year had to start with Nisan. This would mean that the Passover was the first major festival in this liturgical year. That seemed fitting since it celebrated the birth of the Hebrew people as a nation, the time of their transition from slavery to freedom, from being *no* people, to being God's chosen people.*

---

*Discovering when the Jews of antiquity began their liturgical year is not easy, for there was more than one starting place in Jewish history. Because the premise upon which this book is organized depends on it, I will use the liturgical year that begins with the month of Nisan and ends either with the month of Adar I or Adar II. I need, therefore, to state my reasons for adopting this starting place. I find that some parts of Judaism are not familiar with a Jewish year that begins in the spring, despite the fact that it conforms to the directives found in the Torah itself. I have cited that Torah text in the body of the book. While this starting place is largely ignored in Judaism today, this practice alone demonstrates how the writers of the synoptic gospels related the memory of Jesus to the ongoing worship life of the synagogue. It is essential, therefore, for me to demonstrate the accuracy of this premise in this footnote.

There is evidence in Jewish history for at least three distinct starting places for the Jewish year. The early Christians, I will suggest, followed one of these three, that later actually fell into general disuse in Judaism.

The familiar Jewish starting point for their liturgical and calendar year is Rosh Hashanah, which occurs on the first day of the month of Tishri (roughly in late September to mid-October) and which is actually called by the Jewish people "New Year's Day."

A second starting point for which some evidence can be found came out of the agricultural cycle of the Jewish people. In this practice the new year began after the harvest festival of Sukkoth had been completed, the grain stored, and the work of preparing the land for the next season was set to begin. This would mean the new year began probably at the end of the month of Tishri, since Sukkoth was observed from the fifteenth day to the twenty-second day of that month. To start the new year at this point clearly seemed to make sense among some segments of Jewish people. *(continued)*

Assuming, then, that the book of Genesis began to be read in the synagogue on the first Sabbath of Nisan, we can chart the approximate time that the other books of the Torah would begin and end. The book of Deuteronomy would conclude the Torah readings for the year in the final month, called Adar. We are also aware that in some parts of the Jewish world, especially among the Jews of the diaspora, a three-year cycle of readings replaced the one-year cycle of the more traditional synagogue. We see some evi-

---

(continued from previous page)

There was, however, a third starting point to the Jewish year that appears to have developed during that period of time in Jewish history that has been called the Babylonian Exile. It was in that exile that the Torah was expanded to its present length by a group of people called "The Priestly Writers."

The exile did not end in a single return, but in waves of returns over a period of about two hundred years. The Torah in its expanded form was carried by the returnees in one of their later returns. A reference in the Book of Nehemiah (Chapter 8) tells us of Ezra, the priest and scribe, reading a new version of the law to the people and gaining from them the pledge to be governed by this law. That was the basis for establishing the new covenant. There are some who think that this text reveals a reference to the expanded Torah in more or less the form that we have it today.

Inside this version of the Torah there were indications that the Jews in the exile had adopted a new calendar, which like the calendar of the Babylonians, among whom they had lived for so long, began in the spring of the year. This meant that according to this calendar the first month of the Jewish year had now become the month of Nisan, which comes in our Gregorian calendar in late March to early April. This shift in when the Jewish year began also meant that now the first major festival of their liturgical year to be celebrated would be the Passover, a Nisan 15 festival, falling always between the second and third Sabbaths of that month. Because the Jews began the day at sundown, not at 12 midnight, some parts of the Western world suggest that Passover was 14 and 15 Nisan. Perhaps it was even because Christianity came to be identified with this starting point for the Jewish year, that it was largely abandoned by Jewish worshippers as the centuries rolled by in favor of one of the two fall dates. A scholar like Ailene Guilding has shown us conclusively, in her book entitled *The Fourth Gospel and Jewish Worship: A Study of the Relationship of St. John's Gospel to the Ancient Jewish Lectionary System,* that both a spring and fall date for the beginning of the annual Torah readings can be demonstrated to have been present throughout the first century when the gospel of John was written. Michael Goulder, another scholar of both the Hebrew texts and the New Testament in his two books *The Evangelists' Calendar* and *Midrash and Lection in Matthew* has also demonstrated, again conclusively, that a Jewish calendar year beginning with Nisan was the practice of Jewish communities, which ultimately produced Mark, Matthew and Luke. I have, therefore, assumed this practice in the development of my thesis in this book.

dence of that tradition, I believe, in the Fourth Gospel, which may have been composed in Ephesus in Asia Minor. The three synoptic gospels, Mark, Matthew and Luke, appear, however, to reflect the annual cycle that ran from Nisan to Adar.

Following the reading of the law, according to the clue found in Acts 13, came readings from "the prophets." The Jews had two groups of prophets. One group was called the "former prophets" and the other was called the "latter prophets." The former prophets were made up of the books of the Bible from Joshua to II Kings.* From this portion of scripture Jewish worshippers would read the story of Israel after the death of Moses, their founding prophet. In some sense, the New Testament book of Acts reflects the Christian version of the "former prophets," for Acts purports to tell the story of Christianity after the death of Jesus, its founder.

Next, the synagogue liturgy would include a reading from the "latter prophets." They were four in number: Isaiah, Jeremiah, Ezekiel and what the Jews called "The Book of the Twelve."** Christians call these twelve the "minor prophets," and they constitute the last twelve books of the Old Testament, as Christians organize the Hebrew Scriptures, the books from Hosea to Malachi. I hasten to assert that the word "minor" refers to the length of these books, not to the significance of their message. These latter prophets tended to be read on a rotating four-year cycle. If we count the writings of the minor prophets as a single book (they

---

*Joshua, Judges, I and II Samuel, and I and II Kings. The Books of Chronicles were not included, since they were added to the biblical texts late in Jewish history.

**The book of Daniel was not included since it was a second century BCE work (ca. 166–165 BCE) and was not regarded as in the same category as the other prophets. Daniel was a late addition to the Hebrew Bible and belongs more properly to the Apocrypha, not in the Old Testament.

were all on a single scroll), then each of the four latter prophets would be about the same length and would provide something akin to a chapter per Sabbath over a four-year rotation.

In synagogue worship, psalms may have been recited or sung between the lessons to break up the periods of passive listening. When the long Torah reading and the shorter lessons from the former prophets and the latter prophets were complete, the leader of the synagogue would either himself* expound on these lessons or, as was the case in the book of Acts, invite a guest in the congregation, perhaps a visiting itinerant evangelist, to bring wisdom to illumine the texts of the day. That is what Paul did and his sermon is recorded in the book of Acts. I do not mean to suggest that the words that appear in Acts are the literal words Paul spoke; I would suggest, rather, that the author of Acts intended the passage to be similar to the kind of Christian preaching that went on at that time. It would have represented the kind of activity that the followers of Jesus did when they were still members of and thus participants in synagogue worship. This insight, which suggests that the story of Jesus was passed on primarily in the synagogue, opens to us a window into the oral period of Christian history and reveals the context in which the story of Jesus was repeated and thus preserved. It was not a random process in which parents told their children about Jesus, or neighbors passed on Jesus stories over the back fence, or people in the marketplace related stories of Jesus to one another. That kind of oral tradition would have resulted in little more than a few anecdotal episodes that stand out in everyone's family history—defining stories, embarrassing stories, or survival stories. One would certainly not get a cohesive

---

*There were no "herself" synagogue leaders.

pattern, such as the one revealed in the gospels, just from anecdotal recollections.

If this analysis is accurate, as I think it is, several things follow
as conclusions. First, we have to face the fact that the content of
our present gospels was probably "preached" before being "written." It also follows that "texts" for these Jesus "sermons" that
make up much of the gospels would have been found in the Sabbath
Torah lessons or in the readings from the prophets. So over the Sabbaths between the end of Jesus' life and the writing of the last of
the four gospels, the memory of Jesus—his life, his deeds, and his
teaching—was kept alive primarily in the synagogues. Sabbath by
Sabbath, month by month, and year by year, the life of Jesus was
orally transmitted by the followers of Jesus against the background
of the Sabbath scripture readings in the synagogue and thus in the
context of the liturgical worship forms of first-century Judaism.
That is, I believe, what gave original Christianity its external form.

Now, if that can be demonstrated to be accurate, and once
again, I think it can be, then the case builds as other things become
obvious. The first is that as Jesus was remembered in the synagogues, inevitably his memory would have been wrapped inside
the Hebrew scriptures. We should, therefore, be able to discern the
imprint of those scriptures on the memory of Jesus as that memory
was recalled in the gospels. As a corollary to this insight, it would
also mean that the gospels are themselves deeply Jewish books
and thus capable of having their nuances clearly understood only
by minds that share a similar Jewish background and life. Jewish
hearts would hear echoes of things to which non-Jewish hearts
would be oblivious.

The second thing that this insight would inevitably mean is that
if Christianity ever moved out of the Jewish world in which it was

born, and its gospels ever came to be read primarily by those who did not understand its Jewish background, its Jewish symbols, its Jewish scriptures and its liturgical practices, these gospels would inevitably be misunderstood and misread. It would probably be assumed by non-Jewish readers that the Jesus tradition recorded in the gospels was the account of something that occurred in literal history, that the words attributed to Jesus were words literally spoken by him. That was, in fact, exactly what happened in Christian history.

Under the influence of Paul, Christianity began to move first from traditional Judaism, practiced in traditional synagogues, to the synagogues of the diaspora—that is, the dispersion. By this I mean the synagogues serving Jewish members in the urban centers around the Mediterranean Sea, where resident Jews had, almost inevitably, begun to interact with non-Jewish people and non-Jewish cultures. These Jews inevitably had become less cultic and more cosmopolitan. In this new model, these synagogues began to attract those who came to be called "Gentile proselytes." It was through the response of these "Gentile proselytes" to the message of Jesus that Christianity transitioned into becoming ultimately a Gentile movement. As noted earlier, somewhere in the latter years of the ninth decade a split occurred between the synagogue and the followers of Jesus. The Orthodox party of Judaism thought of those followers as "Jewish revisionists" and excommunicated them from the synagogue. In the ninth chapter of the Fourth Gospel we can sense and feel the pain of that split and can even see the signs of the hostility it caused.* Once that split had occurred, Christian-

---

*Once again I refer to the story of the man born blind who was expelled from the synagogue. The dialogue in that narrative reeks of pain.

ity began to move more and more into the Gentile world. By about the year 150 CE, and that is obviously an arbitrary date,* there were hardly any Jews left in the Christian movement. From that day to some point after the end of World War II, the only people who read the New Testament were Gentiles, who had no understanding of and no appreciation for the original Jewish context of the gospels.

Absent that context, these Gentiles began to literalize the Jesus stories, a practice which the original writers of the gospels could never have imagined. They had been relating Jesus to the Hebrew scriptures and incorporating his memory into Jewish liturgical practices. They were writing Jewish interpretations of the Jesus experience, not biographical accounts or historical tales. Christian literalism or fundamentalism, which comes today in both a Catholic and a Protestant form, is thus nothing more than a "Gentile heresy." It is the result of a misunderstanding of the Jewish message, born in the period of Christian history that I now call the "Gentile captivity" of the Christian church! When encountering gospel phrases such as Jesus being referred to as "the lamb of God who takes away the sin of the world," first-century Jews would have known that this was a reference straight out of the Yom Kippur observance on Tishri 10. Such Jews would never have imagined that these very familiar Jewish liturgical words could ever be so distorted that they would someday become the basis of something called "substitutionary atonement," which did little more than expand guilt into being the primary coin of the Christian

---

*The conflict in the middle of the second century CE with a man named Marcion, who wanted to remove all things Jewish from Christianity, occurred about this time and therefore seems to give the year 150 CE some credibility as a date by which time Christianity had become overwhelmingly Gentile.

realm. Moses stories, Elijah stories, and familiar texts from the Hebrew scriptures that were wrapped around the memory of Jesus were no longer understood by Gentile leaders as interpretive tales, but as actual events. So literalism abounded and people assumed that the original attempt of the gospel writers was to relate the history of what had actually happened in Jesus' life. Nothing could have been further from the minds of whoever actually wrote Mark, Matthew, Luke, and even John.

There is another interpretive tool that today's reader of the gospels must understand. If the Hebrew scriptures were read in Sabbath day worship in the synagogue and their images were wrapped around the meaning of Jesus, then what was it that organized synagogue worship? Did the same thing that organized the synagogue year also organize the memory of Jesus and thus the writing of the synoptic gospels? I believe that case can also be made, and to the discovery of that organizing principle we turn next.

CHAPTER 4

Discovering the Clue
That Organized the
Synoptic Gospels

THE CLUE THAT BROKE OPEN the Jewishness of the gospels for me, and thus set me to the task of writing this book, came to light in a rather mundane conversation. The year was 1991. I was at Magdalen College of Oxford University in the United Kingdom on a study leave. Oxford had given me the title "scholar in residence." I was working with the assistant dean at Magdalen College, a young priest named Peter Eaton, who would someday become the bishop of the diocese of Southeast Florida in Miami.

My agenda on that study leave was to explore the birth narratives of the New Testament. There are two magical birth narratives in the New Testament. One is in Matthew, where a star announces Jesus' birth and Oriental magi follow that star to Bethlehem to present their gifts of gold, frankincense and myrrh. The second is in Luke, where angels break through the midnight sky to sing to hillside shepherds about the birth of Jesus. Both stories were probably the products of the ninth decade with Luke coming near the end of that decade or even in the early tenth decade. Both stories were designed to introduce the miraculous virgin birth into the developing Christian tradition.

I had long been convinced that none of this material could possibly have been literal history, but I could not say what it was, what it meant, or how these narratives had come to be developed. At that particular moment, I was engaged in an offhand and quite informal conversation with the dean of Magdalen College, a young and brilliant New Testament scholar named the Reverend Dr. Jeffrey John. Jeffrey was also destined for future greatness and would later play a crucial role in the Church of England's struggle over gay rights. Now, however, he was at the beginning of his career at Oxford University. My question to him was not planned; it just came up in a conversation over a cup of tea, a pause in a day of study. I simply asked my friend to recommend the best books that I could read on the birth narratives. His response was not to answer my request, but to make a pronouncement that startled me. "The birth narratives are nothing but haggadic midrash," he said, sounding quite authoritative.

While I was adjusting to his answer, he continued: "Are you not familiar with the work of Michael Goulder?" I was not only not familiar with the work of Michael Goulder, but I had never even heard of the man. Jeffrey described Goulder's work briefly, saying that he regarded the three synoptic gospels as Jewish liturgical documents, written primarily for use in the synagogue, and filled with Old Testament content and references. It was a point of view that I had not encountered before.

Intrigued, I went that day to an Oxford bookstore seeking to purchase a Goulder book. Only one was in stock. It was entitled: *Luke: A New Paradigm.** It was in two volumes, published by Sheffield Academic Press. It was also probably the most expensive book I had ever encountered. The price was £80, which in that day translated to about $160! I purchased it and began reading it that evening. It was one of the most difficult books I had ever tried to read. It was heavily footnoted. Many times a page would be less than half-filled with Goulder's text, only to be followed by his extensive notes. When Goulder quoted from the Old Testament, he did so in Hebrew, without translation. When he quoted from the New Testament, he did so in Greek, again without translation. It would take me two years before I had completed my first reading of that book.

Soon after purchasing this work on Luke, I went to the Bodleian Library at Oxford, one of the great libraries of the world, to see what books its shelves contained by Michael Goulder. My search was rewarded. I checked out his very early book entitled *Type and Ministry in Acts,*** and his later, better-known volumes in which he spelled out his liturgical theory of gospel formation. I tackled these books at once. First I read *The Evangelists' Calendar.* Second, *Midrash and Lection in Matthew.**** I finished both books quickly, and that experience was for me like finding the missing piece in a complicated puzzle, the presence of which caused everything else to fall into place.

So enthusiastic was I about this man's work that I immediately contacted Professor Goulder. He was teaching New Testament at

---

*See bibliography for details.

**See bibliography for details.

***See bibliography for details.

the University of Birmingham in the U.K. He agreed to see me, and I went for what would be the first of many visits. Working with him was for me the beginning of a whole new way of understanding the gospels in general and the synoptic gospels in particular.

I had long been fascinated with the Jewish background to the Jesus story. That was reflected in my second book, *This Hebrew Lord,** which strangely enough is still in print some forty-two years after its original publication. That book in turn was the catalyst for a life-changing dialogue that I conducted with Richmond's Rabbi Jack Daniel Spiro, which seemed to electrify that lovely, conservative southern city. It also enabled me to be ready to see the Jewishness of Jesus as a major aspect of my study. Throughout my career I have pursued this theme by reading books on this subject written by such luminaries as Samuel Sandmel, Krister Stendahl, Geza Vermes, Paul Van Buren, Moses Maimonides, Abraham Joshua Heschel, Martin Buber, Moses Mendelsohn, Amy-Jill Levine and many others.** I was thus predisposed to look for the meaning of Jesus inside the Jewish frame of reference that had produced him. I was also eager to see how those Jewish ideas had evolved in their Christian, and thus increasingly non-Jewish, setting. So it was that Goulder's work fitted into my own life path and study so beautifully. It fed my own interests deeply and significantly.

Michael and I in time came to have some serious disagreements. He had started his career as a priest in the Church of England with an academic interest. He was successful in that career to the point that he was even talked about as a serious possibility to be named the Anglican bishop of Hong Kong. He turned that possi-

---

*See bibliography for details.

**See bibliography for details.

bility down, however, because his natural bent was toward higher education, not the institutional church. His academic career led him more and more beyond where the church was willing to go in its thinking, so in 1981 he resigned his ordination, proclaiming that he was no longer a Christian. He began to define himself as a "non-aggressive atheist." Most church leaders simply dismissed him at this point. What he did for me, however, was to give my faith a new context that would mark my career path for the rest of my days. Michael Goulder's work was the key on which my life and study were destined to turn.

As much as I gained from him, Michael and I would come to dramatically different understandings of the gospels and certainly to different conclusions. Nonetheless, I want, and need, to tip my hat in deep appreciation to Professor Goulder and to acknowledge my intellectual debt to him. I also want to acknowledge publicly that my understanding of the synoptic gospels in general, and of Matthew's gospel in particular, owes much to Michael Goulder's scholarship. I have driven my study beyond Goulder and the conclusions in this book are my own, not his, but clearly he was the person who put me on this path, and I am grateful to him for that. This is also why I have designated him in this book as one of my three great mentors, to whom this book is dedicated "in memoriam."

The Goulder conclusion, namely that the liturgical life of the synagogue was the organizing principle of the three synoptic gospels, seems like an obvious assumption to me now. So in this book, I will seek to apply that assumption to Matthew's gospel in particular. I believe that it will illumine this gospel, and through it, Christianity itself, in dramatic new ways.

Christianity began as a movement within the synagogue, as we saw in the previous chapter. Its first adherents were synagogue-worshipping Jews who had come to see in the Jewish Jesus not only the fulfillment of the Jewish scriptures, but also the long-awaited "messiah" about whom, they believed, these scriptures spoke. This in turn meant that the synagogue had to have been the context in which, of necessity, the words of Jesus as well as the narratives about Jesus lived in that oral period before gospels came to be written. The data to support these conclusions are to my mind now overwhelming.

When the written gospels first appeared, Jesus had already been integrated into and wrapped inside the Hebrew scriptures. Indeed these scriptures had been applied to him over and over again. All of these things could not have happened anywhere else except in the synagogue. Books in that day had to be hand-copied, so they were prohibitively expensive. Few individuals actually owned books. They tended to be instead community property. There was no Gideon Society to place a copy of the scriptures into one's hotel or motel room. The only place, therefore, where people could hear the Hebrew scriptures read and the only place where people could listen as these scriptures were expounded was in the synagogue. The only place where they could hear or study the Torah was in the synagogue. The gospels had to be products of the synagogue, written by Jewish people who lived their lives inside the rhythm of synagogue worship. They were written from a Jewish perspective inside a Jewish worldview and based on sacred writings with which only a Jew would be conversant. Why anyone ever proposed a different starting place is the question we need to ask. The gospels of Mark, Matthew, Luke, and even John* were, therefore, liturgical documents, born in

---

*John is, however, quite different based as it appears to be on a three-year liturgical cycle not a one-year cycle. I developed this theme in my book *The Fourth Gospel: Tales of a Jewish Mystic*. See Bibliography for details.

the synagogue and designed to be read there along with the Hebrew scriptures. These gospels reflected the liturgical year of the synagogue, and that fact is crucial to their understanding.

If, as I shall argue in this book, Matthew's gospel was written to provide Jesus stories for the Sabbaths and holy days of the Jewish year, how would we ever understand that without an awareness of the basic shape and structure of the Jewish liturgical year? Yet how many Christians know much of anything about the liturgical year of the Jews? We might know something about the season of Passover. After all, grocery stores advertise Lenten diets and Passover diets together. If we have Jewish friends we might know the words "Rosh Hashanah" and "Yom Kippur," but few would know what these days mean to the Jews or how these days were and are observed in Jewish practice. Beyond that, show me the Christian who knows the meaning of Shavuot, Sukkoth or Dedication. Given this ignorance, what would it mean for us to say that the gospels are liturgical books formed in the synagogue? Most Christians are not knowledgeable about things Jewish. Some, indeed more than will admit it, are actually prejudiced, sometimes not even consciously, against all things Jewish. Yet until we see the gospels as Jewish books based on a knowledge of the Jewish scriptures and the patterns of worship well known in Jewish liturgical circles, I submit we will never find the key that will unlock the treasures that the gospels contain.

In this chapter, therefore, as I continue to provide the groundwork for this book's thesis, I want to outline briefly, but in order, the major holy days in the Jewish liturgical calendar. I hope my readers will keep both the order and the content of these days in mind, for in so doing, I believe, they will discover the key to the pattern developed in each of the synoptic gospels.

The first great observance in the Jewish liturgical year that I am following is Passover, which celebrates the beginning of the Jewish nation, the moment when the Jews came out of Egypt and began to fulfill their national destiny. We will see, as this book develops, how early Christians correlated the crucifixion of Jesus with the killing of the paschal lamb. This had the effect of linking the final, climactic moment of the Christian story with the first great celebration of the Jewish liturgical year. So the end of the Christian story was told against the background of the first festival of the Jewish liturgical year. This dislocating fact has for centuries both confused and hidden from Christian eyes just how closely the gospels follow the synagogue's liturgical pattern. Once we adjust to that difficulty, however, the Jewish year flows with integrity and intensity, and the Jesus story tracks that year magnificently. I will return to this time of difficulty again. I hope you will recognize it when I do.

The second great celebration of this Jewish year comes fifty days after Passover and for that reason is called Pentecost, since *pente* means "fifty." The celebration has other names, however. It is often called Weeks because it comes seven weeks and one day after Passover. Its Jewish name is Shavuot, which is Hebrew for the word "weeks." This was the time when the Jews recalled Moses receiving the Torah from God on Mt. Sinai. It was normally observed as a twenty-four-hour vigil and it comes in the Gregorian calendar somewhere near the end of May or the first part of June.

The third great Jewish liturgical celebration, which does not come until late September or early October, is the one I have previously mentioned called Rosh Hashanah, or the Jewish New Year. On this day, liturgically, the Jewish people thought about the end of history and prayed for the coming of the messiah to inaugurate the kingdom of God on earth. It was fixed by the Torah on the first day of the seventh month of the Jewish year. It was, in fact, the first of three great Jewish observances that were and still are closely related and that are celebrated in quick succession during that same month. Ten days after Rosh Hashanah, and thus on Tishri 10, comes Yom Kippur, the Day of Atonement. Far more than most of us realize, Christianity's doctrine of atonement was shaped by this day. More accurately, as I will argue later in this book, the Christian conception of atonement was shaped, not so much by Yom Kippur itself, as by Gentile ignorance of the Jewish meaning of this day. Rosh Hashanah and Yom Kippur combined to form what the Jews called the High Holy Days.

The third Tishri festival, the fifth of the major Jewish celebrations, occurred on the eight days between Tishri 15 and 22. Called Sukkoth, it was the harvest festival of the Jewish year, a kind of Jewish Thanksgiving Day celebration. Although now overshadowed by other celebrations Sukkoth was at the time of Jesus probably the most anticipated and the most enjoyed holy day of the Jewish year.

In the Jewish month of Kislev, which corresponds roughly with our month of December, and thus comes in the darkness of winter, the Jews observe a later-developed festival that they call Dedication. You may be more familiar with the name Hanukkah, which is nothing but the Jewish word for "dedication." It was and is a "festival of light" telling the story of how the light of "true worship" was restored to the Temple. Like Sukkoth, Dedication-Hanukkah was an eight-day celebration. It originated in the second century BCE, rising out of that period of history known as the time of the Maccabees.

About three months then pass until the Jews were back to the first month of their year in the calendar we are following, Nisan, and with this their liturgical journey started all over again. Then Passover returned and the cycle was repeated. The liturgical year for first-century Jews thus flowed with an annual rhythm that should not surprise Christians, for the liturgical year of the church, with its seasons of Advent, Christmas, Epiphany, Lent, Easter and Pentecost, does exactly the same thing.

There were two other minor observances in the liturgical year of the synagogue that deserve a brief mention. The first is the 9th of Ab, which comes in the late summer and which marked the fall of Jerusalem and the Temple to the Babylonians in the sixth century BCE. The little book of Lamentations was written to be used liturgically on that day. The other was the feast of Purim, a feast that was observed in the month of Adar (February/March in the Gregorian calendar). Purim celebrated the deliverance of the Jews from the threat of genocide at the hands of the Persians in the fifth century BCE. The biblical book of Esther was written to be used on that day. Please note that the Jews saw their scriptures as something being regularly created. These texts did not come as the revelations of God, but rather out of the history of the Jewish people, and they were always born in the service of liturgy.

These, then, are the major days that formed the outline of the liturgical year of the synagogue that I will be following. We will return to them many times in the course of this book. I will argue that the gospel of Matthew has organized its Jesus material around this liturgical year of the synagogue. It is a simple suggestion and an easily identified possibility. It is, however, revolutionary in its ability to open our gospels to new meaning.

This was Michael Goulder's great insight. Now it is also mine. I hope that by the end of this book it will also be yours.

One final introductory thing needs to be done before we delve into Matthew. We need to see Matthew's dependency on Mark and how the liturgical connections between the memory of Jesus and the liturgical practice of the synagogue came to be tied together. To that story we now turn, and with it we will end this introductory section.

CHAPTER 5

Matthew's Dependency on Mark

E ACH OF THE THREE SYNOPTIC GOSPELS begins with references to the Hebrew scriptures. Mark says that the gospel
of Jesus starts in the prophets Isaiah and Malachi. Matthew opens with a genealogy of Jesus' ancestors beginning
with Abraham, which he has derived substantially from I Chronicles 1–9. Luke opens with the story of the birth of John the Baptist,
which is based very clearly on the account in the book of Genesis
of the birth of Isaac (Gen. 18:9–15). That is but the beginning of
what will be a gospel pattern. The story of Jesus is grounded in
and shaped by the Hebrew scriptures.

We will follow Matthew's story line in this book, but that
moves us into following Mark's story line as well, since Mark
was the first of the three synoptic gospels to be written. Matthew and Luke both first leaned heavily on Mark and then both
expanded Mark. Matthew incorporated about ninety percent of

Mark directly into his gospel. Luke was a little less dependent, but he still copied about fifty percent of Mark. Both Matthew and Luke are also about forty percent larger than Mark, and the additions to Mark from both are primarily in the beginning of each of their gospels. Matthew was more traditionally Jewish than Mark and his changes were normally to cover things of great importance to the people in Matthew's synagogue, which many, but not all, believe to have been located in Antioch.

Luke was written, perhaps in Caesarea, for a less traditionally Jewish worshipping community. Luke's congregation was more cosmopolitan and tended to be made up of diaspora Jews—that is, Jews far removed from Jerusalem both physically and emotionally. More and more they were mingling with Gentile proselytes. Where Matthew would emphasize Jewish celebrations that were twenty-four-hour vigils or eight-day observances, Luke would tend to collapse those time periods into a theme for a single day. His community appears to have moved beyond many of the cultic practices of the Jewish people, which were still important to Matthew.

All of the synoptic gospels connected the crucifixion of Jesus with the Passover tradition of the Jews. As we shall see as our story unfolds, this connection appears to be a liturgical connection more than a historical connection. That idea usually startles people, for to separate the crucifixion from the season of Passover is almost unheard of for them. The gospels themselves portray Jesus as journeying up to Jerusalem at the time of the crucifixion for the purpose of observing Passover there. That connection is deeply embedded in the minds of believers. Liturgy has reinforced that connection for twenty-one centuries. There are, however, hints in the gospel that this connection is not a matter of history, and we shall look at those later.

Once Passover and the crucifixion are firmly tied together liturgically in our minds, we can roll the earliest gospel, Mark, backward over the rest of the liturgical year of the Jews. As we do so, two things quickly become obvious. First, there is an appropriate Jesus story (the transfiguration) in exactly the place where the observance of Dedication-Hanukkah comes in the Jewish liturgical year. Second, there is an appropriate Jesus story first for the harvest season of Sukkoth (Mark 4), then for Yom Kippur (Mark 1:40–2:12) and, finally, for Rosh Hashanah (Mark 1:1–13). John the Baptist appears to speak the Rosh Hashanah message that the kingdom of God is at hand and to call the people to repentance. So the first gospel reveals a liturgical order for telling the story of Jesus, but it runs only from Rosh Hashanah to Passover.

This fact also suggests why it was that both Matthew and Luke felt the need to expand Mark. Mark had provided Jesus stories for only six and a half months of the year. The growing communities of Christians wanted to have Jesus stories for the whole twelve months. That is also why both Matthew and Luke appear to front-end load Mark. They wanted to cover the time that Mark had omitted, namely the time of the Jewish year that came after Passover, but before Rosh Hashanah. The differences between Matthew and Luke can be explained in that Matthew was writing for a more traditional Jewish congregation and Luke for a more dispersed and increasingly Gentile-oriented congregation.

Before we can fully enter into a study of Matthew, we need, therefore, to embrace the reality of the primacy of Mark in Matthew's text and the fact that Mark is the gospel writer who first used the liturgical year of the Jews as his organizing guide when relating the story of Jesus. All of this, I submit, serves to reflect that period of history when the story of Jesus was repeated orally in the life of the synagogue.

Jesus was "preached" in the synagogues long before people thought about organizing the details of his life in some biographical pattern. This pattern would also mean that rather than being told in a chronological narrative, the Jesus story was related to the Jewish scripture and unfurled against the liturgical year of the synagogue. It also reflected the tradition of Jewish storytelling. That is why it becomes so obvious that, as long as the Christian community was made up primarily of Jewish followers of Jesus, they would understand how to read their gospels, but when the Christian community ceased to be Jewish, that understanding would be lost.

In this book I will try to recapture the Jewish meaning of the gospels. Linking the Jewish liturgy and the Jesus story was the insight that made it possible for me to escape the cruel and meaningless literalism inside which the words of the Bible had been captured in Christian practice. That literalism cannot be sustained in our century. Can we lift the burden of literalism from the way we read the Bible? Is there anything of substance left when we do? I think we can and I think there is. I also am convinced that we must. So I invite you to read on.

PART II

From After Passover to Shavuot: Birth to Early Ministry

CHAPTER 6

Genealogy and Birth

MATTHEW'S GOSPEL HAD A DOUBLE CLIMAX. The first climax was the crucifixion of Jesus, which he related to the Passover celebration (Matt. 26:20–27:66). The second climax was his Easter narrative, in which two appearance stories were recounted, one at the tomb in Jerusalem that focused on the women (Matt. 28:1–15), and the other on a mountaintop in Galilee that focused on the disciples (Matt. 28:16–20). Matthew related these two Easter stories to the two Sabbaths after Passover. Since Passover came after the second Sabbath of Nisan, this meant that Matthew's two Easter stories were attached to the third and fourth Sabbaths of Nisan. I will treat the crucifixion and Easter stories in great detail in their proper places at the conclusion of Jesus' life. I want to mention them here at the beginning only to help us be clear on how the Jesus story, as Matthew would tell it, related to the liturgical calendar of the synagogue.

For Jewish worshippers Adar, the last month of the Jewish year in the pattern that we are following, flowed rather quietly into Nisan, the first month of the new year. The first two Sabbaths of Nisan served to set the stage for Passover, the celebration of the birth of the Hebrew nation, which began at sundown and continued until the evening of the fifteenth day of Nisan.

From Passover to the next great Jewish celebration, Shavuot, as noted earlier, there were fifty days or seven weeks and thus seven Sabbaths, plus a day. Matthew would use the first two of these Sabbaths to tell his story of Easter, and thus to conclude the story of Jesus' life. He would then take the next five Sabbaths in which to introduce Jesus before he composed his account of the Shavuot celebration. Shavuot, you will recall, was the time when the Jews remembered the moment in their history when God delivered the Torah, the law, to Moses on Mt. Sinai.

On those five Sabbaths available to him before the onset of Shavuot, Matthew relates five Jesus stories that lay the groundwork for his entire gospel. They are:

1. The genealogy and the birth of Jesus (Matt. 1:1–25)
2. The wise men and Herod (Matt. 2:1–23)
3. John the Baptist and the baptism of Jesus (Matt. 3:1–23)
4. The story of the temptation (Matt. 4:1–11)
5. The beginning of Jesus' public ministry (Matt. 4:11–25)

We turn now to examine the first of these five introductory Jesus stories. It is the dramatic narrative of Jesus' birth to a virgin named Mary.

As noted earlier, Matthew is the first Christian writer who suggests that Jesus had a miraculous or virgin birth. There is no hint of such an idea in any earlier texts. Paul, who wrote between the years 51–64, records nothing that might suggest a miraculous birth for Jesus. All that he says about Jesus' origins is found in two places, neither of which suggests anything that might be called supernatural. The first is a single verse in Galatians; the second is a single verse in Romans. In Galatians, Paul says that Jesus was "born of a woman" like everyone else and was born "under the law" like every other Jew (Gal. 4:4). In Romans, Paul writes that Jesus was "descended from the house of David, according to the flesh" (Romans 1:3). Even the word for "woman" in the Galatians text (*gunaikos,* from which we get the word "gynecology") has within it no hint of virginity. I think it is fair to say that either Paul had never heard of the miraculous birth tradition, or he dismissed it as a tradition unworthy of passing on. That the story of Jesus' miraculous birth simply had not yet developed appears to me to be the most likely explanation.

When we look at Mark, the first gospel, this conclusion is strengthened. First, Mark's gospel also contains no story of a miraculous virgin birth. When Jesus makes his first appearance in the pages of Mark he is a fully human, adult male who comes to be baptized. It was for Mark in his baptism, not in his conception, that Jesus became infused with the Holy Spirit and was declared by a heavenly voice to be God's "son" (Mark 1:1–11). Second, Mark relates a story just a little later (Mark 3:20–31) which seems to indicate that no story of a miraculous birth was known to this author, once again suggesting that this tradition had not yet been created. In this story the behavior of Jesus' mother is quite revealing. She is embarrassed by Jesus' public actions and by the enmity that he is engendering. So together with Jesus' brothers, who are named in Mark as James, Joseph, Judas, and Simon (Mark 6:3), Jesus' mother moves to take him out of the public arena. They are concerned that he is "beside himself." That was a Jewish way of saying that they thought he was "out of his mind," or mentally disturbed. Such an attitude would hardly be what one would expect from a woman who, as later sources would suggest, had been told that she would be the "virgin mother" of the "son of God." An experience like that at conception would not normally lead a mother to think that her special child, when grown, would be mentally deranged! The conclusion once again is clear: The tradition of Jesus having had a miraculous or virgin birth was simply unknown prior to Matthew's decision to include it in his gospel in the middle years of the ninth decade. Indeed, the virgin birth of Jesus appears to be a creation of the author of the gospel of Matthew.

Now, having entertained that possibility, we are driven to ask what might have motivated Matthew to develop this story. The idea of a virgin birth was simply unknown in the Jewish scriptures. Supernatural births were noted, but they were normally found there in only two varieties. First, there were post-menopausal conceptions, such as is found in the story of Abraham and Sarah, both of whom were beyond ninety years of age and childless until angelic visitors informed the unbelieving couple on their way to Sodom and Gomorrah that Sarah would bear a child to be named Isaac (Gen. 18:9–15). The second kind of special birth in the Hebrew scriptures was that of "barrenness" being overcome in order for a pregnancy to occur. That is what happened in the story of Hannah, who gave birth to Samuel (I Sam. 1:1–20), and in the case of the nameless wife of Manoah, who gave birth to Samson (Judg. 13:1–22). In a world where the intricacies of reproduction were clearly not part of human knowledge and in which patriarchy reigned supreme, the inability to conceive was assumed to be the woman's fault. God had closed up the woman's womb—that was the way infertility was understood (I Sam. 1:5). No one at this time knew anything of low sperm count in the male. So the power of God to overcome the natural boundaries of either menopause or the inability to conceive was the only way the Hebrew scriptures had ever explained the birth of a special life.

The idea of a virgin birth was a distinctly Greek or Mediterranean concept, widely known and claimed for heroic figures in that part of the ancient world.*

Matthew, the most Jewish of the gospel writers, nonetheless opted for this Mediterranean myth rather than either of the Hebrew possibilities. He sought, however, to ground this idea in the Hebrew scriptures by basing his birth story on a weak and obscure text from Isaiah.

What drove Matthew to do this? To what pressure was he responding? What charges against the Christian movement forced him to rise to Jesus' defense? The answer to these questions is found, I believe, in other parts of the New Testament, which appear to be defending Jesus against the charges of being base-born—that is, of being illegitimate. Matthew himself alluded to this charge in his portrayal of Joseph, who upon discovering Mary's pregnancy, believed her to have violated her pledge to him in the betrothal and so he decided to "put her away"—that is, to return her to her father's house as "damaged goods." Only then, according to the story, did Joseph receive the message from God that he could take Mary as his wife, for the child in her womb was holy; this child was "of God" and not from an act of unfaithfulness. The image of conception in Matthew's mind was that of the Holy Spirit hovering over the womb

---

*Candidates for the concept of virgin birth ranged from mythology (Romulus and Remus) to history (Alexander the Great).

of Mary in order to bring forth in her a new creation, just as in the Jewish story of creation the Holy Spirit had hovered over the chaos to bring forth life in the first creation (Gen. 1:1–3).

Matthew is, however, not the only gospel writer to hint that illegitimacy was being charged against Jesus. In Mark, after Jesus had taught in the synagogue in Nazareth, the amazed crowd of locals was publicly wondering from whence had come the wisdom he displayed. The words Mark attributes to a voice in the crowd are these: "Is not this the carpenter, the son of Mary?" (Mark 6:3). Please note that in this text Jesus is "the carpenter." A father named Joseph, who might be the carpenter, had not yet been mentioned in any Christian source. The words "the son of Mary" are, however, the crucial words for us to notice. In Jewish society, to refer to a grown man as the son of a woman was to cast public aspersions on the legitimacy of his birth. A final reference to this same idea is found in the Fourth Gospel, admittedly written after Matthew, but it nonetheless reveals that this debate about Jesus' paternity was still abroad. Once again this charge came from an anonymous voice in the crowd. A discussion about Jesus' origins is being held, when this voice says to Jesus: "We were not born of fornication!" (John 8:41). The clear implication is that the one speaking believes Jesus was a creation of fornication, so whispers about the legitimacy of Jesus' life and the source of his paternity were obviously part of the debate in early Christianity.

Against these spoken and unspoken charges Matthew felt a need to rise to Jesus' defense. That is what appears to be the background to the first biblical narrative that attributes a miraculous or supernatural birth to Jesus. We next have to look at the way Matthew addresses this subject. It was, to say the least, a strange, multi-level defense.

First, Matthew has an angel say, in a dream to Joseph, that this child is indeed holy, the offspring of the Holy Spirit. Second, Matthew adds that his birth is actually the fulfillment of the scriptures. It is in this second task that his reasoning process appears to be weak indeed, requiring a third strange assertion. We trace that process.

First of all, the text that Matthew chooses in order to show that this birth is in fact the "fulfillment" of the prophets is misquoted. Was this deliberate or accidental? Matthew appears to be a learned scribe. That makes an accidental misquoting of the text improbable. Matthew, nonetheless, claims that the text reads: "Behold, a virgin will conceive." There are two things wrong with Matthew's rendition. First, the word "virgin" is not in the Isaiah text (Isa. 7:14). The Hebrew word Isaiah uses that Matthew has translated "virgin" is *almah*, which means simply "woman." There is no connotation of virginity in this word at all. Isaiah does not use the word *bethulah*, which is the Hebrew word for "virgin."

Second, the tense in Isaiah's text is a present tense, not a future tense. Isaiah does not say "will conceive"; he says, rather, "is with child." So in this text Isaiah is saying "a woman is with child," which has a distinctly different meaning from the words "a virgin will conceive."

Once we begin to examine that text in any depth, including its context, still other problems emerge which render it not competent to do what Matthew is asking it to do. When Isaiah was writing this passage, the historical situation in Judah was this. The city of Jerusalem was under siege from the armies of the kings of both Syria and the Northern Kingdom of Israel. Those kings with their armies had surrounded Jerusalem and were demanding the surrender of Judah. Ahaz, the king of Judah, reigning in Jerusalem, was out in the midst of that siege, inspecting the battlements in his city's walls. He was obviously quaking in his boots at the possibility of being conquered by these invaders, who were intent upon deposing him from his throne. On this inspection trip, he is confronted by the prophet Isaiah, who informs him that Jerusalem will not fall to his enemies. Ahaz is unconvinced. Isaiah says to the king: "Ask a sign of the Lord your God; whether it be as deep as Sheol or as high as heaven" (Isa. 7:11). A sign from God is meant to convince King Ahaz. Ahaz, however, refuses to ask for a divine sign. Isaiah then says that God will give him a sign whether he wants it or not. "Behold, a woman is with child" (Isa. 7:14), he says. A footnote in the Revised Standard Version of the Bible informs the reader that this is the proper translation, though the RSV makes it appear to be a future event by translating the verb as "will conceive" instead of "is with." Given that the pregnancy of this woman was to be the sign that Jerusalem would not fall, it would make no sense for this sign to be about a birth some eight hundred years in the future. The verse probably refers to the wife of Ahaz, who was about to give birth to Hezekiah, the heir to the throne. That son's birth would thus be a sign of the continuity of the kingdom. This would be somewhat like the chant in the Middle Ages announcing the death of a monarch: "The king is dead, long live the king." The nation endures in the continuity of its royal family. Isaiah goes on to say that before this soon-to-be-born child knows how to distinguish right from wrong, the two attacking kings, Pekah of Syria and Resin of Israel, will be long gone (Isa. 7:16). At what age does a child discern the difference between right and wrong? Many child psychiatrists place that at before age two. Whatever the actual timing might be, surely Isaiah was not referring to a messianic child who would be born centuries later in Jewish history. It is a weak argument that Matthew is developing, and he must know that he is placing the burden of proof on a text that cannot support his thesis. He decides, therefore, to buttress his argument with yet another line of defense. We watch the wheels in his mind turning.

Matthew decides to introduce the story of Jesus' virgin birth with a seventeen-verse genealogy, designed to trace Jesus' tribal origins and to lay out the background for Jesus' messianic credentials. To do so, he goes all the way back to Abraham, the presumed father of the Jewish nation. Abraham, if he was a person of history at all and not part of tribal mythology, would have lived, according to our best estimates, some 1,850 years before the Common Era. Was this ancestry chart then ever meant to have been understood as an accurate genealogical record? Of course not! No records existed that were capable of tracing the lineage of Jesus or anyone else through some 1,850 years from Abraham to David to the exile to Jesus. To put it in another perspective, that would be like one of us living in the twenty-first century claiming the ability to trace our lineage through a single line back in time to the year 250 CE, an unimaginable task even with modern records. Why then does Matthew open his virgin birth story with this genealogy? His agenda, I believe, is revealed in the fact that he places four women into this genealogy. This was unheard of in that patriarchal world, when people did not know that a woman had an egg cell and thus a genetic role in reproduction. Women in that era were thought of as serving the reproductive process only by being "incubators" for the male seed. So the inclusion of women in this genealogy was both startling and unprecedented.

The next thing we notice about these four women is that they are all clearly known in the Hebrew scriptures. The Jews would have read or heard their stories when these narratives came up in the regular synagogue readings. These were not anonymous women.

Finally, when today one reads or hears their stories from the Bible itself, two other things pop out. First, all of them are Gentiles, not Jews. Second, all of them are, by the standards of that day, sexually compromised women. We need to listen briefly to their stories in order to grasp the narrative power that their names contain.

The first of these women is Tamar, the daughter-in-law of Judah, one of the twelve sons of Jacob. Judah's descendants would form the tribe of Judah and produce the royal house of King David. Tamar's story can be found in the Torah in Genesis 38. Tamar is a Canaanite woman who marries Judah's son Er. When Er dies suddenly, Tamar, according to the law of the Jews, has to marry Er's brother Onan. Onan, however, refuses to impregnate her and thus also to raise up children to Er. Next, however, Onan also dies suddenly.* The only other son in Judah's family, and thus the one who must now marry his brother's widow, is Shelah, who is but a child, perhaps only about five years of age. He has no desire to take on his two brothers' widow. So Judah sends Tamar back to her father's house with the promise that he will send for her when Shelah comes of age, a promise that is quickly forgotten. The years pass, bringing with them more inevitable life changes, among which are that Shelah grows up and that Judah's wife dies, making him a widower. This news traveled, as news always does—in this case, to the village of Emaim, where Tamar is living in shame in her father's house.

---

*The text actually says God killed him. See Genesis 38:8.

Next the news gets around that Judah is going to shear his flocks, which are grazing in Timman just beyond the village where Tamar is living. One cannot get to those grazing lands without going past the gate of Tamar's village, so this clever woman develops an audacious plan. She removes the clothes that mark her as a widow and puts on clothes that proclaim her to be a prostitute, including a veil covering her face, and then she takes up a position, sitting by the gate of her village, as if to solicit business.

When Judah comes by, he sees this prostitute and decides to avail himself of her services. They negotiate and arrive at a mutually acceptable price, a lamb from Judah's flock. He agrees to have this lamb delivered by one of his servants the next day. Tamar, still unrecognized by her father-in-law, demands some insurance, something valuable left with her to guarantee the future delivery of the lamb. These items are to be returned when the debt is paid. They agree that the guarantee shall be Judah's rope, his staff and his signet ring. The bargain is thus struck, and Judah and Tamar go off for their tryst.

The next day Judah, true to his word, sends a servant to Tamar's village with a lamb on his shoulders to be delivered to the woman. He does not find her in what he had assumed was her regular position by the gate. He inquires about the prostitute who solicited business at the village gate and is told that there is no such person. He conducts some further inquiries but gains no clues as to her identity, her whereabouts or even her existence. So the servant returns with the lamb still in tow. Judah, not wanting to be embarrassed, decides to charge his now-lost possessions off to "business expenses" and does not pursue the matter further.

Several months later, the rumor comes to Judah's ears that his son's widow, Tamar, is expecting a child. Confident that she has become a harlot and that this child is the fruit of some adulterous relationship, Judah demands that his family's honor be restored by having Tamar put to death, the normal punishment for adultery. She is to be burned at the stake. As Tamar is brought forth, however, to be put to the flames, she brings the rope, the staff and the signet ring with her. She lays them rather dramatically before Judah and says: "I am pregnant by the owner of these possessions" (Gen. 38:25). Judah recognizes them as his own, recalls that he has not offered her to his now-grown son Shelah, and repents. He not only declares Tamar to be more righteous than himself, but he also takes Tamar into his harem as one of his wives, becoming her protector. In time, she bears twin boys and names them Perez and Zerah. It is through Perez, Matthew says, that the line that produced Jesus of Nazareth traveled. What is Matthew saying? Tamar's pregnancy by her father-in-law, Judah, was, by the standards of his day, an act of incest. Yet Matthew in this genealogy says that the line that produced Jesus flowed through the incest of Tamar! Certainly, that is a strange note to place into a genealogy and a strange note on which to introduce the story of Jesus' miraculous birth.

The second woman in Matthew's genealogy continues this strangeness. Her name is Rahab. Her story is told in the book of Joshua, chapters 2 and 6. A citizen of the Canaanite city of Jericho, she is known as "Rahab the prostitute." She appears to operate a "house of pleasure" that is literally built into the wall around the city of Jericho. Indeed, a window in Rahab's house is a window in the protective wall around Jericho. Joshua sends spies into Jericho to search out the land before he begins his campaign to conquer it. The spies go directly to the house of Rahab. When the word gets around that spies are in the city, a search for them begins. Rahab protects these spies by hiding them under some stalks of flax on her rooftop, telling their pursuers that the men had been there, but that they had departed before the city's gates were closed at dusk on that day. These spies might be caught, she adds, if the authorities pursue them. They leave immediately to do so.

Then Rahab strikes a deal with the spies in exchange for her protection. She will help them escape that day, but if Joshua's army invades Jericho, Rahab will gather all of her family into her home. The house will be identified by a red cord hanging in the window. All those who are found in that house will be spared. The deal is agreed to, and then Rahab, under cover of darkness, lets the spies down in a basket from her window in the wall and they return to the army of Joshua.

When in time Jericho does fall to Joshua's army, Rahab and all her relatives are spared. Rahab appears to have married a man named Salmon. Was he one of the spies? We do not know, but the marriage issues in a son named Boaz. Again we ask: What is Matthew trying to communicate when he says that the line that produced Jesus of Nazareth traveled through the incest of Tamar and then through the prostitution of Rahab?

The strangeness of the women in the genealogy continues with woman number three. She is a Moabite named Ruth, and her story is told in the book of Ruth. A Jewish couple, Naomi and Elimelech, with their sons Mahlon and Chilion, move to Moab in search of work during a downtime in the Hebrew economy. While there the two boys marry Moabite women, Ruth and Orpah. Then tragedy strikes and the three Jewish males in the family, Elimelech, Mahlon, and Chilion, all die, leaving a non-viable family of a Jewish mother-in-law and her two Moabite daughters-in-law. Naomi recognizes the hopelessness of their situation and urges her daughters-in-law to return to their families to live under the protection of their fathers. Her own plan of survival would then be to return to Judah and live among her own relatives or her deceased husband's relatives. One daughter-in-law, Orpah, agrees, but Ruth refuses and in moving words, frequently used today in weddings, she says to Naomi: "Entreat me not to leave you, or to return from following after you. For where you go I will go, and where you lodge I will lodge; your people will be my people and your God, my God. Where you die I will die, and there will I be buried" (Ruth 1:16–17).*

So the two single and vulnerable women return to the land of Judah and find a shack in which to live. It is near the fields owned by a man named Boaz, the son of Rahab, whom Naomi knows is distantly related to her deceased husband. Jewish law required that the landowners had to leave some part of the crop in the fields to be "gleaned" by the poor. Each day Ruth goes into Boaz' fields and gathers enough grain to bake a small loaf of bread that will keep the two of them alive for another day. So faithful is Ruth in caring for her mother-in-law that she comes to the attention of Boaz, who then instructs his workers not only to leave some grain on the land for Ruth to gather, but also to provide her with water and not to molest her. Naomi is told of these things, and she realizes that her plan is working.

At the end of the harvest season, a celebration is planned. Naomi instructs Ruth that she must go to the celebration, where wine is sure to flow, and to flow freely. Ruth is also instructed by Naomi to bathe in the river, to put on her best dress and to wear whatever perfume she can find. An act of seduction is clearly being

---

*One wonders if this would still be used at a wedding if the couple recognized that Ruth was saying these words to her mother-in-law!

planned. Ruth is told to wait for the proper moment at the celebration to act, a moment that is sure to come. By midnight Boaz has drunk so much wine that he lies down on the floor and is soon fast asleep. This is the moment! Ruth gets a pillow to put under his head and a blanket to spread over his sleeping body. Then with all things in readiness, she climbs under his blanket with him.

When Boaz wakes the next morning, he finds this woman sleeping beside him. "Who are you?" he asks. "Marry me," she responds, "for you are next of kin." Boaz is not convinced. Surely there must be a relative of closer kin than he, he suggests. If he were to marry her, he would get all of her assets and her liabilities, which included the care of Naomi. He locates a person who is closer in kinship than he, but this person declines the honor. So Boaz, seduced by Ruth, then does the honorable thing. He marries her and they produce a son whose name is Obed. Matthew's genealogy is proclaiming that the line that produced Jesus has flowed through the incest of Tamar, the prostitution of Rahab and the seduction of Ruth! What is Matthew seeking to communicate?

The fourth woman continues to build the strangeness of whatever Matthew's agenda was. She is not named in the genealogy, being referred to only as "the wife of Uriah the Hittite," but we all know that her name was Bathsheba, a name that means "daughter of Sheba," a nation in the southeast part of Arabia. Her story is told in II Samuel, chapter 11.

David's army had gone to war against the Ammonites under the command of his captain, a man named Joab. David, for some reason, was not in the field of battle. One afternoon he walked out onto his rooftop, which, because of the size of David's home, was higher than any other rooftop in Jerusalem. Below him, in what she thought was the privacy of her own rooftop, was an exquisitely beautiful woman taking a bath. David, smitten by this woman's charms, sent a message to her inviting her to come to the palace to have a tryst with the king. Bathsheba came. Whether she was free *not* to come is the real question, but she came. They had a lover's moment together and when it was over she returned to her house. Perhaps for King David this was neither the first nor the last of a series of similar encounters, so Bathsheba quickly faded from his mind. Then one day, David received a written message marked "for the king's eyes only." This message informed the king that Bathsheba was expecting David's child.

David squirmed at first, suggesting that surely since she was married, it might be her husband's child. Bathsheba replied that her husband was in King David's army and that he had not been home for months. There was no way this baby was not fathered by the king, she said. David then decided to grant Uriah, her husband, a furlough, so that "he might bring King David a firsthand report on how the battle was going," expecting him while on leave to stay in his own home and make love to his wife. Then they could claim that "the baby just came early." Uriah, however, who appears to have been a very gung-ho soldier, thought it inappropriate to enjoy his home and his marriage bed while his comrades were fighting, bleeding and dying on the battlefield. So he ostentatiously set up a tent in the street outside his home and slept there each night.

Frustrated in his attempts to create a cover-up, King David then sent orders to Captain Joab by the hand of Uriah, to mount a flying wedge attack against the Ammonite city of Rabbah and to put Uriah at the point of the wedge. The plan worked, and Uriah was killed. Joab then sent a message to the king that his "problem was solved." The child of this adulterous relationship died, but David nonetheless took Bathsheba into his harem as his wife and in time a second child was born of this union. His name was Solomon. Matthew's point was now complete. The line that produced Jesus of Nazareth flowed through the incest of Tamar, the prostitution of Rahab, the seduction of Ruth and the adultery of Bathsheba! That is the way that this gospel writer decided to introduce his story of the miraculous or virgin birth of Jesus. We can certainly speculate on why he adopted this method of telling his story, but to me it seems clear and its message is profound.

Matthew had experienced a "God presence" in Jesus of Nazareth. He was convinced that Jesus' origins were of God and were therefore holy. He knew, as a scribe, that the text he used from Isaiah, and on the basis of which he had asserted the holiness of Jesus, was a weak one that really did not support his contention. So he introduced in this very creative way the story of Jesus' virgin birth, a narrative which he knew had nothing to do with biology. He prefaced it with a genealogical chart of Jesus' ancestors. He obviously also knew that this genealogy was not literal history. When the two are put together, however, Matthew's message becomes obvious. We have experienced the presence of God in the life of Jesus, he was asserting. We believe that Jesus is from God, that God is in some sense the source, the father of his life. Even if that argument is not sustainable in any literal way, Matthew was saying, it makes no difference, because God can bring holiness out of any human symbol of brokenness, inadequacy, or even evil. God can bring holiness out of incest, prostitution, seduction, and adultery. So let the enemies of the Jesus movement rail! Let them try to assassinate Jesus' character by suggesting that he was base-born—we know better. We know God was in Christ and we know that God can work through any set of human circumstances to bring holiness out of life.

It was a profound message, a true message, but obviously not a message that was meant to be literalized. Matthew, the author of this gospel, surely knew this. The largely Jewish audience for which the gospel of Matthew was originally written also knew this. They were familiar with the narratives in the Bible about each of these so-called shady ladies of Matthew's genealogy. It would not have occurred to his readers to think that either the genealogy or the story of the virgin birth was literal history.

As long as the Christian movement was made up primarily of Jews, the implicit, non-literal meaning of Matthew's birth narrative was clear. By the year 150 of the Common Era, however, there were few Jews left in the Christian movement, which had become an almost completely Gentile church. These Gentile Christians had neither a knowledge of Jewish symbols nor a familiarity with the Jewish scriptures, so they assumed that these opening chapters reflected a literal account of how Jesus came to be born. From the year 150 on, literalism, a Gentile heresy, became established as the only proper way to read the gospels; from that point on, Christians read the gospel texts as if they were describing literal events that actually occurred in history. A revolution in biblical scholarship that started in the early 1800s began the slow but certain decline of this way of understanding the New Testament. In the late twentieth century some movements began to appear that were designed to bring Judaism and Christianity into a deeper relationship by recognizing their mutual interdependence.

When the Jewish background of the gospels began to be redis-covered, their original meaning gradually emerged into the clear sunlight and biblical literalism began to fade. We will see this theme of Jewishness in Matthew's text again and again. We will discover a Jewish way to read his stories. Illumined by Jewish eyes and Jewish understandings, these narratives are very different from what we have been taught for so long. In that difference lies my hope that these stories will begin to make new sense to the educated world of the twenty-first century, a sense to which contemporary people might be willing to listen once again. That, however, will never be the case so long as biblical literalism continues to be taken seriously by anyone.

CHAPTER 7

Joseph: Myth or History?

s soon as Matthew decided to present Jesus as the
product of a God-induced miraculous birth, he confronted the necessity of producing a character who will
play the culturally demanded role of his earthly father.
The role of the father in a patriarchal society was to protect the
child. A mother and child without a male protector were deeply
vulnerable. The father also served in this society to legitimize the
child by claiming him as his own, which was accomplished symbolically in the act of naming the child. These are the reasons that
Matthew moves immediately to introduce us to the man named
Joseph.

We begin by establishing a number of biblical facts about this
man—facts that, surprisingly, seem not to be generally known. First,
this Joseph receives absolutely no mention in any Christian writing before Matthew introduces him into the Christian story at the
same time that he introduces the account of Jesus' miraculous or

virgin birth. This means that there is no mention of this Joseph in the Christian tradition until the middle of the ninth decade, or some fifty-five years after the life of Jesus has come to an end. Prior to this first mention in Matthew the name Joseph, so far as we know, has never been uttered by anyone as the name of a member of the immediate family of Jesus. This fact alone raises questions about the historicity of Joseph. Second, Joseph disappears from the Christian story as soon as the birth narratives are complete. The earthly father of Jesus appears in no gospel story of the adult Jesus of Nazareth. Joseph, the father of Jesus, is thus a character found in the birth narratives of the gospels alone. There are three later references to him, one in Matthew (13:55) and two in John (1:45 and 6:42), but the figure himself never appears in any subsequent text once the birth narratives are complete. Throughout Christian history attempts have been made to explain this intriguing absence. The most popular of these theories is the suggestion that Joseph died while Jesus was but a child. That would certainly account for his sudden and complete disappearance from the text. This possibility has seemed credible to many because Joseph has typically been portrayed in Christian art as a man much older than Mary.

This concept of Joseph's advanced age is so assumed and undebated that it has to have had a specific point of origin. A search yields the following results. In the early to middle years of the second century (about 115 CE), an apocryphal gospel entitled the Proto-Evangelium of James, or the Proto-Gospel of James, appeared. This book purported to tell the story of the childhood of Mary and how she was prepared from her birth to be the bearer of the Christ child. Her vocation was to provide the womb, which was to give birth to the promised messiah. In this mythological story from this apocryphal gospel, Mary was raised from infancy by a group of holy women who assisted her in the fulfillment of her holy vocation. All went well until Mary entered puberty and the cultural necessity in Jewish society that every woman must come under the protection of a male had to be served. This protective male role was generally played by either a father or a husband. In Mary's case, a father was out: There was no reference to a father in the Mary tradition until much later in Christianity, when the prophetess Anna, mentioned in Luke's gospel (Luke 2:36), was said to be the mother of Mary, and the name Joachim was later adopted for her husband (thus Mary's father). Today both names stretch historical credibility significantly.

In any case, when the Proto-Gospel of James was written, a father figure who might have offered Mary male protection was simply not available. This meant that the holy women who were raising Mary had to seek a husband for her. He would, however, have to be a unique husband, for his role in this developing drama was determined to be that of protecting Mary's virginity so that she could fulfill her God-given vocation to be the virgin mother of the son of God. So these women decided to search for a husband for Mary only among elderly men, perhaps widowed men who had already raised their children. The prospective grooms also had to be too old to have any interest in sex. I don't know how old that is, but it's old! Through a series of wondrous signs, which included the sprouting of leaves and flowers from his staff, a man named Joseph was chosen to be the husband of Mary. This then is the historical origin of the idea that Joseph was a much older man. With this idea so well established in the tradition, it lent credibility to the suggestion that Joseph might have died when Jesus was still an infant or a very young child.*

---

*There is the story in Luke of Mary and Joseph taking the twelve-year-old Jesus up to Jerusalem. That story, however, appears to be based on Samuel being taken up to Shiloh and is generally dismissed as reflecting history. It is also technically part of Luke's birth narrative.

I would, however, like to suggest a different possibility, one that I feel is far more credible. I suggest that Joseph never lived, that there never was a man named Joseph who served as the earthly father of Jesus. Some people will surely gasp at this suggestion, but I urge those who might be tempted to do so to hold your minds open to this possibility while I develop this idea based on a Jewish understanding of Matthew's Joseph story.

I begin with a question. If Joseph is nothing more than a literary character, as I am proposing, are there any compelling Jewish reasons why Matthew might have wanted to name his literary creation Joseph? Well, yes there are, but only people with a deep understanding of Jewish history would be in a position to discover that symbolic connection. It would inevitably go up and over the minds of Gentiles, who were not familiar with the intricacies of Jewish history.

Those who were familiar with Jewish history, however, would know that the Hebrew nation had never been a fully united people. Evidence of a deep division was writ large in their history. This division became apparent after the death of King Solomon, when ten of the twelve tribes of Israel seceded from the tribe of Judah to form the Northern Kingdom, which then was called Israel. The seeds of this division had always been present, however, and its origins had been written into an ancient story in the book of Genesis (see Gen. 29). In that story the patriarch Jacob was said to have had two wives, who were also sisters. Both were the daughters of Laban, a nephew of Abraham. One of these two sisters was named Leah, and she was the mother of Judah. The other was named Rachel, and she was the mother of Joseph. The descendants of Judah grew to become the dominant tribe in the south, while the descendants of Joseph grew to become the dominant tribe of the north. There had always been a fierce rivalry between them.

The two competitive and divergent parts of this nation had been kept together during the reigns of Kings Saul, David and Solomon. When Solomon died, however, his son Rehoboam could not keep the kingdom united. There was first secession and then a civil war, and the northern tribes, dominated by the descendants of Joseph, successfully established their independence from the southern tribe of Judah, out of which came the royal family that produced both David and Solomon, and over which the house of David was to reign for about four hundred years, with Jerusalem as its capital. There were now two Hebrew nations, the Northern Kingdom, sometimes called Israel, and the Southern Kingdom, sometimes called Judah, and later Judea. The major patriarchs of the two Hebrew nations were thus Judah and Joseph.

With that history in mind, now look again at Matthew's genealogy and at his story of the birth of Jesus, into which he introduces the character named Joseph as the earthly father of Jesus. In the genealogy Matthew establishes the connection between Jesus and the tribe of Judah. Jesus is descended from the royal line of the house of David, who was Judah's king. Thus Jesus' Judean credentials have been established. One of the messiah's roles in Jewish mythology was to bring the children of Israel back together into a single nation. How better could Matthew symbolize that than to suggest that even though the messiah was a member of the tribe of Judah, he had been protected and legitimized by a man named Joseph; and thus the two Jewish patriarchs w e united in Jesus. In this manner, one of the messianic tasks had been symbolically accomplished in the birth narrative itself.

If my readers have journeyed with me this far, then we are ready to ask a second question. If Matthew created the character Joseph out of whole cloth, where did he get the details that he used to build Joseph's biography? To answer that question, we turn to the first two chapters in Matthew's gospel, for that is the primary place in the Bible where we are given any biographical data about this Joseph. There we learn three things: First, Joseph has a father named Jacob (Matt. 1:1b). This is a detail that occurs in Matthew alone, because in Luke's genealogy, Joseph's father is named Heli (Luke 3:23), which is the only other non-Matthean detail about Joseph in the Bible. Second, in Matthew's narrative God communicates to this Joseph only through dreams. In a dream Joseph is told to take Mary as his wife because the child is holy (Matt. 1:20). In a dream he is told to flee from Herod (Matt. 2:12). In a dream he is told when it is safe to return to his house in Bethlehem (Matt. 2:19–20). In a dream he is then told that Bethlehem is now also not safe, so he must go to Galilee and to the city of Nazareth (Matt. 2:22). This Joseph is thus overwhelmingly identified with dreams. Third, the role that this Joseph will play in the drama of salvation is to save "the child of promise" from death at the hands of Herod and he does this by fleeing down to Egypt (Matt. 2:13).

Now turn with me back to the story of the patriarch Joseph as told in the book of Genesis (37–50). There we learn three things about this Joseph, who is popularly identified by his coat of many colors, given him by his doting father (Gen. 37:3).* First, this Joseph has a father named Jacob (Gen. 37:1, 2). Second, this Joseph is overwhelmingly identified with dreams. He dreams of his superior role in the future of his family (Gen. 37:5). He is called "the dreamer" by his brothers (Gen. 37:19). He gains access to the pharaoh by being the interpreter of the dreams of the

---

*A Broadway musical entitled *Joseph and the Amazing Technicolor Dreamcoat,* with music by Andrew Lloyd Webber and lyrics by Tim Rice, opened in 1982.

pharaoh's baker and the pharaoh's butler (Gen. 40). He rides into political power in Egypt as the interpreter of the dreams of the pharaoh himself (Gen. 41). Dreams are part of this Joseph's identity. Third, his role in the drama of salvation is to save "the chosen people," the "people of the covenant," from death, in this case death by starvation, which threatened them because of a famine. How does he save them? He saves them by taking them down to Egypt (Gen. 45).

Does anyone really think that these connections are just coincidental? Is it not more likely that Matthew has quite consciously shaped his character, Joseph, after the pattern of the patriarch Joseph? I believe that this is not just highly probable, but is in fact abundantly clear. Matthew is writing his gospel some two to three generations after the crucifixion. He is writing as a Jew to a community that is primarily Jewish. He is interpreting Jesus through the lens of the Jewish scriptures. His readers would understand the symbols he employed. They would not be tempted to think he was writing a researched historical treatise, and they certainly would not read this narrative as if it represented literal history!

That, however, is what happened after the Christian church became an almost completely Gentile movement. There were no longer any Jewish people in the Christian movement who understood how Jews created their sacred stories. As noted earlier, from around the year 150 CE only Gentiles read, interpreted and wrote commentaries on these Jesus stories of antiquity, and they did so with a profound ignorance of things Jewish. In addition, they were increasingly infected by a rising tide of hostility toward all things Jewish, which meant that they were not motivated even to look into the Jewish background of these narratives. Instead, out of both their ignorance and their prejudice, they decided that the material in the gospels was literal history and literal biography. That Gentile heresy has served to blind Christians for centuries to the essential meaning and point of the Jesus story. When this distorting literalism is lifted from these sacred texts, new understandings became possible. Joseph was a literary character created by Matthew to symbolize the messianic task of binding the Jewish nation into one united people by bringing together the divided tribes of the Hebrew people in the birth of Jesus. The Jewish readers of his gospel would recognize that as a messianic expectation being fulfilled. The Gentile readers would have no clue.

Once this Jewish division was overcome, the messiah's next task would be to bring together all the peoples of the world—Jew and Samaritan, Jew and Gentile. Paul, who wrote some twenty-one to thirty-four years before Matthew, had alluded to this same messianic theme when he wrote that in Christ there is no longer Jew nor Greek, male nor female, bond nor free (Gal. 3:28). To bring all people into oneness will be a major Christian theme in Matthew's gospel, and this theme will be fulfilled in the later books of Luke, Acts and John. It is to this day the major thrust of the Christian faith.

CHAPTER 8

The Magi and Their Gifts: An Original Sermon?

MATTHEW HAS PRESENTED the birth of Jesus under a series of highly stylized symbols, from "shady ladies" in the genealogy to "virgin purity" in the birth itself. He has introduced Joseph into this narrative to serve the messianic role of bringing together the divided Hebrew nation, the Judah tribes and the Joseph tribes, into one whole. Now, in the third phase of his infancy narrative, Matthew will begin to introduce the impact of this Jesus on the whole world. He does this through a tale filled with magical symbols that his Jewish readers would understand as "the fulfillment of scripture," but which his later Gentile readers would for centuries assume was literal history and would misunderstand completely. We turn now to that story with its star in the east, its journeying magi, and its highly symbolic gifts of gold, frankincense and myrrh.

The story begins with a star shining with an unearthly brightness. What gives this star its special meaning for Matthew is that, as a cosmic sign, its light is seen all over the world. It sends a universal message. The brightness of this star transcends every national boundary, including especially the boundary that separates the people of Israel from the people the Jews called the Gentiles. This star is also said to attract the Gentile world to seek its meaning, as the wise men do when they are drawn by its light to search for the newborn king of the Jews. When they find him, they present him with highly meaningful gifts.

Did Matthew think that these new details in his story were literally true? Of course not! That possibility never entered his mind. It would not enter ours either, if we would but stop for a moment to ask realistic questions about the narrative. Does a star in the sky ever announce events that occur on earth? Perhaps that idea was possible when human beings believed that the universe consisted of three tiers, with the earth at its center, and heaven, the domain of God, just above the sky. If God sat on a throne beyond the sky, then the stars were little more than divine lanterns hung out for human beings to see and to interpret. Astrology was born in that mind-set. I suppose, under that ancient belief system, it would be conceivable that God could or would hang out a new star to announce a birth of cosmic proportions. Even if that had once been thought of as common wisdom in history, however, the Copernican revolution in the sixteenth century put an end to that possibility forever.* Today we try to embrace the vastness of space and the distances between the stars and the galaxies that our minds cannot fully fathom. We know the material of which stars are made. We also know that

---

*Nicolaus Copernicus, a Polish monk, was the first to suggest that the earth actually revolved around the sun. Galileo built on his work.

the light we see today from the stars was emitted millions of years ago and only now has come into our range of vision. If God had wanted to use the light of a star to announce the birth of Jesus, God would have had to hang that star out in the east literally millions of years in advance. To literalize that star in the eastern sky is to participate in astrophysical non-sense. That is, however, but the beginning of the non-sense that biblical literalism forces us to assume.

Next we ask, Could a star wander through the sky so slowly that wise men could follow it? That might be conceivable if we assumed that God or one of God's angels could pull that star on a string across the roof of the earth, which would be the floor of heaven, to guide these wise men to their destination. We are told, however, in Matthew's story that the star did not lead them to the Christ child. It rather led them to the palace of King Herod (Matt. 2:1, 2). Did the star get lost? No, Matthew was saying, it simply needed to be reprogrammed by Jewish scripture in order to get back on the right track (Matt. 2:3–6, a passage we will look at later). Reading the Bible literally requires the suspension of all reason. What kind of people, we might also ask, would it be who, upon seeing a new star in the sky, would immediately interpret that star as announcing the birth of a new king of the Jews, and therefore set out at once on a journey to an unknown destination to pay homage to that infant king? Did they keep not only the camels nearby to transport them, but also a supply of gold, frankincense and myrrh, just in case these gifts were needed for this purpose?

No, that is not how the world operates, so we are driven by rationality out of our biblical literalism to entertain other conclusions. There never was a star in the east. That is a fact. All of those planetarium programs designed to give astronomical content to this story show just how seductive literal interpretations of the Bible can be.* There were also no wise men. There was no journey. There were no gifts. All the content of this mythological story was a product not of history, but of the rich imagination of the author of the gospel we call Matthew. His purpose in developing this story was clear. He had found in the life of Jesus of Nazareth one who was for him "the light of the world," one who could draw all people into a sense of oneness as they came into the meaning of this Christ; and he sensed that this would also draw people into new dimensions of their own humanity. Since in his mind this Jesus was destined to change the entire world, that world needed to glimpse this new light at the moment of his birth, feel drawn into his presence, and thus be compelled to seek out new understandings of what it means to be human. They needed to acknowledge the presence of this Jesus with appropriate symbols of the messianic claims. Jesus, Matthew would later say, was the son of a carpenter (Matt. 13:55), but it is not those human details that are important. What Matthew wanted to convey through his birth narrative was the meaning of humanity itself and to suggest that the relationship of the human to the divine is to be found in Jesus. The birth story played the role in Matthew's gospel that the overture plays in an opera. The musical themes that would be developed later are introduced in the overture. The overture is filled with hints of things to come.

---

*When I was a student at the University of North Carolina in Chapel Hill, the Morehead Planetarium, during the Christmas season, regularly offered a program in which the presenters tried to locate the star of Bethlehem in the astrophysical world. Professor Alexei Filippenko, a noted astrophysicist at the University of California at Berkeley, also makes a reference to what might have been the star of Bethlehem in his course on the origins of the universe.

Did Matthew create these symbols himself? Did he create them out of nothing more than the richness of his imagination? Or did he have a source from which he drew his details? When we examined the Joseph story in the previous chapter, it became obvious that he had drawn details out of the Hebrew scriptures. Can we successfully search these same scriptures for the origins of Matthew's story of the wise men? I think we can.

Recall our study of where the Christian story resided during the silent years between the death of Jesus in 30 CE and the birth of the gospels between 72 and 100 CE. We accept the fact that the locale of the oral tradition had to have been the synagogue, which was the only place that the stories from the Hebrew scriptures could have been systematically related to the memory of Jesus. So the interpretive task in the study of the gospels is to determine which parts of the Hebrew scriptures provided the content and the images of the gospel stories. Some key common words in the story of the wise men, words like "kings," "camels," "gold" and "frankincense," lead us to a passage in the book of Isaiah where we find these same words. My supposition is that the story of the wise men, as told in Matthew, was born as a sermon preached in the synagogue by one of the followers of Jesus on a text found in Isaiah 60. We thus enter that doorway and begin our exploration.

Isaiah 60 invites its readers to "arise, shine, for your light has come, and the glory of the Lord has risen upon you" (Isa. 60:1). It goes on to describe the darkness that will cover the earth and its people before that new light appears (Isa. 60:2). When that light does appear, however, nations will come to it, and "kings" will be drawn "to the brightness of God's rising" (Isa. 60:3). Next it suggests that these kings will come on camels. They will come from "Midian and Ephah," and "those from Sheba will come"

(Isa. 60:6). Guess what this text says they will bring with them? "They shall bring gold and frankincense, and they shall proclaim the praise of the Lord" (Isa. 60:6).

Is this not a rather obvious and reasonable connection? Kings shall come to your light. They will come on camels. They will come from Sheba and they will bring gold and frankincense. Do we not have in this Isaiah passage the basic images of Matthew's story of the wise men? Those raised in a tradition of literalism will, however, immediately respond, "Where's the myrrh? Two out of three gifts might be little more than a coincidence." Not so, we respond; the myrrh is there, if one knows how to read the Jewish scriptures—that is, through the lens of Jewish history.

The Isaiah text says that the royal visitors will come from several destinations, including quite specifically the land of Sheba. Sheba was a nation located near the present-day country of Yemen. As soon as the name Sheba was heard, Jewish minds of the first century would have begun to scan their knowledge of the Hebrew scriptures. "Is there not another story in our sacred text," they might have wondered, "about another royal visitor from Sheba who also traveled to pay homage to another king of the Jews?" Their minds would then have fastened on a visit of the queen of Sheba to King Solomon as described in I Kings (10:1–13). The queen of Sheba was drawn to make this journey, according to the story, by the fame of Solomon and his wisdom. "She came to test him with hard questions," says the text. She came with a great retinue and "with camels" bearing "spices, gold, and precious stones." It was the spices, however, that stood out in this text. "A very great quantity of spices," it says. The story concludes with these words: "Never again came such an abundance of spices as those which the queen of Sheba gave to King Solomon." Then Solomon, the text said, "gave to the queen of Sheba all that she desired, whatever she asked, besides that which was given her by the bounty of King Solomon" (I Kings 10:13). This was the biblical text from which the myrrh entered Matthew's story.

Myrrh was the primary spice known and used in the Middle East at that time, and thus it would have been assumed to be paramount among "the spices" that the queen of Sheba brought to King Solomon. Myrrh was a sweet-smelling resin gathered from a Middle Eastern bush. It was used in that region of the world as a kind of deodorant. Baths were infrequent and myrrh was used to blunt body odors. Myrrh was also associated with death among the Jews. The Jews did not embalm their dead. That was an Egyptian practice. The Jews wrapped the deceased in burial cloths sprinkled liberally with myrrh to repress the odor of decaying flesh. Jewish burial took place fairly soon after death. In a story told only in the Fourth Gospel, we learn that Jesus waited for two days after Lazarus had died before responding to Martha's message. When Jesus arrived in Bethany, "Lazarus had been in the tomb for four days" (John 11:1–17). This indicates that there was little time in the land of the Jews between a person's death and that person's burial. Recall that after the crucifixion, which the biblical text tells us brought death to Jesus at 3:00 P.M., he was buried before sundown in the tomb of Joseph of Arimathea (Matt. 27:57). So it was that myrrh came to be associated with death.

That brief study of Isaiah 60 changes how we look at the symbols Matthew built into his story of the wise men. The star in the east was "the brightness of God's rising" (Isa. 60:3). The kings came on camels. Although in Matthew the magi are never called kings and no camels are ever mentioned, over the centuries we have conflated Matthew's story with the *source* of his story in Isaiah; we sing "We Three Kings,"* and we assume that the wise men traveled by camel. Jesus was to be king of the universe, making gold an appropriate gift. He was to be the life in whom God was experienced to be present, making frankincense an appropriate gift. He was to accomplish his purpose through his death on the cross, making myrrh an appropriate gift.

When this sermon was first preached on this Isaiah text in the synagogue, it interpreted Jesus' life in a profound way. Matthew, I believe, simply adopted it for his birth story. Matthew did not intend or expect his story of the journey of the gift-bearing magi led by a star to be seen as literal history. His concern was to communicate, using familiar scriptures and symbols, that Jesus was born to bring together both Jew and Gentile. The Gentiles would thus follow a guiding star to find the promised messiah of the Jews. This star would lead them first to the palace of King Herod, where they would have to consult the Jewish scriptures to find their ultimate destination (Matt. 2:3–6). The prophet Micah was the one who provided the answer found in the sacred text. If Jesus was to be the heir to the throne of David, he must be born in David's city, the place of David's birth. So Micah wrote, and Matthew quoted: "You, Bethlehem, little among the clans of Judah, from you shall come forth for me one who is to be the ruler of Israel" (Micah 5:2). Micah was undoubtedly envisioning the birth of a new David. Bethlehem, which had been David's birthplace some two hundred years before Micah wrote, would someday produce his successor, a new David. The messiah had to be David's heir, so he must come

---

*The hymn "We Three Kings" is in almost every Christian hymnal. The words and music are by John Henry Hopkins (1820–1891).

forth from David's city. That idea was thus placed by the prophet into Jewish expectations and was picked up in Matthew's story.

Was Jesus actually born in Bethlehem? Of course not! He was presumably a child of Nazareth, as Mark's gospel suggests (Mark 1:9). Messianic dreams, however, would move his birthplace to Bethlehem and connect his birth with cosmic signs, including a star in the east that would lead Gentiles into the worship of a Jewish messiah.

Matthew's birth narrative is now complete. It is time to move on to the story of the adult Jesus. In that story the portrait of Jesus as messiah will continue to emerge, "fulfilling the scriptures" time after time.

CHAPTER 9

Herod and Pharaoh; Jesus and Moses

IDDEN AWAY IN MATTHEW'S STORY of Jesus' miraculous virgin birth is another strange story that I have thus far ignored. This story connects King Herod to the wise men and ultimately to the fleeing of the "holy family" into Egypt (Matt. 2:7–18). No hint of this particular narrative occurs anywhere else in the New Testament. For Matthew, however, it was a necessary link between the story of Jesus' birth and those of his baptism and his temptation in the wilderness. All three accounts serve to force the story of Jesus into the mold of the story of Moses. That connection would have been quickly recognized by the Jewish readers for whom Matthew's gospel was written. To this underlying theme of Jesus as the "new Moses" or as the "prophet of whom Moses spoke" we now turn.

The wise men, Matthew tells us, in their pursuit of the newborn king of the Jews, were led by a star, not to the birthplace of Jesus, but to the palace of King Herod. If this star were meant to be understood literally, then we would have to conclude that it had a malfunction in its GPS mechanism! Literalism, however, was not Matthew's purpose. He was painting a portrait of how Gentiles had learned of Jesus' birth. The star announced it, he said—but before these Gentile magi could find Jesus, they had to be guided by Jewish scripture.

This was not a prejudiced statement of religious superiority, as some now suggest. We need to note that Matthew tells us time after time that even the Jews must follow this same procedure. So Matthew has Herod, in response to the wise men's inquiry, consult his sages and scripture scholars, who point these magi to their destination in Bethlehem.

So, guided by the Hebrew scriptures, the magi—now following that newly reappeared star—are guided to Bethlehem. There the star stops and bathes in its light the house in which, according to Matthew's gospel, Joseph, Mary and the newly born Christ child are living. There these wise men do obeisance, offer worship and present their symbolic gifts of gold, frankincense and myrrh before departing (Matt. 2:10–12). They do not, however, return to inform Herod of the child's location, as Herod had requested them to do (Matt. 2:8). This detail is the one that sets up the Moses connection.

When it slowly dawns on Herod in Mathew's story that these eastern stargazers are not returning, he is said to have fallen into a furious rage and to have dispatched his troops to Bethlehem with orders to kill all the male children up to two years of age. When that dark deed is completed, Matthew proclaims that the words of Jeremiah have been fulfilled anew (Jer. 31:15). The prophet had declared that Rachel, the mother of Joseph, and therefore the tribal matriarch of the Joseph tribes that formed the Northern Kingdom, had wept with loud lamentations when the Northern Kingdom had been overrun and destroyed by the forces of Assyria around the year 721 BCE. Now their children were being destroyed again. It was an interesting application of the words from Jeremiah to the life of Jesus.

Was this slaughter of innocent children an event that literally happened? Once again the answer is: "Of course not!" Matthew was not writing history. We need to say that over and over to break the prison of literalness in which these words have been forced to live for so long. The idea that a wandering star led the wise men to King Herod, who then led them to the writings of the prophet Micah, which then led them to Bethlehem, is a beautifully dramatic, theological, interpretive wonder! It is everything *but* history. The idea that a reigning monarch, feeling a threat to his throne from one the wise men called the newborn "king of the Jews," would have deputized these absolute strangers to be his intelligence gatherers and to go to Bethlehem to search for this child, whose birth the star had announced, involves behavior that is not just irrational, but literally absurd. The suggestion that Herod, if this story were literal, would have had no clue which house the wise men had entered with their gifts and over which this guiding star had stopped to shine its light is preposterous. Bethlehem was a village of a few hundred people. If you have ever lived in a town that small, you surely recognize that if something like this had actually happened, everyone in that village would have known exactly which structure had housed the child who was the recipient of celestial recognition. King Herod could have gone directly to that house with no difficulty. There was no need for a killing rampage against all the male babies of the village. Obviously, however, Matthew had another thought in mind. He was interpreting the life

of Jesus in terms of the sacred story of the Jews. The idea that a
wicked king would try to stamp out God's promised deliverer in
his infancy was a story familiar to the Jewish people.

This narrative represented Matthew's first reference to the figure of Moses, on whom he intended to pattern his Jesus story.
When Moses was born, says the book of Exodus, a new king arose
in Egypt, "who did not know Joseph" (Exod. 1:8) and who, therefore, did not appreciate Joseph's role in preventing starvation in the
land of Egypt. This new Egyptian ruler's concern was only with
the threat that this rapidly multiplying group of Hebrew underclass
or slave people might seek to topple Egyptian rule.

To counter this perceived threat, the book of Exodus tells us, the
pharaoh issued a decree that every boy child born in the growing
Hebrew population was to be put to death (Exod. 1:15, 16). The
infant boys were to be thrown by the midwife who delivered them
into the waters of the Nile River. According to that Exodus narrative, the baby Moses escaped this fate by being placed alive into
the Nile in a basket made from bulrushes and lined with bitumen
and pitch so that it would float on the water. His sister, Miriam,
was assigned the task of hiding in the reeds along the river bank
to watch over and to protect the child (Exod. 2:1–10). That legend
then suggested that the pharaoh's daughter, who came to bathe
in the Nile River, saw the child and recognized him as a Hebrew
baby. Taking pity, she drew him out. Miriam then immediately
materialized out of the reeds and offered to find a Hebrew woman
who could wet-nurse the child that the pharaoh's daughter was
presumably planning to raise as her own. The pharaoh's daughter
accepted this offer, and Miriam went to get Moses' mother to serve
as her own child's wet nurse. It is a lovely legend, but clearly it is
not history. Speculation through the ages, however, has suggested

that there may be a germ of truth behind it. No less a person than Sigmund Freud proposed, in one of his books, that Moses may have been the illegitimate child of the pharaoh's daughter by a Hebrew slave.* Freud developed this theory by suggesting that when Moses later decided to intervene in a conflict in which an Egyptian over-lord was beating a Hebrew worker, what he was doing was choos-ing his Hebrew heritage over his royal upbringing. This possible choice of the slave identity by an "Egyptian prince" raised in the pharaoh's palace became the experience, Freud argued, through which the Hebrew people got their powerful sense of being God's elect, God's chosen.

Be that as it may, in the folklore surrounding the founder of the Jewish nation was this narrative about a wicked king who had tried to kill Moses, God's promised deliverer, while still in his infancy, only to have this future leader miraculously spared. Mat-thew quite obviously took that familiar Jewish story and wrapped it around the infant Jesus. By repeating that story from the life cycle of Moses, now about the infant Jesus, Matthew was signal-ing that his gospel was about another person who was destined to be "the deliverer of his people." So once again a wicked king, this time named Herod, tried to extinguish a special life in its infancy and thus to thwart God's plan for that life. Every Jewish reader of Matthew's gospel would have recognized this as a Moses story.

Matthew inserts this story into his birth narrative of Jesus to plant an interpretive seed. He will use the life of Moses as a model to which he will link the story of Jesus. As soon as the birth nar-rative is complete, Matthew picks up that interpretive clue again, developing it fully in his opening narrative about the adult Jesus.

Moses and Monotheism. See bibliography for details.

This includes the stories of his baptism and of his temptation in the wilderness. Both will reflect Moses and his role in Jewish history. When those stories are complete, Matthew will then have Jesus inaugurate his public ministry. He will also, at that exact time, have arrived at the Jewish celebration of Shavuot, and Matthew's portrait of Jesus as the new Moses will be complete.

To these later "Moses touches" we now turn, as Matthew's gospel unfolds. Here we will discern the pattern and discover the style of this author. He is not writing history. He is painting a portrait. We must read this story not as one reads a book but as one "reads" a portrait, seeing its interpretive meaning.

CHAPTER 10

The Baptism of Jesus:
Moses Relived

ONE OF THE MOST DRAMATIC STORIES in the Hebrew Bible is the account of the children of Israel crossing what most translators call the Red Sea (Exod. 14:10–31). Artists have painted this scene countless times. Sunday school teachers have taught it. Children have imagined it. In 1956 a Hollywood film produced by Cecil B. DeMille turned this story into a blockbuster motion picture that won a number of awards. It was entitled *The Ten Commandments*.* That film has been rerun so many times on television during Lent or Holy Week that most people, unknowingly, get their images of this biblical story, not from the Bible, but from this motion picture. What we have done is to literalize the DeMille film while thinking that

---

The Ten Commandments produced in 1956 was actually a remake of a DeMille film from 1923, before sound had been added to the art of filmmaking. The 1956 film starred Charlton Heston as Moses.

we are literalizing the biblical story! This makes dismantling and interpreting the story of the Red Sea crossing that much more difficult. If we are going to understand the story of Jesus' baptism, however, we must revisit the account of the Red Sea crossing, because the two are deeply related. Here are some facts about this biblical narrative.

First, if Moses and the Hebrew people literally crossed the Red Sea, they went far out of their way. The Red Sea not only empties into the Indian Ocean, but its location also means that the escaping slaves were traveling in the wrong direction, since the Red Sea is several hundred miles south of the land of Goshen, where the Bible says that most of the Hebrew people lived. Second, the Red Sea is about two hundred miles wide. The biblical text suggests that the Hebrew people crossed it in a little more than twenty-four hours. That means that this crowd of refugees—some elderly, some infants, some pregnant and some children—even at the Red Sea's narrowest point, would have had to travel at a rate that would be a literal impossibility. Third, the words "Red Sea" never occur in the text. That is a King James mistranslation that has been carried forward through the years. The words used in Hebrew are *Yam Suph, yam* meaning "sea" and *suph* meaning "reeds." The reference is probably to a region far to the north of the actual Red Sea and on a direct path toward their destination, which they believed was their promised homeland—the Promised Land—occupied at that time by a host of other tribes, including the Canaanites and the Jebusites.

The Sea of Reeds was a mass of swampy land between Africa and the Arabian Peninsula. If there is a germ of historical truth in this narrative, it is that the slave people, traveling with little more than the clothes on their backs, were able to navigate this swampland successfully, though with great difficulty, while the Egyptian army of the pharaoh, with its horse-drawn iron chariots and its soldiers clad in heavy armor and carrying weighty weapons, sank into the mire, thus allowing the slave people to get beyond their reach. As the story was told and retold over the period of some 250 to 300 years before it was written down, it grew in grandiosity and in supernaturalness, becoming a favorite national tale of the early history of the Hebrew people. What the story indicated to them was that God was present with God's people to deliver them from peril.

Because most of us today are not generally familiar with the Old Testament scriptures, we are also not aware that the splitting of various bodies of water to allow special people to cross over on dry land is retold in the Hebrew Bible on three additional occasions.

Joshua, Moses' successor, repeated the Moses water-crossing miracle when he was said to have been able to cross over the flooded waters of the Jordan River on dry land with all the people who had traveled from Egypt, and thus to reach the Promised Land, their destination (Josh. 3:14–17). To the Hebrew people this new water-crossing story meant that the God who had been with Moses had not abandoned them, now that Moses, God's special servant, was dead, but that this God was still present with Joshua. It was a story that built security among the people in a time of transition. It was Red Sea II.

This theme was repeated in the biblical narratives about two other great leaders of the Hebrew people. The first of these was a man named Elijah, who is called "the father of the prophets." Near the end of Elijah's life he is said to have journeyed with his chosen successor, Elisha, into the wilderness to a pre-appointed place, where he was destined to have a rendezvous with God. To get to this wilderness location, however, the two of them had to cross the Jordan River. At the river's edge, and in the presence of "fifty men of the sons of the prophets," Elijah took his mantle, rolled it up and struck the waters of the Jordan River with it. In this action, Elijah was seen as one who was endowed with Moses' power. The waters of the river were immediately parted and Elijah and Elisha crossed over on dry land (II Kings 2:6–8). It was Red Sea III.

It was on that far side of the Jordan that we are told Elijah ascended into heaven in a magical fiery chariot drawn by magical fiery horses, leaving his mantle on the ground (II Kings 2:9–12). Elisha, now alone, grasped Elijah's mantle and started his return trip, no longer as Elijah's apprentice, but now as his successor. Coming once again to the Jordan River, Elisha repeated Elijah's behavior. He rolled up Elijah's mantle and, striking the waters of the river with it, watched the waters part again. Then Elisha walked across the river on dry land (II Kings 2:13–14). It was Red Sea IV! The author of II Kings allowed the aforementioned "sons of the prophets" to interpret this narrative, and they did so with the words: "Behold, now the spirit of Elijah rests on Elisha" (II Kings 2:15). The message from this new parting of the waters story was clear. God was still with the people even after Elijah had been taken from them, and now God was clearly with Elisha. The transition had been successful!

The author of Matthew's gospel, as well as its first readers, would have known about these parting of the waters traditions in the sacred stories of the Hebrew people. They would, therefore, have understood the background to Matthew's story of Jesus' baptism. It would be those who were not raised in or schooled by these Hebrew traditions that would later think that the story of Jesus' baptism was told as a remembered event in history.

In his first adult story of Jesus, Matthew brought this central figure to the edge of the waters of the Jordan River (Matt. 3:13). Matthew was convinced that Jesus was the one to whom Moses had pointed. He was also convinced that "a person greater than Moses" was here. So watch how he tells his story.

When Jesus steps into the waters of the Jordan River to be baptized by John, it is not the waters of that river that are parted. That would be far too mundane—that had already been done on three different occasions in the Hebrew story; four if one counts the parting of the Red Sea! Jesus, rather, at his baptism, parts the heavens (Matt. 3:16). Now, what are the heavens in Matthew's mind? Read the creation story as told in chapter 1 of Genesis. On the second day in the creation story, we are told, God said: " 'Let there be a firmament in the midst of the waters, and let it separate the waters from the waters.' And so God made the firmament and separated the waters which were under the firmament from the waters which were above the firmament. And it was so. And God called the firmament heaven" (Gen. 1:6–8).

When Jesus was baptized, Matthew says, God opened the firmament that separated the waters above from the waters below. That is, the heavenly waters were parted. All Moses could do was to part the waters of the Red Sea. All Joshua, Elijah and Elisha could do was to part the waters of the Jordan River. The "new and greater Moses," as Matthew seeks to portray Jesus, could part the heavenly waters, which then poured down upon him as the Holy Spirit (Matt. 3:16). "Living water" is always a symbol of the Holy Spirit in Jewish thought. Matthew is identifying Jesus as one who had been "God-infused." The message of his earlier birth story, about God entering Jesus at conception, has now been completed when God enters him anew and publically at his baptism. This life, which Matthew will continue to pattern after Moses, is in fact a life in which God will be experienced as present. Mark, who began his gospel with the baptism experience of divine infusion, has been trumped by Matthew, who says that the baptism simply *confirms* what his miraculous birth had already proclaimed. God is the source of this life. God is present in this life. God will be encountered through this life. Matthew has incorporated many Hebrew themes into his narrative of Jesus' origins. Now he concludes his baptismal narrative by having a "voice from heaven" interpret the meaning of this story. The voice says: "This is my beloved son, in whom I am well pleased" (Matt. 3:17). The words echo the prophet we call II Isaiah, who, when his mythical figure, who will be known as "the Servant" or "the Suffering Servant," emerges on the stage of history, has God say: "Behold my servant, whom I uphold, my chosen in whom my soul delights; I have put my Spirit upon him" (Isa. 42:1).

That is the meaning of Jesus' baptism for Matthew. By including the baptism account, Matthew is solidifying Jesus' Mosaic identity. The new Moses can also split waters, but the waters he splits are the heavenly waters beyond the firmament. The voice of God has validated Jesus, just as the voices of the sons of the prophets had validated Elisha. The messiah is now ready to begin his career.

Before describing that career, however, Matthew relates one additional Moses story. It will be the last narrative before Matthew arrives at the synagogue celebration of Shavuot, but it will be essential to the Moses-like portrait of Jesus that Matthew is painting.

CHAPTER 11

Into the Wilderness:
Forty Days, Not Forty Years

THE BAPTISM IS COMPLETE. Jesus has been linked with two important Moses stories: the wrath of a wicked king who tried to destroy him at birth, and the narrative of splitting the waters. The story of Jesus' baptism, as told by Matthew, is Red Sea V, but greatly enhanced. Splitting the waters of the Red Sea can hardly be compared with splitting the firmament that separated the heavenly water from the waters below. Clearly, Matthew is not writing a literal story, and those familiar with Jewish scriptures and the Jewish storytelling tradition would be completely aware of and understanding of that fact. This story is yet another example of the fact that it takes Jewish eyes to get the intended message from Jewish scriptures.

When one is familiar with these scriptures, one does not need to ask what comes next in Matthew's story. He is clearly following a

script. Read the ancient story line. The covenant people had successfully escaped Egypt through the Red Sea. Then, we learn, they wan-
dered in the wilderness for "forty years" (Num. 13:33). Why so long
a time? The Bible's rationale is a bit complicated. First we are told
that it was punishment. The people had complained so frequently
and were so rebellious that God thought it would be best to allow
the escaping generation to die before the next generation settled into
the Promised Land. Forty years would take care of that, since forty
years was about the average life expectancy in that period of history.
There was, however, also a positive reason. The Hebrews needed
time to discover what it meant to be "the people chosen of God."
They did not yet know what was required of the "members of the
covenant." They had to be tried and tested in the wilderness before
they could arrive at their promised destination (Num. 14). They
had to eat manna "for forty years" before they could reach the land
"flowing with milk and honey" (Exod. 16:35, 33:3).

Centuries after that, the gospel tradition, which had begun in
Mark and then was being developed and expanded in Matthew,
was intent on making the career of Jesus parallel the career of
Moses and the Hebrew people. Jesus' baptism in the Jordan River
became his Red Sea experience, as we saw in the previous chapter.
Now Jesus' forty days in the wilderness will parallel Israel's forty
years in the wilderness. Like the people of Israel, Jesus had to learn
what it meant to be chosen. He had to go into the wilderness to
discover what it meant to be messiah.

Matthew is the first gospel writer to describe the content of
Jesus' temptations (Matt. 4:1–11). All Mark had related about the
wilderness experience was that Jesus was "in the wilderness for
forty days, being tempted by Satan" (Mark 1:13). Matthew will

now proceed to tell us just exactly what those temptations were.*
From where do you suppose Matthew got the content of the three
temptations? If one is familiar with the Hebrew scriptures, one
recognizes immediately that he took them out of the Moses narrative. All of his original readers would have recognized that fact, for
they would have known that Moses faced three trials during the
wilderness years of Israel's history. The first of Moses' trials had
to do with the shortage of food. Moses prayed to God, and God
answered him with "manna" from heaven (Exod. 16:35). Heavenly
bread would fall upon them. Over the years the story would be
altered so that neither God nor the people had to violate the Sabbath restriction against work by sending the bread or by gathering it on the Sabbath, but the story itself endured. God answered
Moses' first crisis with bread.

The second crisis that confronted Moses came with the shortage
of water, which occurred near a place called Massah or Meribah
(Exod. 17:7). The people murmured against Moses, saying: "There
is no god among us," and demanding a sign. Moses struck the
rock at Meribah with the same rod with which he had struck the
Nile when the plagues began, and life-giving water flowed from
that struck rock. The people had put the Lord to the "proof" or to
the "test," which this second crisis story claimed was a sin. Moses
would later be forbidden to enter the Promised Land because he
had "put God to the test" (Num. 20:10–13). This explanation was

---

*Here again we run into the Q hypothesis. Q subscribers tell us that the content of the tempta-
tions was Q material since it is also in Luke, though Luke changes the order of the temptations, reversing the second and third. It seems to me far easier, and far better, to assume that
Luke had Matthew as well as Mark in front of him when he wrote. Theories based on support
by a lost source are inherently suspect. I have no interest in attacking the Q hypothesis. I simply want to register that I am not convinced of it. Indeed I feel no need for it.

repeated later in the Hebrew scriptures to make it perfectly clear (see Deut. 6:16 and Ps. 106:14).

The third trial or crisis for Moses in the wilderness came when he was delayed on Mt. Sinai prior to returning to the people with the two tablets of stone on which the commandments were written. The people, anxious about Moses' long absence and feeling in that absence the absence of God, prevailed upon Aaron, Moses' brother and the high priest, to make for them a god they could see and worship. Aaron complied by melting their golden earrings, necklaces and bracelets, and fashioning them into the image of a calf. The people then built an altar to this golden calf and began to worship it as "the god who brought us out of the land of Egypt" (Exod. 32:1–6). The people had turned from God to the worship of something other than God.

The author of Matthew's gospel and the people for whom he wrote this gospel were familiar with these stories in the Torah. They would have understood that Matthew was still weaving Moses stories around Jesus; they would have recognized that Matthew was portraying the three temptations of Jesus as similar to the trials or crises in Moses' life. The first temptation of Jesus in the wilderness had to do with the shortage of food. Does that not sound familiar? Jesus was hungry, just as the people of Israel had been hungry in the wilderness. The tempter came to him, saying: "If you are the messiah, the son of God," use your power. In Moses' day God had sent bread from heaven. You now make bread from these stones. Jesus responded by rejecting the temptation. "Man [and woman] does not live by bread alone," he said, "but by every word which proceeds out of the mouth of God" (Matt. 4:4). Round one in this struggle with the tempter goes to Jesus.

The second temptation was to put God to the test. Again it sounds familiar. The devil, we are told, took Jesus to the pinnacle of the Temple (Matt. 4:5). Presumably that was in Jerusalem, so the geography of the wilderness has been compromised, which is another indication that Matthew did not understand this story to be literal. In this new setting, the devil speaks again: "If you are the son of God, throw yourself down" from this pinnacle. Trust the scriptures, the devil adds, quoting from the psalm in which the psalmist writes: "God will give his angels charge of you to guard you in all your ways. On their hands, they will bear you up, lest you dash your foot against a stone" (Ps. 91:11–12). From this Matthean text, the understanding has come that even the devil can quote scripture, which suggests that quoting the Bible literally does not affect either truth or reality, a lesson fundamentalists have never learned! Jesus, however, once more passes the test and indicates that he understands the Moses background on display here: "You do not tempt [or put to the test] the Lord your God," he answers, quoting Deuteronomy, which says: "You shall not put the Lord your God to the test, as you tested God at Massah"—that is, Meribah (Deut. 6:16). Round two to Jesus!

The Moses-like struggle goes on. The third temptation comes out of the golden calf episode. It is the temptation to worship something other than God. The devil, according to Matthew's story, now takes Jesus to the top of a very tall mountain, from which, presumably, he can see all the nations of the world. The devil then says to him: "All these, I will give you, if you but bow down and worship me" (Matt. 4:8–9). Jesus, still quoting Deuteronomy (6:1–13), using a passage that describes all that God has given God's people—cities, houses, cisterns, vineyards and olive trees—responds: "You shall worship the Lord your God, and him only will you serve" (Matt. 4:10). Round three, a unanimous decision for Jesus!

The temptations are over. The devil is banished and Jesus, who quoted Moses in his time of trial (assuming, as did his generation, that Moses had authored the books of Genesis, Exodus, Leviticus, Numbers and Deuteronomy), is ready now to emerge out of the wilderness. His life is set on a path; his vocation is formed. His role to be messiah is still intact. Like Moses, he is now ready to proceed with his earthly vocation. Matthew has woven the figure of Moses deeply into his portrait of Jesus. As usual, he has done so with an eye toward the Jewish calendar. The Jewish world for which this passage was written was about to celebrate Shavuot, the day that recalled that moment in this nation's history when God had given the Torah to Moses on Mt. Sinai. Now this Sinai image of Moses needs to be incorporated into Jesus. That is exactly what Matthew will accomplish when he has Jesus deliver the Sermon on the Mount. It is a new Moses on a new mountain, not with a new Torah, but with a new interpretation of the Torah. This narrative will dominate Matthew's next section.

Matthew has provided Jesus stories for all seven of the Sabbaths between Passover and Shavuot. The first two were his Easter stories. Next came Jesus' ancestry and birth, the wise men and Herod, the baptism in the River Jordan and the forty days of wilderness temptation. Now for his fifth and final Sabbath he has Jesus come out of the temptation experience resolved as to who he is and what his life means. This calls for a bit of stage-setting on Matthew's part: He offers the arrest of John the Baptist as the signal for Jesus to step forward and to present himself as messiah. Matthew has Jesus call two sets of brothers into discipleship, Andrew and Peter,

James and John. Next he portrays Jesus as moving quickly about Galilee, preaching the gospel of the kingdom of God and healing sicknesses and other infirmities. His fame begins to spread. Great crowds start following him. They come, Matthew tells us, from Galilee, Decapolis, Jerusalem, Judea and from beyond the Jordan. That is, they are both Jews and Gentiles. Matthew will have Jesus respond to these crowds as the celebration called Shavuot dawns. The traditions and the liturgies of the synagogue are still organizing Matthew's story.

PART III

Shavuot and the Sermon on the Mount: Sinai Revisited

CHAPTER 12

Jesus' Return
to the Symbolic Sinai

MATTHEW HAS NOW REACHED the first major celebration of the Jewish liturgical year since Passover and he uses it as the background to relate the climax of his initial correlation between Moses and the adult Jesus. It forms one of the most familiar parts of the New Testament, known and quoted both inside the life of the church and throughout our increasingly secular society. We call it the Sermon on the Mount. Harry S. Truman, president of the United States from 1945 to 1953, who was denigrated by critics for his lack of formal education, responded to these charges with the claim that his presidency was guided by nothing else than the Sermon on the Mount.*

---

*Every problem, President Truman asserted, could be solved if the words of the Sermon on the Mount were applied to it.

First, some facts about the Sermon on the Mount need to be stated. Though this episode is drawn with both beauty and intensity in Matthew's gospel, there is no other reference to the Sermon on the Mount elsewhere in the New Testament. Mark, as we have noted, is Matthew's primary written source, but Mark never alludes to the Sermon on the Mount. Luke, who writes after Matthew and who may have had access to Matthew, includes in his gospel some of the teachings of Jesus that Matthew says were delivered in the Sermon on the Mount, but Luke makes these sayings a part of a much smaller and by comparison almost pedestrian "Sermon on the Plains." Other parts of this sermon Luke scatters in other places in his narrative. Still other parts he simply omits. So if Luke did have access to Matthew, he did not view the material in Matthew's Sermon on the Mount as having any kind of unique integrity. If Luke did *not* have access to Matthew, then both Matthew and Luke must have had access to that hypothetical, now-lost source Q.

If the Q hypothesis turns out to be true, and certainly the majority of American New Testament scholars continue to affirm it, then we are driven to the conclusion that Matthew and Luke used this material in radically different ways. This would mean, at the very least, that the form, if not the content, that the Sermon on the Mount assumes in Matthew's gospel is the creation of that gospel's author alone. This in turn would strongly argue against the Sermon on the Mount ever having been a literal event in the life of the Jesus of history. There are other data, which I shall allude to from time to time in this book, that push me rather relentlessly away from the Q hypothesis, but I do not want to be distracted by that argument. I simply will not assume it, and my reasons will be apparent as this story unfolds.*

---

*I find it difficult to understand why New Testament scholars hold so tightly to a thesis based on the existence of a document that no one has ever seen.

When I look at the Sermon on the Mount, I see a dramatic portrayal of Jesus clearly in an interpretive role. He is the new Moses, being placed on a new mountain, to deliver a new interpretation of the Torah. The three chapters in Matthew that constitute "the Sermon" (5, 6, 7) are stylized, unique and deeply symbolic. It is clear to me that this passage is an artistic creation. It is simply too deeply Jewish not to be. It is too influenced by the liturgical life of the synagogue and too beautifully outlined to have occurred literally. It bears all the markings of a developed literary device. It also presents too studied a contrast between Moses and Jesus to have been original with Jesus. It is not a self-portrait or a self-revelation. It is, I am convinced, the creation of the author of Matthew's gospel. So I conclude, with some confidence, that Jesus never preached this sermon, and that neither Matthew nor his original readers ever assumed that a literal interpretation was a possibility. With these conclusions stated, let me proceed to lay out the reasons behind them.

If the liturgical year of the Jews in the Torah began with the month of Nisan in the early spring of the year, as the book of Leviticus asserts (Lev. 23:24), then the first great festival of the Jewish liturgical year in the time frame we are considering was the celebration of their birth as a nation and as a people. This is what Passover represents. If it is also true that Jesus' crucifixion was linked very early in Christian history with the Passover celebration, as I have previously suggested, and as all four gospels in one way or another assert, then the link between the telling of the Jesus story and the celebration of the great events of Jewish history in the liturgical year of the synagogue must have been established very early. If that link was fixed in the crucifixion-Passover connection, then we could expect to see a correlation in the gospels between the telling of the Jesus story and the annual flow of the synagogue's other observances of its holy days.

The first holy day after Passover was called Pentecost, or Shavuot. As we have seen, the name Pentecost referred to the fifty days
that came after Passover and before Shavuot. Passover in the biblical story was the liturgy that celebrated the escape from Egypt. It
was followed in Jewish history by a long period of wilderness wandering, before this band of escaping slaves would enter, conquer,
and settle in what they called the Promised Land. It was, therefore,
in the nomadic wilderness period that their sense of being "the
people of the covenant" developed.

As we saw in chapter 3, these former slave people, like all denigrated minorities, had thought of themselves while in Egypt as
no people. Now, in the post-slavery wilderness years, they had
come to think of themselves as God's especially chosen people.
The major aspect in their experience of being embraced in a covenant relationship with God was the moment they believed that
they had been given by God the law of God, known as the Torah.
In response to that gift of the law, which marked God's special
relationship to the group of former slaves, something was clearly
required of them, namely their adoration of and obedience to the
Torah. Mutuality is the essence of the covenant.

The story of how the Torah was given to the people and how
the people committed themselves to obey the Torah, indeed to bind
the Torah onto their hearts, was a dramatic part of this people's
history and folklore. In the Hebrew scriptures it is told in great
detail (Exod. 19–20).

It took place on Mt. Sinai in the wilderness. Moses stood in
the center of this story as God's mouthpiece. The Torah was said
to have been personally dictated by God to Moses on top of that
mountain. Moses then read the Torah, which begins with what
we call the Ten Commandments, to the people, and the people in

turn agreed to be governed by these laws. This was such a great and pivotal day in Jewish history that it had to be remembered and renewed annually. That sort of remembrance/renewal is exactly what liturgy is created to do. So into the liturgical year, fifty days after Passover, the Jewish festival of Shavuot was established. Once each year, the Jewish people in solemn worship would renew the Sinai covenant.

Shavuot was observed with a liturgy that took the form of a twenty-four-hour vigil. This vigil was divided into eight three-hour segments, during which the Jewish worshippers would, among other things, read the Torah lesson from the book of Exodus that described the original Sinai experience.

The biblical background for this Sinai story was a conversation between Moses and his father-in-law, Jethro, who was described as "a priest of Midian" (Exod. 18:13–33). Jethro, observing Moses in his role as adjudicator of disputes among the people, suggested that his task of judging and deciding all the controversies of the citizens was more than one leader could or should do. He recommended to Moses that he divide the people into groups of one thousand with a wise man—one who "fears God," is "trustworthy" and "who hates a bribe"—designated as the judge over any disputes that might arise in that group of a thousand. Next, Jethro continued, these groups of one thousand should be subdivided into groups of one hundred, with leaders appointed over each lot of one hundred. Finally, those groups of one hundred should be subdivided into groups of ten, with leaders appointed to judge the disputes that arose among that lot of ten. Moses would then have to adjudicate only those disputes which could not be settled at the ten level, the hundred level, or the thousand level. It was a kind of appellate court system, with Moses as the court of last appeal.

For this plan to become operative, however, Moses and the people had to face the problem of subjectivity. By what standard would these lesser judges make their decisions? Only Moses had talked directly with God and knew, thereby, the law and the will of God. An objective standard had to come down from God on high, and through Moses to the people, or subjectivity would destroy the system. That is exactly what is described in Exodus 19 and in the entire Sinai experience.

The biblical signs surrounding the giving of the law were dramatic. The people were to prepare rigorously for this anticipated divine-human encounter. The book of Exodus dates the Sinai experience as occurring on "the third moon" after they had escaped Egypt (Exod. 19:1). Moses had gone up Mt. Sinai beforehand to work out all the details with God. The people were instructed to wash their garments in order to be ready "on the third day" (Exod. 19:10–11). The promise was that God would become visible to them on that day. On pain of death, the people were instructed to keep a proper distance from the mountain until a loud blast of the shofar, a ram's horn, invited them to come forward. All was in a high state of readiness.

On the third day, the book of Exodus says, there was thunder and lightning. A great dark cloud covered Mt. Sinai. Then came the blast of the shofar, and the people trembled with fear. As Moses led them to the foot of the mountain, Mt. Sinai was wrapped in smoke and fire and the mountain itself quaked. God then called Moses to come up the mountain. The priests were told to await consecration, and Aaron, the high priest, was told to accompany Moses on his upward journey. The high priest first, and then the lower ranks of the priesthood, had to be validated. Their authority rested on this validation.

When all of this preparation was complete, God spoke, says the text (Exod. 20:16b). The law thus came from God through Moses to Aaron and the priests. In that manner the law was written down, objectified and revealed. Those who judged the people must judge according to that single standard of the revealed Torah. It began with the great moral principles that we call the Ten Commandments, but it finally stretched out into the intimate details that governed the lives of the people until it covered almost every conceivable human experience: kosher dietary laws, Sabbath day restrictions, circumcision requirements, purity rites and many, many more. The Torah was thought to spell out God's will for God's people in every conceivable set of circumstances. Thus it formed the heart of Judaism, the heart of the Jews' covenant with God. This *meaning* of the covenant was that which had to be renewed liturgically each year, and that was what the twenty-four-hour vigil at Shavuot was all about. Shavuot bound the people of Israel to God in a solemn act of renewal once a year, by an act in which the promise to be obedient to the covenant was included. That is how liturgy functions.

A twenty-four-hour vigil needs to have substantial content to carry the people through so long a concentrated time of worship. So the Jews wrote a psalm to be used at this vigil, a hymn to the beauty and wonder of the law. A psalm for a twenty-four-hour service has to be very long indeed. Psalm 119 meets that requirement and is today the longest psalm in the psalter. Though most of us have never understood the reason for its length, its structure reveals that it was written to be the psalm for a twenty-four-hour vigil. It could be divided into an introductory stanza, plus seven segments of three stanzas each, so that each of the eight three-hour segments of the twenty-four-hour vigil had a portion of that psalm specifically for its use. The words of this psalm exalted the law, the Torah, again and again. "Thou hast demanded thy precepts [thy law] to be kept diligently" (Ps. 119:4). "I will praise thee with an upright heart, when I learn thy righteous ordinances [thy law]" (Ps. 119:7). "Teach me thy statutes [thy law]. Make me understand thy precepts [thy law]" (Ps. 119:26–27). "Spare my life that I may keep the testimonies [the law] of thy mouth" (Ps. 119:88). "O Lord, thy word [thy law] is firmly fixed in the heavens" (Ps. 119:89). "Thy hands have made and fashioned me; give me understanding that I may learn thy commandments" (Ps. 119:73).

The theme of this Shavuot psalm is relentless. God's law rules. The call to the people is to obey. God has spoken. Matthew, as the scribal head of the synagogue of the Jewish followers of Jesus, knew this background and this history, as did the members of his congregation, who first heard this gospel read to them.

Look now at Psalm 119. Its introductory stanza has eight verses. The first two of these eight verses begin with the word "blessed." Now look at Matthew's Sermon on the Mount. It begins with an eight-verse introductory stanza. Each of the eight verses begins with the word "blessed." We call those verses "the Beatitudes" (Matt. 5:3–10). This is our first hint that Matthew is going to use Psalm 119 as the basis upon which to build his Sermon on the Mount.

The hints quickly compound. The first of Matthew's eight verses of his introductory stanza reads: "Blessed are the poor in spirit." The reward these poor in spirit shall receive is "the kingdom of heaven." The last verse of this introductory stanza says: "Blessed are those who are persecuted for righteousness' sake," and to them Jesus promises the same reward: "For theirs is the kingdom of heaven." Then, in verse 11, Matthew has Jesus begin eight commentaries on each of the eight beatitudes, one commentary to be read at each of the three hours of the twenty-four-hour vigil. He does this, however, in reverse order. That is, his first commentary is on the eighth beatitude (see Matt. 5:11–20), his second commentary is on the seventh beatitude, and so on he goes until he has reached his last commentary, which is on the first beatitude.

In the Sermon on the Mount, Matthew also has Jesus do a commentary on each of the Ten Commandments. Jesus' message clearly drives each commandment beneath the level of the literal command—that is, it is not sufficient to keep the sixth commandment just by refraining from the literal act of murder. You must, says Jesus, listen to the law against murder in the innermost levels of your life, for it is also a call not to be angry, not to judge another, not to insult. It is not enough to refrain from the act of adultery, as the seventh commandment says. The law pierces the interior of life until it reaches one's level of motivation. It journeys to the source of one's lust, one's desire to use another rather than to love another. It is not enough to refrain from swearing by the name of God (taking the name of God in vain). You are not to swear at all, for your word must be all that is necessary. Matthew has Jesus continue until all the commandments are covered in a new way. Making God's name sacred, reserving the word "God" for God alone, keeping the Sabbath inviolate, honoring one's elders, not stealing, not bearing false witness, and not coveting. All are covered in the eight commentaries on the eight beatitudes. This is not a spontaneously delivered sermon on a mountaintop. This is a beautifully crafted interpretation of Jesus as the new Moses. It is organized around the psalm used at Shavuot. It is an interpretive portrait of Jesus set against a liturgical celebration.

To say it yet again, and in the bluntest language possible, Jesus never preached the Sermon on the Mount. It is a creation of Matthew, the gospel writer, who is interpreting the life of Jesus to a synagogue community as they go through the liturgical year of the Jews. It is Matthew spelling out his understanding of Jesus as the new Moses.

Matthew has been building the theme for some time. This is why he placed a Moses story into the birth narrative of Jesus, making both Moses and Jesus the spared agents of God when a wicked ruler tried to destroy both at birth. This was why he likened the baptism of Jesus to the Red Sea experience of Moses. Both split the waters; Moses at the Red Sea, Jesus the heavenly waters. This is why he portrays both Moses and Jesus as having been tempted in the wilderness and why he makes the content of the temptations of Jesus identical with the content of the crises that Moses faced. In the Sermon on the Mount, Matthew reaches the grand crescendo of this theme. Jesus in the Sermon on the Mount is made to revisit the story of Moses on Mt. Sinai.

There is no doubt that this gospel is not eyewitness reporting. Matthew is not recording things that actually happened; he is interpreting, through the lens of synagogue worship, the power of the Jesus experience. He is using the language of worship, which all of the Jewish followers of Jesus, who made up Matthew's congregation, would have understood. We must learn to read this gospel as its author intended it to be read. It is a Jewish book, and its Jewish readers would have read it properly. As we proceed through Matthew's gospel, this will become apparent on every page.

CHAPTER 13

The Lord's Prayer:
Taught by Jesus or
Composed by the Church?

I F MY CONTENTION THAT THE JESUS OF HISTORY never
preached the Sermon on the Mount is true, then there are
some ancillary things that fall out as collateral damage or
that are unanticipated consequences of that insight. One of
them is the divine authorship of the Lord's Prayer.

Matthew's Sermon on the Mount is where the Lord's Prayer is
introduced (Matt. 6:9–13). There is a second, shorter version of
that prayer found in the later gospel of Luke (Luke 11:2–4), but
Matthew's reference to it is first, and it appears to me to be primary. Its presence in Luke, however, raises once again the question
of sources. Who got what from whom? The evidence for me points
to the fact that Luke copied his version of the Lord's Prayer from
Matthew. Here too I see no reason to postulate the lost source Q.

As has been outlined in earlier chapters, it is my thesis that the three synoptic gospels, Mark, Matthew and Luke, were developed as "liturgical documents," based on the worship life in the synagogue. This thesis serves to weaken dramatically, if not to destroy totally, the argument upon which the Q hypothesis rests. That is also the firmly held and well-documented position of one who has been my mentor, Michael D. Goulder, and it is supported by the work of other scholars, including Austin Farrer.* My dissatisfaction with the Q hypothesis began to form when I embraced the fact that Matthew had constructed the Sermon on the Mount to be used as a Christian way of observing Shavuot. It reached a new level of intensity when I came to realize that Jesus was not the author of the prayer we call the Lord's Prayer. So it is to that prayer that I now turn my attention. It is all but universally used in Christian worship, and frequently it is introduced with these false and misleading words: "And now, as our Savior Christ has taught us, we are bold to say: Our Father," etc.

There is no mention of a prayer taught by Jesus to his disciples, and thus enjoined to them to pray, found in any Christian writing before Matthew, whose text was composed in the middle years of the ninth decade. Is it likely that a "Jesus prayer," enjoined on his followers to pray, would be referenced nowhere in Christian writing for the fifty-five or so years after Jesus' earthly life had come to an end before Matthew first mentioned it?

Paul, who wrote all of his authentic epistles** between the years 51 and 64, never alluded to anything that was called the Lord's Prayer. If the claim is accurate that this prayer carried the impri-

---

*The works of both Austin Farrer and Michael Goulder on which this statement rests are found in the bibliography.

**I refer my readers back to the discussion of Pauline authorship found in chapter 2.

matur of Jesus himself, would Paul have declined to reference it in any way?

These questions become even more provocative when we recognize that Mark, the earliest gospel, which today is normally dated about the year 72 CE, and on which Matthew leaned so heavily, likewise does not include any reference to a prayer taught to his disciples by Jesus. To make this biblical analysis complete, we need also to note that when the last gospel to be written, John, appeared near the end of the first century (95–100 CE), there was again no reference to a special prayer taught by Jesus. Would this final gospel writer have omitted a Jesus prayer if he had known about it? If he did omit it, would that not suggest that it was not authentic and that it did not go back to Jesus? These are questions that the biblical facts raise, yet most Christians appear unaware of the facts and thus unconcerned by the questions.

In Matthew's gospel, the Lord's Prayer is introduced into the Christian tradition simply as a part of this author's commentary on the fourth beatitude: "Blessed are those who hunger and thirst after righteousness, for they shall be satisfied." For the Jews, "righteousness" was a synonym for God's kingdom. To hunger for righteousness was to hunger for the coming of the kingdom of God. That connection between righteousness and the coming of the kingdom of God is one with which the Jewish readers of this gospel would have been thoroughly familiar. The prophet Isaiah referred to Israel as "God's vineyard," where "righteousness"—that is, God's kingdom—is to be established (Isa. 5:7). Later, that same prophet writes that God shows the divine self "present" and holy in the manifestation of "righteousness" (Isa. 5:16).

Matthew first introduces the word "righteousness" into his story at the time of Jesus' baptism. John the Baptist, who in early Christian writing is made to view himself as a figure quite secondary to Jesus, is said to have objected to doing the baptism of Jesus, saying: "I have need to be baptized of you, and do you come to me?" To these words, Matthew's Jesus replies that his baptism is a necessary step to "fulfill all righteousness" (Matt. 3:14). By this Matthew is asserting that Jesus' baptism at the hands of John the Baptist is a means of establishing the kingdom of God. Later, but still in the Sermon on the Mount, Matthew portrays Jesus as exhorting his followers not to be anxious about what they are to eat, to drink or to wear, insisting that they rather spend their time "seeking God's kingdom and God's righteousness" (Matt. 6:33).

"Righteousness" is a word that the deeply Jewish Paul uses frequently in his epistles. Though we will not look at specific examples here, it is worth noting that every time he uses "righteousness," it refers to the kingdom of God.

This context helps us see that when Matthew has Jesus say, "Blessed are those who hunger and thirst after righteousness" (Matt. 5:16), he is referring to those who are living in a tradition of anticipating the arrival of the kingdom of heaven*—that is, those who are spending their lives preparing themselves for that kingdom's arrival by fasting, praying and studying the Torah. In the mind of Matthew the kingdom of heaven is present and becomes visible when God's righteousness is lived out in human history or when God's life is experienced as present in human life.

The earliest Christian prayer recorded in the New Testament is thus not the Lord's Prayer, but a prayer for Jesus to come and in his second coming to establish God's kingdom. That was the meaning present when Paul closed his first epistle to the Corinthians with

---

*Matthew generally refers to the kingdom of *God* as the kingdom of *heaven* because, I believe, of the Jewish reluctance to speak the name God.

the words "Our Lord, come" (I Cor. 16:22). The book of Revelation, with which the New Testament closes, has Jesus in its final chapter promising to "come soon." The prayer of the people in response to this promise is "Amen, come Lord Jesus" (Rev. 22:20).

It is with this understanding that Matthew introduces the Lord's Prayer as part of his commentary on the beatitude that pronounces as "blessed" those who "hunger and thirst" after righteousness. They are the ones who yearn for the kingdom of God to dawn in human history. This is also the setting in which Matthew has Jesus say things about the nature of prayer itself. The Lord's Prayer in Matthew's Sermon on the Mount serves, then, as an example of Jesus' teaching on prayer. We turn now to the Matthean context in which the Lord's Prayer is first mentioned.

Matthew has Jesus begin this section of the sermon by describing the proper prayer attitude. Jesus is portrayed as exhorting his followers to observe a particular tradition when praying. Prayers for the kingdom are not to be done for show, he says. One does not pray in order to be "seen of others" (Matt. 6:5b). So do not do your praying on the street corners, but in the privacy of your own room (Matt. 6:6). Next, Matthew has Jesus say that prayers should not be the stringing together of pious phrases and empty words (Matt. 6:7). Jesus reminds his listeners that God knows their needs before they ask. It is an elementary assertion, but one that so often is neither assumed in prayer nor acted upon. Prayer is thus for Jesus *not* the activity of reminding God about what it is that we need, or what it is that we want God to do.

This is the moment in the Sermon on the Mount that Matthew has Jesus say, "Pray then like this," and then the words of the Lord's Prayer follow (Matt. 6:9). This prayer, which is above all else a prayer for the kingdom of God to come in human history, begins by addressing itself to the one who is beyond all limits. That is what it means to say, "Our Father, who art in heaven." Heaven, in its primary meaning, was never a place located somewhere above the sky, but an expression of the limitlessness of God. God's kingdom is, therefore, not a physical realm, but an experience of God's presence. The kingdom thus becomes that moment in which the life and reality of God become visible in another person or in an event of history.

This prayer then moves on to express the human yearning to be sustained until the kingdom of God arrives. That is what it means to pray, "Give us this day our daily bread" (Matt. 6:11). It is also what this prayer means when it says, "Do not bring us to the test"—or, to use the more familiar, but less accurate, words, "Lead us not into temptation" (Matt. 6:13). This is an expression of the human yearning to be ready to greet the messianic age and not to miss its arrival in our blindness.

In this prayer Jesus has already, and quite obviously, been cast in the role of the messiah, whose task it is to inaugurate the kingdom of God. In all likelihood, then, this prayer is based on an understanding of Jesus that surely had not been worked out by his disciples until well after the defining experiences of his crucifixion and his resurrection, through which his followers had to walk before their hearts and minds could finally recognize his meaning. Had the disciples known prior to his execution who he was, then surely they would not have forsaken him when he was arrested, as Mark tells us so clearly that they all did (Mark 14:50). Nor would the indelible record of the denial of Jesus by Peter have occurred (Matt. 26:69b), to say nothing of the story of one of his own acting as the traitor (Matt. 26:47). Those were certainly not the deeds of a group of disciples who had already come to believe that in Jesus' death and resurrection the kingdom of God would be made manifest!

So it becomes obvious that the Lord's Prayer is the creation of the church and never was taught us by Jesus. It reveals that his followers, well after his death, have realized that in the life of Jesus they had seen the meaning of God's kingdom and now waited in joyful anticipation for his "second coming," when God's kingdom would be fully realized.

To complete this biblical analysis of the prayer we have been taught to call the Lord's Prayer, we need to go back for a moment to the one place in the Bible that gives us a second version of this prayer, namely the gospel of Luke. The words Luke uses are recognizably similar, but they are not identical. In its entirety, Luke's version of the Lord's Prayer reads as follows:

Father,
Hallowed be thy name.
Thy kingdom come.
Give us each day our daily bread and
Forgive us our sins, as we forgive
Everyone who is indebted to us;
And lead us not into temptation. (Luke 11:2–4)

That is Luke's version. It is stark, direct, and abbreviated.

When one finds in Matthew and Luke two similar but not identical versions of the same prayer, some explanation must account for their similarity. Did Luke, who wrote perhaps as late as a decade after Matthew, simply shorten Matthew's version? If he did that, why? Is it not a rather bold act to shorten a prayer that, as

Matthew has told us, Jesus taught his disciples to pray? Or did Matthew and Luke both draw on the common Q source? If these are the only options, then we must ask which one of the two is the more likely and thus the more accurate. Did Luke edit out the more deeply Jewish elements of this prayer in order to make it have a stronger appeal to his more cosmopolitan and less Jewish audience? Or did Matthew heighten the Jewish elements and the Jewish understanding of these words in order to satisfy his purpose in telling the story of Jesus to his Jewish audience?

Is there perhaps a better alternative? Is it part of Matthew's agenda to present to his world a deeply Jewish messiah who would ultimately, as his gospel does, call Jews and Gentiles to step into a new kind of humanity? If the entire Sermon on the Mount was designed by Matthew to give Christian form to a twenty-four-hour Jewish vigil called Shavuot, would he not have wanted to present this prayer in a distinctively Jewish manner? If Luke, and his more "worldly" congregation, had given up such things as twenty-four-hour vigils and eight-day festivals, would he not have tended to edit and even to truncate those long and traditional Jewish liturgies? Does this not suggest Luke's dependency on Matthew as well as on Mark?

Luke's understanding of Pentecost was clearly different from Matthew's. For Matthew, Pentecost was the celebration of the Sinai experience from the book of Exodus, in which Moses received the Torah from God. The Torah was still regarded by him as the greatest gift God had given to the Jews. By the time Luke wrote, however, the Holy Spirit, not the Torah, was thought of as the greatest gift that God had given to God's people, so Luke changed the meaning of Pentecost from the giving of the Torah to the giving of the Spirit (Acts 2). In that context, the

Lord's Prayer in Matthew, which focused on praying for the kingdom of God to come, would in Luke be changed inevitably into a prayer for the church, which was thought of as the place through which the kingdom of God would emerge. That would occur, Luke thought, in and through the mission of a Spirit-filled community called to embrace and convert the world. The Lord's Prayer thus did not have the same meaning for Luke that it had had when Matthew introduced it. By the time the Fourth Gospel was written (95–100), the second coming of Jesus had been explicitly identified with Jesus breathing the Holy Spirit directly into the lives of his disciples (John 20:19b). Perhaps that is why the Lord's Prayer, a prayer for the kingdom to come soon, never occurs in that gospel. It did not fit into the author's understanding of the meaning of Jesus.

So my conclusion regarding the Lord's Prayer is that Jesus never composed it, nor did he ever enjoin upon his disciples the words of this prayer. Yet, while I accept that conclusion, I cannot stop with it, for it does not mean that this prayer has no value for us. It does mean, however, that we must come to see this prayer in an entirely different way.

"Our Father, who art in heaven" means that God cannot be limited by human creeds, doctrines or dogmas. It means that we must seek to define "the holy" beyond the theistic definitions that we have for so long used so uncritically.

"Hallowed be thy name" means that the ultimate, the mystical, the ineffable can never be captured in human words. Perhaps we need to learn from the Jews that if one speaks the name of God, one is pretending that one is able to know and to define God, which is the beginning of human idolatry. That is when we begin to create God in our own image, while pretending it is the other way around. Perhaps we need to heed the warning of Xenophanes, a sixth-century BCE Greek philosopher, who wrote that "if horses had gods they would look like horses."* We walk into the mystery of God; we do not define that mystery.

"Thy kingdom come" means that our eyes must be trained to see the divine inside the human. It means that the kingdom of God comes when we are empowered to live fully, to love wastefully and to be all that we are capable of being. It means that the work of the kingdom of God is the work of enhancing human wholeness; it is not the work of denigrating humanity or proclaiming the doctrine of original sin and human "fallenness." It then also precludes us from offering Jesus as the prescription for our guilt, which seems to mark so much of the contemporary understanding of Christianity. It means that the work of the kingdom of God is done when the eyes of the blind are opened to see reality undistorted by religious propaganda and the ears of the deaf are opened to listen to truth even when it threatens our religious security. It means that the limbs of the twisted, the crippled and the broken will be able to leap with joy as new humanity breaks in upon us without the distortions of our tribal past. It means that the voices of those once muted by fear can sing as they watch all the life-denying prejudices that separate human beings into destructive camps fade away and die. That will be the time when the kingdom of God becomes visible, and that will be when God's righteousness—for which, without always knowing it, human beings have both hungered and thirsted—will finally be revealed.

That will thus become the moment when we are finally able to

---

*Xenophanes appears to be known for little more than this one statement. I haven't been able to track down the exact source of this quote, but the universal attribution seems to be to Xenophanes.

pray the essentially Christian prayer. The distinction of being the earliest prayer in the gospels, I repeat, was not the Lord's Prayer, but the prayer "Come, Lord Jesus!" Come and establish the realm of God in each one of us. Show us what it means to live, not for our survival, but for a higher purpose, for that will be the moment in which we will finally learn that to be human and to be Christian are one and the same thing.

PART IV

Rosh Hashanah
and Yom Kippur:
Miracles and Teaching

CHAPTER 14

Jesus' Journey from Shavuot to Rosh Hashanah

ROSH HASHANAH, one of the great celebrations of the Jewish year, occurs on the first day of Tishri, the seventh month in the Jewish calendar as stated in the book of Leviticus. It is called Jewish New Year's Day and it is true that, in an earlier period of Jewish history, this New Year's Day did actually mark the beginning of the Jewish year.

There is no question as to how Rosh Hashanah was celebrated in early Judaism. It was the holy day to which Jewish hopes for the coming of the messianic kingdom were fastened. The Rosh Hashanah ritual was described in the book of Leviticus in this way: "On the first day of the seventh month you shall observe a day of solemn rest, a memorial proclaimed with the blast of trumpets, a holy convocation. You shall do no laborious work; and you shall present an offering by fire to the Lord" (Lev. 23:24). In time, as the idea of a coming messiah who would usher in the kingdom of God developed, Rosh Hashanah increasingly became the focus of that development. When Rosh Hashanah was observed in the synagogue, a particular passage from the Hebrew scriptures became intimately associated with it: Isaiah 34–35. In that passage the prophet talked about the signs that would accompany the arrival of the messianic kingdom.* The day on which the kingdom would arrive was called simply "the Day of the Lord." For Isaiah this day would be preceded by the violence that would accompany the end of the world. The rivers would be turned into pitch; the soil into brimstone (Isa. 34:9). The land would be burned by day and night (Isa. 34:10). The powers of this world would be destroyed. The text reads: "All its princes shall be nothing. Thorns shall grow over its strongholds, nettles and thistles in its fortresses" (Isa. 34:12–13). The land would no longer be a place fit for human life, so only animals would possess it (Isa. 34:13b–15). All of this would precede the arrival of the kingdom of God.

Then the prophet began to describe the dawning of that kingdom:

The wilderness and the dry land shall be glad.
The desert will rejoice and blossom,
Like the crocus, it shall blossom abundantly.
And rejoice with joy and singing . . .
For God will come and save you!

And when, says Isaiah, God comes at the end of time to establish that kingdom:

The eyes of the blind shall be opened,
And the ears of the deaf unstopped;

---

*This passage is from the writings of the prophet we today call I Isaiah, which constitutes chapters 1–39 of Isaiah.

Then shall the lame leap like the hart,
And the tongue of the dumb [mute] sing for joy. (Isa. 35:1–6)

It was a grand vision.

Over the years all these elements were incorporated into the celebration of Rosh Hashanah. The blowing of the ram's horn was said to herald the arrival of the New Year. When that shofar blast was heard, the people gathered. The message of Rosh Hashanah was then proclaimed: "The kingdom of God is drawing near. Repent, prepare to greet the day of the Lord."

As messianic thinking developed, the tradition grew that Elijah would come to precede the messiah, so Elijah also became associated with Rosh Hashanah. The prophet Malachi cemented this identification when he wrote: "Behold, I send my messenger to prepare the way before me" (Mal. 3:1). Then, shortly afterward, Malachi added: "Behold, I will send you Elijah, before the great and dreadful day of the Lord comes" (Mal. 4:5).

Mark, writing the first gospel, knew well the messianic imagery of the Hebrew scriptures, including Elijah's role. Mark opened his narrative with words that were deliberately designed to make clear the identification of John the Baptist with the role of Elijah, preparing the way for the messiah's coming. Mark clothed John the Baptist in camel's hair with a leather girdle around his waist (Mark 1:6). In the Old Testament Elijah had been described as wearing "a garment of hair with a girdle of leather about his loins" (II Kings 1:8). Mark located John the Baptist in the wilderness out of which Elijah had emerged (Mark 1:3). Finally, Mark gave John the Baptist the diet of the wilderness: "locusts and wild honey" (Mark 1:6). The John the Baptist we meet in the Bible was quite obviously not the John the Baptist of history, but rather the John the Baptist who had been incorporated into Christian messianic thinking. Clearly, John the Baptist had been assigned to the Elijah role by the time the first gospel was written.

Although the text does not say so, it becomes obvious when one studies Mark that his gospel begins with the festival of Rosh Hashanah. That is the holy day that would have come to mind for Jewish worshippers hearing about John's role as the new Elijah, preparing the way for the messiah to come. John's voice in Mark thus replaces the shofar, proclaiming that the kingdom of God is drawing near in the person of Jesus, perhaps is even at hand; and John urges the people to prepare, to be in readiness to greet the kingdom (Mark 1:2–4).

Mark, in building his image of the Baptist, also drew from the "Suffering Servant" passages in the book we call II Isaiah (40–55). John became, in the words made familiar by George Frideric Handel's oratorio *Messiah*, the voice crying in the wilderness, "prepare the way of the Lord, make straight in the desert a highway for our God" (Isa. 40:3–4). All the liturgical signs of Rosh Hashanah are present in the first chapter of Mark. That is why it is clear that the first gospel writer began his gospel with a Jesus story tied closely to this Jewish New Year celebration. It is also obvious, when Mark's gospel is read in its entirety, that he ended his gospel with a Jesus story tied closely to the Jewish observance of Passover (Mark 14:17–15:47).

Let me pause to re-emphasize this point for just a minute. If the opening of Mark's gospel was written against the background of the celebration of Rosh Hashanah, and if the closing of Mark's gospel was written against the background of the celebration of Passover, then is it not obvious that the Jewish liturgical year from Rosh Hashanah to Passover was the organizing principle for Mark's gospel? If that conclusion is valid, then one interpretive task before us is to seek to find Jesus stories in Mark's gospel that are appropriate to Yom Kippur, Sukkoth and Dedication-Hanukkah, which are the three great liturgical days that fall between Rosh Hashanah and Passover. I believe that this can be done; indeed, I chronicled those stories in an earlier book, published under the title *Liberating the Gospels: Reading the Bible with Jewish Eyes.** I shall now refer to them, but quite briefly, to form continuity. I will later describe them more fully as Matthew's gospel develops them anew.

Shortly after Mark's opening with the John the Baptist–Elijah story, he portrays Jesus in a series of cleansing, healing stories that would be appropriate for Yom Kippur, the Day of Atonement, which comes in the Jewish calendar just ten days after Rosh Hashanah. They are, in quick succession, the story of the man in the synagogue with an unclean spirit (Mark 1:21–28), the banishment of a fever (Mark 1:29–31), the cleansing of a leper (Mark 1:40–44) and the healing of the paralytic (Mark 2:1–12). Then, in what is perhaps the clearest Yom Kippur story of all, Mark relates the call of the Jewish man named Levi into discipleship from his job as a collector of taxes from the Jews by the Roman government (Mark 2:13–17). A Jew, working for the oppressive and alien Gentile Romans, and in that service abusing his own people, was "unclean" on every level. For Jesus to enter that evil and unclean world and to lift Levi out of it, making Levi whole, clean and even a disciple, and in the process not becoming unclean himself, was exactly the meaning of Yom Kippur. So this Yom Kippur story comes in Mark's gospel at exactly the proper time, following quickly on his Rosh Hashanah lesson.

---

*See bibliography for details.

As we continue to read Mark, we come next to a long parable about the harvest (Mark 4:1–25). That parable is followed by a series of other harvest-related episodes, all appropriate for the harvest festival of Sukkoth, or what might be called Jewish Thanksgiving. As was noted in chapter 4, this holy day falls five days after Yom Kippur in the Jewish liturgical calendar. Also called both Tabernacles and Booths, Sukkoth lasts for eight days, from Tishri 15 to Tishri 22.

The next festival in the Jewish liturgical year comes weeks later. Known as Dedication, today it tends to be called Hanukkah, as we saw earlier. Dedication-Hanukkah, which comes in the dead of winter, also lasts for eight days. It celebrates the return of the light of God to the Temple. It was established in the Jewish calendars, not from the Torah, but from the time of the Maccabees (second century BCE). If we roam the pages of Mark's gospel, assigning lessons from this gospel to the Sabbaths between Sukkoth and Dedication, we would come in exactly the right moment to chapter 9, in which Mark tells a story about the light of God coming not to the Temple, but to Jesus. We call this narrative the transfiguration. In that story Jesus is being presented as the new Temple, the new meeting place between God and human life under whom both Moses, the giver of the Torah, and Elijah, the father of the prophets, are subsumed. It is the perfect Jesus narrative for the festival of Dedication. So as we trace Mark's story, it becomes more and more obvious that the organizing principle underlying this gospel is not the remembered life of the Jesus of history, but the liturgical year of the first-century synagogue.

As was noted earlier, Mark is considerably shorter than either Matthew or Luke—in fact, about forty percent shorter. Have you ever wondered why both Matthew and Luke felt a compelling need to expand Mark? Perhaps we have now found the answer. Mark, as was suggested in chapter 5, is a liturgical book designed to give us Jesus stories from Rosh Hashanah to Passover. That is only six and a half months of the Jewish year. Matthew and Luke both seem to have felt a compelling need to provide Jesus stories for use in the synagogue on *all* of the Sabbaths of the Jewish liturgical year. Each, therefore, had to expand Mark to accomplish that goal.

Why then, given their common use of Mark and their common desire to cover the whole liturgical year, are Matthew and Luke so different? That too seems clear when one examines the congregations for which these two authors wrote their expansions of Mark. Matthew wrote for a traditionally Jewish synagogue made up of Jewish disciples of Jesus, probably in Antioch of Syria. Luke, on the other hand, wrote for a more cosmopolitan synagogue, possibly in the city of Caesarea, made up of dispersed Jews—that is, Jews living among Gentiles, where Gentile proselytes were beginning to enter the life of the synagogue.

If this pattern of the liturgical year as the organizing principle behind at least the first three gospels is now becoming apparent to us, is it not probable that in the early Christian church, made up as it was primarily of Jews, those people would have recognized this liturgical pattern as the norm? Is it not equally probable that when the Christian church became predominantly a Gentile movement in the second century, this liturgical knowledge would have been lost on those who had no concept of what synagogue worship was all about or how it was organized? That fact would have made it almost impossible for later Gentile Christians to see the original pattern of the early gospels. Without that key to how the synoptic gospels were organized, is it not almost inevitable that they would have misunderstood the gospels and then have begun to assume that they were reading literal history written by eyewitnesses? We are beginning to open up the Jewishness of the gospels, and with that insight we can also begin to dispel the literalness in which the gospels have been trapped for most of Christian history.

Now, listen carefully as I seek to bring this insight out of Mark, where it originated, and into our study of Matthew, who is so dependent on Mark. Since our study of Mark reveals that he began his gospel with a Jesus story related to the Rosh Hashanah celebration, would that not also be the moment when, for Mark, Jesus stepped out of the shadows and into the public arena? So Mark had Jesus being introduced by John the Baptist, both in his proclamation and in his act of baptizing Jesus. By attaching the beginning of Jesus' public life to Rosh Hashanah, Mark limited his story; as we have seen, he filled only half the calendar year. If Matthew wanted to expand Mark to cover the entire year, he had to fill the Sabbaths from Passover to Rosh Hashanah, or from the middle of the first month of Nisan to the seventh month of Tishri. We have already noted that he took the first two Sabbaths after Passover to tell his two Easter stories. Then he had all the Sabbaths from then until Rosh Hashanah to fill.

In chapters 6 through 13 of this book, we saw how he began this effort. Matthew first added the genealogy and the long and elaborate birth story. That filled chapters 1 and 2 of Matthew. Then he expanded the John the Baptist story by filling us in on the content of John's preaching before he related the story of Jesus' baptism. That filled chapter 3. Then he added the content of the temptations in the wilderness, which, along with the inauguration of Jesus' public career by calling his first disciples and beginning to speak broadly, filled up chapter 4. Then, when he reached the festival of Shavuot, he filled chapters 5, 6, and 7 with the Sermon on the Mount, a Jesus story shaped by this Jewish holy day and modeled on Psalm 119, the psalm of Shavuot.

Following the Sermon on the Mount, Matthew still had two to three months of Sabbaths in the Jewish liturgical year to cover before he arrived at Rosh Hashanah, where he could then pick up Mark's story line. Our next task, therefore, is to examine how Matthew covered this period of time. The supposition that the liturgical year of the Jews is the organizing principle in the development of the three synoptic gospels becomes more and more certain as this study unfolds.

Matthew, however, had a problem that he had to address. First, he had already used John the Baptist in his initial story of Jesus' baptism. What would he do when he got to Rosh Hashanah and could not repeat his use of John the Baptist to articulate the Rosh Hashanah message as Mark had done? His solution to this problem was sheer genius.

Matthew borrowed a page from Hollywood and employed the technique of a flashback. Matthew took an obscure note from Mark's gospel (Mark 1:14), which told us of John the Baptist's imprisonment by Herod, and he combined it with the story of Herod's execution of John (Mark 6:14), making the assumption that there must have been a time of imprisonment between his arrest and his execution. When he arrived at Rosh Hashanah in his narrative, he brought John the Baptist out of prison, not in person, but through messengers, and thus back into his text to create the familiar Rosh Hashanah theme. From prison, Matthew had John send emissaries to Jesus asking him: "Are you the one who is to come [that is, the messiah], or shall we look for another?" (Matt.

11:3). It became for Matthew the perfect Rosh Hashanah story, as we shall see when we arrive there.

In Matthew's gospel the Sabbaths between Shavuot and Rash Hashanah would be covered in chapters 8, 9, 10 and part of 11. In these texts Matthew begins by describing a series of apparently supernatural deeds that come in rapid-fire succession, exhibiting a wide range of healings, as well as one story that must be described as a nature miracle.

So we turn in the next chapter to examine Matthew's understanding of Jesus as a miracle worker. The liturgical calendar moves on.

CHAPTER 15

Matthew's Introduction of Jesus as a Miracle Worker

I N THIS PERIOD OF TRANSITION, as Matthew goes from Shavuot to Rash Hashanah, he introduces an aspect of Jesus' life that, strangely enough, has not been mentioned in this gospel before, namely Jesus as a "worker of miracles." Embrace, first, what this means. Matthew is eight chapters into his gospel before he associates miracles with the memory of Jesus! Most people are not aware of the fact that miracles do not appear in the Christian tradition in any narrative that we can identify until early in the eighth decade, or some forty-two years after the crucifixion, when Mark wrote. A quick analysis of the development of the New Testament, however, will make this abundantly clear.

Paul, the earliest writer in the New Testament, who is believed to have died in 64 CE, never alludes to a miracle, and he gives no evidence that he has ever heard of Jesus as a miracle worker. The second strand of the New Testament to be written is what we call the "pseudo-Pauline epistles"—that is, those epistles that claim to be written by Paul, but clearly are not. One group of those epistles, including II Thessalonians, Colossians, and Ephesians, appears to have been written about a decade after his death, but they still predate the gospels, with the possible exception of Mark. None of these, however, mention miracles in connection with Jesus. Q supporters suggest an early date for that supposedly lost document—certainly a date earlier than Matthew and Luke, to whom they attribute a use of Q material. Since I am not convinced of the Q hypothesis, I am not moved by the proposal of a very early date for Q; but even if the Q document is finally established as both real and early, the fact remains that nowhere in the Q material is there an association of Jesus with miracles.*

Some scholars date the noncanonical gospel of Thomas as earlier than the first of the canonical gospels. I think of two of my colleagues in the Jesus Seminar who hold this position, Robert Funk and Stephen Patterson.** I do not agree with this early dating of the gospel of Thomas, believing it to be rather an early-second-century piece of gnostic writing; but again, even if Funk and Patterson turn out to be correct (and both are brilliant scholars), the gospel of Thomas contains no miracle stories that are associated with the memory of Jesus.

So miracles make their first appearance in the Jesus story only

---

*There is one possible exception to this statement, which I will address later in the text.

**Robert Funk I have identified before, and his books are in my bibliography. Stephen Patterson is the George H. Atkinson Professor of Religious and Ethical Studies at Willamette University in Salem, Oregon. He argues this case in an impressive and well-written book entitled *The Lost Way: How Two Forgotten Gospels Are Rewriting the Story of Christian Origins*. See bibliography for details.

when the gospel of Mark is written, and that means not until the early years of the eighth decade. Mark introduces miracles almost immediately: He offers a series of quick miraculous vignettes as soon as he has completed the story of Jesus' baptism by John and Jesus' temptation by Satan (Mark 1:21b). In the last part of chapter 1 and throughout most of chapter 2, Mark tells story after story of Jesus performing supernatural acts or miracles.

Matthew, on the other hand, waits until transition chapters 8 and 9, the chapters we are about to consider, to introduce the idea that Jesus was a miracle worker. We first must let that fact sink in. If there were actual supernatural miracles to report, would Matthew not have led with that? Furthermore, Matthew's gospel, which appears to have been written some ten to fifteen years after Mark, is not an independent source. The miracle stories that he details come overwhelmingly out of Mark, with only a few editorial changes. If Matthew's stories deal with non-supernatural events, then so do Mark's.

These facts, taken together, force us to consider the possibility that the miracle stories in *all* the gospels might represent something other than supernatural events alleged to have actually happened in time and space. That is quite a different conclusion from the traditional way that the miracle stories have been understood in most of Christian history. Could it therefore be, I am forced to ask, that the miracles attributed to Jesus in the gospel tradition actually meant something quite different to the original Jewish authors, Mark and Matthew, and to their original Jewish audiences? Could it be that thinking of the miracle stories as literal deeds displaying Jesus' supernatural power is one more manifestation of those later Gentile Christians who did not understand the meaning of Jewish writings? We keep these possibilities before us as we focus on the miracles in the gospels in general and the miracles in Matthew's gospel in particular.

The first thing a look at these accounts reveals is that some of the miracle stories in the gospels are reminiscent of miracle stories found earlier in the Hebrew scriptures, wrapped around such Jewish heroes of the past as Moses and Elijah. Miracle stories are also associated with these two people's immediate successors, Joshua and Elisha. It would have been quite easy for Jewish authors to magnify these stories and retell them about Jesus.

A second category of supernatural acts that are attributed to Jesus appear to have arisen out of the Jewish messianic tradition. When the Jews first began to develop the idea of the messiah, the one who would inaugurate the kingdom of God, they populated their dreams of "the age to come" with accounts of human wholeness replacing human brokenness, with healing replacing sickness, and with the power of life overcoming the power of death.

We have already noted the powerful and memorable portrait of the day of the Lord drawn by Isaiah in chapter 35 of his book. There the prophet argued that the day of the Lord would be recognized when the signs of human brokenness being overcome became apparent: sight for the blind, hearing for the deaf, the ability to leap for the lame and the ability to sing for the mute. When Jesus came to be recognized as messiah, these same messianic signs then were wrapped around his memory.

That messianic recognition, however, did not come during Jesus' lifetime. Perhaps that is why no miracles were associated with Jesus until decades after his crucifixion. Jesus as a miracle worker was not a result of eyewitness reporting, then, but of interpretive portrait painting. Jewish followers of Jesus would have understood this, for they knew the sources from which the gospel writers were drawing.

Later Gentile Christians would not recognize or know these sources. That was when the miracle stories came to be thought of as literal events that took place in the life of Jesus. Miracles were never that to the Jewish authors of the gospels.

That is also the source of the thinking that led the humanity of Jesus to be compromised in Christian history. When Charles Wesley wrote his familiar Christian hymn "Hark! the Herald Angels Sing," he could without embarrassment include the words "veiled in flesh the Godhead see; hail, the incarnate deity."* Jesus was thought to be a worker of miracles because he had come to be thought of as "God in disguise." That, I submit, represents a long journey from the way miracles were understood by the original Jewish gospel writers.

With this background in mind we now turn to Matthew's developing gospel and watch how he introduces miracles into his story of Jesus. Matthew has by now completed his Shavuot story. Before he gets to Rosh Hashanah, he must find a way to reintroduce John the Baptist in order to tie his story in with Mark, his primary source. So he has John the Baptist from his prison cell send messengers to Jesus. Please confirm, these messengers say, that you are the messiah. Jesus, in Matthew, never answers this request directly. He simply instructs these messengers to return to John and tell him what they see and hear. Then Matthew quotes Isaiah's signs (Isa. 35) to demonstrate that the kingdom of God is dawning in Jesus. The blind see, the deaf hear, the lame leap, the mute sing. Matthew then adds two other categories: "The dead

---

*This hymn is found in most Christian hymnals and sung in most Christian churches, usually as the final hymn at the major Christmas service. "O Come, All Ye Faithful" is usually the opening hymn at that service. I regard Wesley's works as totally misleading in regards to Jesus' divine nature. "Veiled in flesh" he is not.

are raised up, and the poor have the gospel preached to them" (Matt. 11:7).

This flashback to John the Baptist will be Matthew's Rosh Hashanah story. To make that story effective, however, Matthew has to show that Jesus had already done the things that he will claim as kingdom signs in his response to the question asked by John the Baptist. So Matthew fills the Sabbaths between Shavuot and Rosh Hashanah with Jesus doing the miracles that mark him as messiah.

We look now at Matthew 8:1–9:34 to attempt to understand why Matthew placed all of his references to miracle stories in that particular sequence. While he uses Mark's content, he does not use it in Mark's order.

We see that Jesus cleansed a leper (Matt. 8:1–4), cured the centurion's servant (Matt. 8:5–13), healed Peter's mother-in-law (Matt. 8:18–27), banished the demons from a possessed man (Matt. 8:28–34), restored the withered limbs of a paralytic (Matt. 9:1–8), raised from the dead the synagogue ruler's daughter (Matt. 9:18–26), stopped the flow of blood from a woman (Matt. 9:20–22), restored sight to two blind men (Matt. 9:27–31) and loosened the tongue of the deaf mute, thus enabling him to speak (Matt. 9:32–34). Matthew has thus covered all of Isaiah's signs. It remained for him only to demonstrate that the poor had the gospel preached to them. That Matthew will also cover before we arrive at his John the Baptist flashback.

CHAPTER 16

Matthew's Take on the Work of the Kingdom

ONCE THE PICTURE OF JESUS as a miracle worker has been developed by Matthew, he then completes this segment of his gospel by having Jesus deliver the second of his five extended teaching segments. This segment goes from Matthew 9:34–11:1 and serves to cover the remaining Sabbaths in the transition between Shavuot and Rosh Hashanah.

Scholars over the years have noted Matthew's five extended teaching segments and have offered a variety of explanations for them. The most popular of these explanations was the suggestion that Matthew was trying to emulate the Jewish pattern of the five books of the Torah: Genesis, Exodus, Leviticus, Numbers and Deuteronomy. No matter how these scholars juggled Matthew's five teaching segments, however, they never could quite fit them into the Torah pattern, so this explanation proved not to be persuasive.

Yet somehow these five sections must be related, for Matthew ends each of them in a similar fashion. The first of these teaching segments is what has been called the Sermon on the Mount, which we addressed in chapter 12. Matthew concluded that sermon with these words: "And when Jesus had finished these sayings, the crowd was astonished at his teaching, for he taught as one who had authority and not as their scribes" (Matt. 7:28–29). The second teaching segment, which we will now consider, ends this way: "And when Jesus had finished instructing his twelve disciples, he went on from there to teach and preach in other cities" (Matt. 11:1). The third teaching segment, which we shall look at shortly, ends with these words: "And when Jesus had finished these parables, he went away from there" (Matt. 13:53). The fourth teaching segment ends similarly: "Now when Jesus had finished these sayings, he went away from Galilee and entered the region of Judea" (Matt. 19:1). To complete the cycle, the fifth of Matthew's teaching segments ends in this way: "When Jesus had finished all these sayings, he said to his disciples," and then he proceeds to prepare for the Passover (Matt. 26:1–2). So it becomes clear that these five segments are linked in some way in Matthew's mind. What, however, is that link? I hope we will discover that as this study develops. For now just file in your minds the pattern thus far developed.

The first teaching section, as we saw earlier, is related to the twenty-four-hour vigil known as Shavuot. The second one, we now discover, is related by anticipation to the celebration of Rosh Hashanah, the Jewish New Year. A liturgical pattern is beginning to emerge. The context of this second teaching section is clear. Jesus calls his disciples to him in order to instruct them on the work of the kingdom of God and their place in it, clearly in preparation for Rosh Hashanah. Jesus wants to convey to his disciples the authority that will be required in order to carry out the work of that kingdom to which Rosh Hashanah points. The disciples are to be given the power to heal the sick, cleanse the lepers, cast out demons and raise the dead. They are thus to be the ambassadors of the kingdom. Their message is to be a quite simple one: "The kingdom of heaven is at hand." This is when Matthew gives us the names of the twelve disciples (Matt. 10:2–4). The old Israel had twelve tribes; the new Israel, another name for the kingdom of God, must also have twelve tribes! The disciples are to possess the same signs of the kingdom that Matthew has stated, in the string of miracle stories, belonged to Jesus (Matt. 10:6–8).

There are some restrictions, however, that are placed on these newly appointed ambassadors for the kingdom. They are to go "nowhere among the Gentiles and to enter no town of the Samaritans, but to go, rather, to the lost sheep of the house of Israel" (Matt. 10:5–6). They are also to travel light, to "take no gold nor silver, nor copper in your belts, no bag for your journey, nor two tunics, sandals nor staff" (10:9). They are not to be paid for their labor, but to be supported by the people they are serving, "for the laborer deserves his food" (10:10). It is to be a short and quick missionary campaign. They are to stay where they are welcomed and to depart immediately when they are not welcomed (Matt. 10:11–15).

Matthew's Jesus then goes on to reveal that he is speaking to a future that he will see only as a visionary, for he is no longer describing the time implicit in this gospel's writing. This is one more reason why a literal reading of this text is nonsensical. The events about which Matthew now has Jesus speak happened, not in the life of Jesus, but in the life of the Matthean community for which this gospel was written some fifty-five years after the crucifixion.

Now listen to Jesus' words in that context: "I send you out as sheep in the midst of wolves," he says. "Be wise as serpents and innocent as doves" (Matt. 10:16–17). "They will deliver you up to councils" and "flog you in their synagogues." You will be dragged before governors and kings for my sake. That is when you will have the opportunity to bear witness to the Gentiles. It will be the rejection by the Jews that will enable the Gentiles to enter the kingdom (Matt. 10:16–23).

The descriptions of persecution continue. The disciples, like Jesus, will be persecuted, for "a disciple is not above his [or her] teacher" (Matt. 10:24). He urges them to have no fear. Your enemies, he states, can kill only the body, but not the soul. This is to be the test of the kingdom; and those who remain faithful during the persecution will know that they are precious to God, for even the hairs of their heads are numbered (Matt. 10:31).

Jesus tells them that the knowledge he once had to impart to them in darkness would now be proclaimed from the housetops in the bright light of day (Matt. 10:26–33).

It is a powerful testimony to what the cost of the dawning of the messianic age is and will be. Matthew's community was, at the time of the writing of his gospel, clearly living it. When this teaching segment comes to an end, Matthew will move immediately into celebrating Rosh Hashanah. The liturgical pattern organizing this gospel is still clear!

One final note. As I suggested earlier, one story in this series of Jesus miracles is *not* taken from Mark. That is the story of the healing of the centurion's servant (Matt. 8:5–13). A centurion was a Roman soldier in charge of one hundred men. Hence, he was a Gentile. This miracle, the second in Matthew's string of miraculous acts, fulfills a recognized Matthean emphasis. In the birth narrative, after grounding Jesus in the DNA of Jewish history in the genealogy, Matthew immediately has a star announce his birth to the whole world; and in the persons of the wise men, he draws Gentiles to Jesus at the moment of his birth (Matt. 1, 2). When Matthew reaches the end of his gospel, he will allude to the same meaning; his final words to his disciples are: "Go into all the world" (Matt. 28:15). That is, you must go beyond your tribal boundary to incorporate Gentiles into the coming kingdom. So now into this list of Marcan miracles Matthew inserts a non-Marcan story of a Gentile, who is to be the recipient of one of the messianic acts of healing. Luke also has a version of this story, so those who hold to the Q hypothesis place the story into the Q material. If that is accurate, then this would be the only miraculous deed in the Q material. I believe Matthew got this story from Mark, but from a very different part of Mark, and that Luke then got it from Matthew. So this story serves for me as another nail in the coffin of the Q hypothesis.

In the crucifixion scene in Mark 15, that gospel writer places a centurion beneath the cross to interpret the meaning of Jesus' death. This centurion is a man of great insight and faith. He sees in the limp, deceased body on the cross the presence of God. His words in Mark are: "Truly this man was the son of God" (Mark 15:39).

When Matthew tells his story of the crucifixion, he enhances the portrait of this centurion by surrounding him with others, presumably a group of soldiers. He also adds to his narrative that they were all "filled with awe" (Matt. 27:54). I am convinced by my study that Matthew introduces this same centurion earlier in his gospel and simultaneously gives some content to his cry of faith. All of this is suggested in the story of Jesus healing the centurion's servant.

Look closely at Matthew's account (Matt. 8:5–13). The centurion is described as a man of great faith. He intercedes with

Jesus for his servant, but acknowledges Jesus as the source of healing power—a power so great, the centurion says, that Jesus does not have to go to where the centurion's servant is, but has only to speak the word. The centurion describes what it means to be under military authority. In the military, the superior speaks and the inferior obeys. He ascribes to the words of Jesus ultimate authority to which even sickness will be obedient. Jesus speaks the word and the servant is healed. Of this centurion Matthew has Jesus then say: "Not in Israel have I found such faith" (Matt. 8:10). Matthew thus uses this healing story to have Jesus once again assert the universality of the kingdom. In the kingdom of heaven, Matthew has Jesus say, "many will come from the east and west and sit at the table with Abraham, Isaac, and Jacob in the kingdom of heaven" (Matt. 8:11). The kingdom belongs to no one by birthright. It belongs to all who see God at work in Jesus of Nazareth.

So, in my opinion, Matthew *did* get this story from Mark, but he has edited it and expanded it to suit his purpose. Miracles represent the edited and expanded understanding of the Matthean principle, namely that God is present in Jesus and all people will be united in him. It is a wonderful interpretive portrait. It points to the experience of life expanded and made whole in the presence of Jesus. That experience is literal. The story is not. Matthew calls people to enter that experience. It is not a call to believe in miracles, but a call to enter the one who makes all life whole.

PART V

Yom Kippur: The Challenge of Atonement Theology

CHAPTER 17

Introducing Yom Kippur:
The Day of Atonement

ROSH HASHANAH, the Jewish New Year, the time that focuses on the hope for the coming of the kingdom of God, is now over and the liturgical calendar of the synagogue moves to the next holy day. Matthew moves on with it. Now Yom Kippur, the Day of Atonement, becomes the focus of our attention.

It is crucial that Christians understand Yom Kippur, for this holy day of the Jews has probably influenced Christianity more specifically and more directly than any other season or holy day of the Jewish year. Yet Christians seem to know almost nothing about it. They do know some of the concepts associated with this day, while not being aware of their source. No one goes to a Christian service of worship without running into an ancient Christian hymn called "Agnus Dei." That is the Latin title for the words "lamb of God." The identification of Jesus with the lamb of God was taken directly from the liturgy of Yom Kippur. The Christian fascination with the "cleansing power of the blood of Jesus" is also directly related to Yom Kippur. In the more specifically liturgical churches, the blood of Jesus is said to be consumed in the Eucharist, bringing its cleansing power to our inner lives, out of which our evil deeds arise. In the more evangelical churches with less formal worship patterns, the external cleansing power of the blood of Jesus is celebrated in hymns. Being "washed" or "bathed" in the "blood of Jesus," as those hymns describe, is a sure way to be cleansed from the sins of the flesh, which itself began to be thought of as the source of evil.

Some years ago I was in Belgium doing a series of lectures at the University of Ghent. A Roman Catholic professor of the New Testament gave me a bound volume of European paintings, all on the theme of being "washed in the blood of the lamb," and all revealing a vivid theological imagination. Few, if any, of these artists, however, would have seen a connection between their paintings and Yom Kippur. Yet the connection is not only there, but it is quite direct.

The idea of a "scapegoat," one who bears the punishment earned by another, was also born in Yom Kippur. This is a concept frequently referred to in modern political rhetoric. In the Watergate scandal, during the administration of President Richard Nixon, it was John Dean, the president's counsel, who was designated to be the scapegoat. He refused, however, to cooperate. In the Abu Ghraib scandal, during the second Iraq war, it was a female private first class, Lynndie England, on whom the scandal was blamed. It was, however, ludicrous and unbelievable to think that such a low-level soldier could have planned or carried out this event. Trying to make her the scapegoat was doomed to failure. I would suggest that in neither of these incidents were the principals on either side aware that they were using misunderstood concepts originally born in the Jewish holy day we call Yom Kippur.

Much of the language used in telling the Christian story is directly related to Yom Kippur. One can hardly escape in any Christian worship service some variation of what has become the "mantra" of Christianity: "Jesus died for my sins." That mantra is present overtly and covertly in our hymns, in our prayers and in most of our sermons. The nature of a mantra is to assume that its meaning is self-evident and thus does not ever need to be explained. While these words are constantly repeated, few Christians would be able to articulate what they mean. Fewer still would recognize them as coming, even in this distorted form, from the Jewish Day of Atonement.

Are these various manifestations of Yom Kippur that are present in Christian worship a true reflection of Yom Kippur's meaning? I do not think so, but that conclusion will be developed slowly as I examine the Yom Kippur section of Matthew's gospel.

In this chapter introducing Yom Kippur, I will explore first the history of that holy day, its origins, its meaning and the way it has changed over the centuries. Then I will seek to show the ways that Yom Kippur shaped the memory of Jesus, as it was recorded in the gospel tradition. In the following chapter, I will show how Matthew incorporated the specific synagogue observance of Yom Kippur into his gospel. That will involve us in a discussion of what was called in the New Testament "the only unforgivable sin." Finally, I will look at the development in historic Christianity of what came to be called "atonement theology," which I regard as a total distortion of the meaning of Jesus, based, as I believe it was, on a complete misunderstanding of Yom Kippur.

Does Yom Kippur deserve this much attention? I believe it does. If Christianity is to live as a vital force in the twenty-first century, it will have to break out of the distortions of Yom Kippur that have captured our faith story. Nothing in this book will be more important than freeing Christianity from the shackles of atonement theology.

The word "atonement" made its first appearance in the Bible in the book of Exodus. The story is a moving one that we have already looked at, but briefly and in a different context. In Exodus, Moses has gone up to Mt. Sinai to confer with God on the still evolving content of the Torah. The essence of the law had been distilled into what came to be called the Ten Commandments.

The biblical story tells us that when Moses returned from God with the two tablets of stone in his hands, he found that his people, having lost faith in God, were instead worshipping the golden image of a calf. On seeing this apostasy, Moses exploded in anger. He hurled the two tablets of stone to the ground, smashing them into hundreds of pieces. Moses became in that moment the only person ever to break all Ten Commandments at the same time!

God's anger was also portrayed in this story as off the charts. God, the text tells us, wanted to annihilate the entire nation and then to start all over with a new chosen people, which God proposed to raise up out of the descendants of Moses alone. This account is similar to the story of Noah and the flood, in which God wanted to start the covenant people all over with the descendants of Noah. Moses, doing damage control, confronted his people and called them to repentance, which they readily gave. After this repentance Moses then planned to return to God to negotiate another alternative to annihilation. His words to the people were these: "I will go to the Lord; perhaps I can make *atonement* for you" (Exod. 32:30, emphasis added). That is the moment when "atonement" entered the Jewish vocabulary. At its origin, atonement was about forgiveness, about being given a second chance, about God being willing to carve into stone the Ten Commandments a second time. Later it would be this meaning of atonement that would be incorporated into the liturgical year of the Jews as Yom Kippur, the Day of Atonement.

The next biblical reference to atonement is a Yom Kippur text found in the book of Leviticus, a book probably composed during the Babylonian exile in the sixth to fifth centuries BCE by a group of people called "the priestly writers." It was the desire of the priestly writers to establish faithful patterns of worship for the whole of the Jewish people. So all of the Torah's feasts and fasts were outlined, defined and prescribed in that book. About Yom Kippur, Leviticus states: "On the tenth day of the seventh month is the Day of Atonement; it shall be for you a time of holy convocation, and you shall afflict yourselves and present an offering by fire to the Lord. And you shall do no work on this same day, because it is a day of atonement, to make atonement for you before the Lord your God" (Lev. 23:26–28).

Sacrifices were traditionally part of the early Jewish observance of Yom Kippur. In Leviticus the first animals to be identified for sacrifice at this observance were a bull and two goats (Lev. 16:61). The identification of the particular animals to be used as sacrifices at Yom Kippur, however, was destined to shift and change over the centuries. Sacrifices themselves were even finally curtailed when the Jerusalem Temple was destroyed for the second time. It was known as Solomon's Temple when it was destroyed for the first time by the Babylonians in the early years of the sixth century BCE. It was rebuilt after the exile and embellished by Herod the

Great in the years before the birth of Jesus, only to be destroyed again by the Romans in 70 CE in the midst of the Jewish-Roman war. Matthew was writing his gospel some fifteen years after this Roman destruction. This means that when he wrote, the Temple had ceased to exist. It would have been hard to conduct Temple sacrifices when the Temple was no longer standing.

By the time the gospels were written, they reflected a history quite different from the one they purported to be describing. While Jesus lived before the Romans had destroyed the Temple, the gospels were written *after* that event. The bull and the he-goats used for sacrifices had by this time evolved into being a lamb and a goat. Echoes of both the lamb and the goat of Yom Kippur will be apparent in the Jesus story as each of the gospel writers will tell it.

Yom Kippur, at the time of Jesus, was to the Jews a day of penitence, above all else. It was not unlike the current Christian practice of Lent, only far more intense; it lasted not "forty days and forty nights," but one long twenty-four-hour day. On this single day the people were asked to meditate on their sinfulness in the knowledge that God was a forgiving deity. The source of their misdeeds was not found in something called "original sin," of which the Jews had never heard, but in the dynamic experience of comparing the person each individual knew themselves to be with the person they believed they had the capability of being. They had been created, they believed, in God's image. They were meant to share in God's perfection. Clearly, however, they had failed in that purpose.

If one does not understand that purpose as the goal of human life, one will never grasp the meaning of the animals chosen for sacrifice at the time of Yom Kippur. These animals became symbols of the innate human yearning to share in the perfection of God, at least on this one day of the year. Through that symbolism, people could be reminded of their human destiny. The animals of Yom Kippur, a lamb and a goat, served in this liturgical rite to remind the Jews of this reality.

For that reason the sacrificial animals of Yom Kippur had to be carefully selected and certified to be "perfect" specimens. These creatures could have on their bodies no scratches, bruises or broken bones. No animal could symbolically represent the human yearning for perfection without exhibiting that perfection physically.

Symbols grow and expand over the years, however, and so at some point in Jewish liturgical history the understanding of perfection required an expansion of the role played by the sacrificial animals used in Yom Kippur. Moral perfection was now necessary along with physical perfection. The argument went like this. Animals do not have free will, since they live beneath the level of human freedom; they cannot, therefore, choose to do evil. This meant that they are considered morally pure. So moral perfection was added to physical perfection in these animals, and they became symbols of that enduring human yearning to share in the perfection of God. As the liturgy of Yom Kippur unfolded, the animals served either to cover human evil with their perfection or actually to take human evil away. Two liturgies associated with Yom Kippur were then developed. One was the liturgy of the lamb and the other was the liturgy of the goat. I will describe them briefly, but please know that liturgical details are never identical in practice.

At the time of Yom Kippur, the lamb was taken first and slaughtered sacrificially. Its blood was drained into a proper vessel. Armed with the blood of this lamb, the high priest, after himself undergoing elaborate cleansing rituals, would enter the Holy of Holies, the most sacred part of the Temple, into which no one but the high priest was ever allowed to go, and he only on this one

Day of Atonement. Inside the Holy of Holies was what the Jews believed was the throne of God, called "the mercy seat." This was, Jewish mythology stated, God's dwelling place on earth. The high priest approached the mercy seat to smear on it the blood of the "perfect lamb of God." A worshipper, symbolically approaching God through the blood of the perfect lamb of God, now found a doorway into the perfection of God. This is the origin of the claim for cleansing power to be present in the "blood of the lamb." When Jesus came to be identified with the lamb of Yom Kippur, the blood of Jesus was thought to be the source of cleansing.

The second liturgy of Yom Kippur involved the goat, which was next brought to the high priest in front of the assembly of the people. The goat, also a symbol of the people's yearning for perfection, and thus thought of as the sinless one, was in this liturgy to serve the function of taking upon itself, in an act of symbolic transfer, all the sins of the people.

The high priest would grasp the goat by its horns and, praying aloud, would begin to confess the sins of the people. As he prayed, all the sins of all the people came out of the people, it was believed, and managed to land on the back of this goat. The goat was then perceived of as the "sin bearer" and, as such, was subject to the curses of the assembly; the people then began to call for its death. Something upon which all the sins of all the people had been laid was so evil, they thought, that it should not be allowed to live. In the Yom Kippur liturgy, however, the goat was not killed, at least not at once. Instead it was driven out into the wilderness, carrying away with it the sins of the people, leaving the people, symbolically, cleansed of all their sins and thus enabled to be, at least for a day, "at one with God." The goat had become the "scapegoat." It was the creature victimized because of the sins of others.

Echoes of these Yom Kippur practices appear in the New Testament, sometimes overtly, more often as symbolic interpretive insights. Surely it is out of the Yom Kippur frame of reference that Paul explains the death of Jesus in his first epistle to the Corinthians. Paul writes of the crucifixion: "He died *for our sins,* in accordance with the scriptures" (I Cor. 15:3, emphasis added). Only in Yom Kippur is the idea expressed that one, namely a lamb, could die to cover the sins of the people.

Once aware of this background one becomes sensitive to other references relating Jesus to Yom Kippur. Although they are more covert, they now seem easy to find. First, Mark writes of Jesus that he gave his life as a "ransom" for many (Mark 10:45). That is repeated by Matthew in identical words (Matt. 20:28). That word "ransom" makes best sense as a symbol of Yom Kippur. Second, in the Fourth Gospel there is a story told, which we noted earlier, but once again in a different context, that in order to hasten the deaths of Jesus and the two thieves crucified with him, the authorities ordered their legs to be broken, lest the men linger in life and thus defile the Sabbath, which would begin at sundown. According to John, the legs of the two thieves were broken, but when they came to Jesus they found him deceased already, so they did not break his legs (John 19:31). This was done, says John, "that the scriptures might be fulfilled," and then John quoted Psalm 34: "He keeps all his bones, not one of them is broken" (Ps. 34:20). Is this a reference to the perfection of the lamb of God at Yom Kippur? I think it is.

Third, in both Matthew and his source Mark, in the trial scene Jesus is presented to the crowd by Pilate. The crowd responds not only with curses, but with calls for his death (Matt. 27:22; Mark 15:13, 14). Are these "death to him" cries references drawn from the Yom Kippur treatment of the goat? Is Jesus now thought of as and identified with the "sin bearer"? I think that too is true. I also think a liturgically informed Jewish audience would have recognized these symbols and they would have understood that this was not literal writing, but liturgical writing.

I cite here a further reference, which some may think to be stretching the identification between Jesus and Yom Kippur to the breaking point, but I do not. I refer now to the story recorded in all four gospels of a man named Barabbas and of Pilate's attempt to free Jesus by linking him with Barabbas and allowing the people to choose between the two (Mark 15:6–15; Matt. 27:15–23; Luke 23:13–25; John 18:38–40).

This story suggests that Pilate had a custom of freeing a prisoner at the feast of Passover, as a kind of goodwill gesture to the conquered people. The text calls this an "annual custom." There are many reasons that make viewing this narrative as literal history impossible.

First, as I sought earlier to demonstrate, I do not think that the crucifixion was originally attached to Passover. So a Passover custom attached to the crucifixion cannot be taken literally. Second, I can find no reference to such a "custom" in Roman or Jewish records. This "custom" seems to have been mentioned on this one occasion alone, further calling its historicity into question.

Third, I examined the name Barabbas, a name that every Jew reading this story for the first time would surely have noted immediately. "Bar" is one of the Hebrew words for "son." In Mark, for example, blind Bartimaeus is identified as the son of Timaeus, which is exactly what Bar-Timaeus means (Mark 10:46). In Matthew, following the Caesarea Philippi confession of Peter, Jesus is quoted as saying: "Blessed are you, Simon Bar-Jona, for flesh and blood has not revealed this to you, but my father in heaven" (Matt. 16:17). Simon Bar-Jona means Simon, son of Jonah.

The last half of the name Barabbas is "abba," which is a Hebrew name for "father," or "God." In Mark, Jesus, in a passion story, prays: "Abba, Father, all things are possible for thee. Remove this cup from me" (Mark 14:36). Paul, writing to the Romans about prayer, notes that "we cry 'Abba, Father'" (Rom. 8:15). In Galatians, Paul writes: "God has sent the spirit of his son into our hearts, crying 'Abba, Father'" (Gal. 4:6). So the name of this man we call Barabbas means literally "son of God"! If we were to hear this name as the original Jewish audience of the gospels heard it, we would recognize that in the drama of the crucifixion there were two "sons of God" present in the narrative, Jesus and Barabbas. One of them, Jesus, was sacrificed, and the other, Barabbas, was set free. In the liturgy of Yom Kippur there were two symbolic animals, one of which was sacrificed and the other, on which all the sins of the people had been cast, was set free. Are the gospel writers in their story of Barabbas deliberately setting the story of the passion against the background of Yom Kippur? I would not dismiss that possibility. So we have ample evidence that the liturgy of Yom Kippur was influential in the interpretation of the story of Jesus and his cross, which is just one more testimony to the fact that the liturgy of the synagogue shaped the memory of Jesus.

How did Matthew portray Jesus when he came to the time in his gospel when Yom Kippur was being observed in the synagogue? How did he portray Jesus as cleansing the people of their sins? To that point in Matthew's gospel we next turn.

CHAPTER 18

Demystifying the Unforgivable Sin: Matthew's Story at Yom Kippur

CHAPTER 12 OF MATTHEW'S GOSPEL corresponds with Yom Kippur in the liturgical calendar of the synagogue. How do we know? Because we have already determined that in chapter 11 Matthew relates Jesus to Rosh Hashanah, and we will soon see how in chapter 13 Matthew will relate Jesus to the harvest festival of Sukkoth. Since Yom Kippur comes ten days after Rosh Hashanah and precedes Sukkoth by five days, Matthew's gospel must deal with Yom Kippur between those two chapters—at least it must if the theory that the gospel is organized on the basis of the liturgical year of the synagogue is to be verified. If there is a glaring exception to the rule, the theory on which this entire book is based will fall discredited. So searching for a Yom Kippur–related text between chapter 11 (Rosh Hashanah) and chapter 13 (Sukkoth) gives us the opportunity to test this principle yet again.

What we discover in chapter 12 is both fascinating and revelatory. Chapter 12 presents us with a conflict between religious rules and human fulfillment, and it opens to us a new way to look at and to interpret human sinfulness. The chapter begins with a narrative about what Jesus and his disciples do when they are walking through a field of ripened grain on the Sabbath day. They are hungry and tension develops immediately around the issue of whether satisfying human hunger should be placed above the need to keep the Sabbath day's opposition to the work of harvesting grain (Matt. 12:1–8). The disciples decide that human need trumps religious rules and so they pick the grain and satisfy their hunger. They are then judged by the defenders of the religious rules, who proceed to challenge them.

In the next episode (Matt. 12:9–13), Jesus and his disciples have entered a synagogue. This is holy space and it is still the Sabbath. Inside they confront a man with a withered or paralyzed hand. It is a chronic condition, not a life-threatening emergency. If nothing is done on the Sabbath, the need can still be addressed on the first day of the week. Jesus, again putting human need above religious rules, restores the withered hand. The story concludes by announcing that these two actions so infuriated some religious leaders that they "took counsel against him, how to destroy him" (Matt. 12:14). This hostility causes Matthew to identify Jesus with the words of II Isaiah, a favorite text of the early Christians. It was a text reminiscent of the baptism of Jesus in Mark 1. "Behold my servant, whom I uphold, my chosen, in whom my soul delights; I have put my Spirit upon him, he will bring forth justice to the nations. . . . He will not fail or be discouraged until he has established justice in the earth and the coastlands wait for his law" (Isa. 42:1, 4).

The next episode in this chapter is an account of Jesus healing a man who was both blind and mute, which results once more in conflict with the religious authorities. This time the debate is not about the healing itself, but the source of healing. Did Jesus heal with the power of God, or did he do it with the power of Satan? That is, did good lie behind the healing, or did evil? This leads to Jesus identifying something that came to be called "the unforgivable sin." Matthew defines the unforgivable sin as the taking of that which is good and confusing it with that which is evil (Matt. 12:22–35). This is then followed by the request of the religious leaders for a sign that will authenticate Jesus. To their request, Jesus responds that they will receive no sign except the sign of the prophet Jonah (Matt. 12:38–42). What precipitated this reference to Jonah? Did it just pop up out of the blue? There are sixteen books of the prophets in the Hebrew scriptures. Jonah is a very minor one. Why this Jonah reference? Why here? (We'll come back to this in a minute.)

The chapter then moves on to a generic story of exorcism. An unclean spirit is banished from its victim. Homeless now, this evil spirit wanders through waterless places seeking rest; finding none, it then decides to return to the one from whom it had been banished. Finding this previous home swept and cleaned, but still empty, the evil spirit returns, bringing seven other spirits, all more evil than the original one. The last state of that person becomes worse than the first. This story ends with the words: "So shall it be with this evil generation" (Matt. 12:45).

This chapter then concludes with a narrative about the family of Jesus, his mother and his brothers, coming to speak to him. In

Mark's gospel, from which Matthew took this story, the explanatory note was added that his family thought he was "beside himself" (Mark 5:21) and so they came to take him away. Matthew
omits that detail, but he does not remove the motif of displea-
sure. Jesus, in response, rejects identification with his family and
announces that his real family is not a biologically defined entity;
on the contrary, "whoever does the will of my Father in heaven is
my brother and my mother" (Matt. 12:46–50).

We shall now mine this material to discover the Yom Kippur
motifs included within it, for they are everywhere!

"Where does holiness lie?" is the question Matthew is addressing. Is holiness found in keeping religious rules or in the vision of
human wholeness? Does the rule about Sabbath day observance
take precedence over human hunger? Does the rule about keeping
the Sabbath holy take precedence over the work of healing, which
brings wholeness? When Jesus confronts and cures a man who is
blind and mute, both conditions at that time being thought of as
manifestations of God's punishment on a sinful life, is that a sign
that the kingdom of God is destroying the reign of Satan on earth?
"How could that be?" is the question the religious hierarchy raises.
Jesus is not a validated religious leader in their eyes. Can God or
does God operate outside the boundaries of traditional synagogue
definitions? The religious leaders seem not to think so, for instead
of rejoicing in the presence of this newly restored human life, they
begin a concerted attack on Jesus' credentials. They claim he cures
by demonic, not godly, power. These leaders see goodness, but they
call it evil! Their distortions have become so total that when the
work of the spirit is on display, they define it as the work of Satan.

This is what Jesus pronounces to be the one "unforgivable sin."
Yom Kippur cannot cleanse this sin. It is too deep a distortion. If

one confuses cleanness with uncleanness, if one confuses sickness with health, brokenness with wholeness, the life of God with the life of Satan, then there is no hope of forgiveness. Such a life is lived in total darkness, total uncleanness. No one can be cleansed of sin unless that one has some awareness of sin. No one can come to the light if that person is not aware that he or she lives in darkness. Yom Kippur, with its message of atonement, cannot address this complete distortion of all values.

These critical religious leaders, still worrying about whose religious leadership is authentic, ask Jesus, the challenger of their rules, to provide for them a sign that he is of God and not of Beelzebul, the "prince of the devils." To this challenge Jesus responds that no sign will be given except for "the sign of the prophet Jonah."

Gentile readers of Matthew's gospel generally do not know that one of the popular readings from the prophets associated with the Yom Kippur liturgy was the book of Jonah, so they are surprised that Matthew now turns the conversation to this book. Matthew's original audience, however—the Jews for whom this gospel was written—would not have been surprised at all, for they were familiar with the customs and practices of the synagogue's liturgical patterns. The subject of the book of Jonah was a familiar Yom Kippur theme, because Jonah's "sin" was that he, too, possessed this mistaken identification. Jonah had confused his vision of what is holy with God's vision of what is holy. In the Jonah story, God had called Jonah to make God known among the people of Nineveh, the capital of the Assyrian Empire.

There are indications all over this little book that the story is a parable. It is not and was not ever intended to be read by anyone as a literal story. One indication of this is that the story was written hundreds of years after the decline of the Assyrian Empire.

Nineveh was thus no longer even in existence as a city! Everyone knew that. The liturgical setting for this book is the time of one of the later Jewish returns from Babylonian exile, probably in the later years of the fifth century BCE. A number of generations earlier the Babylonians had conquered Assyria. Then the Persians conquered the Babylonians, making a Jewish return to their homeland possible. The return came in waves over several centuries. Jonah was a parable associated with one of these returns.

The second recognizable sign that the Jonah story is not history is found in its use of exaggeration. The way people of the Middle East in that day informed their audience that a story was not history was to fill it with exaggerated details. The Western technique designed to accomplish the same thing is to begin the story with the words "Once upon a time." Jewish readers were not fooled by these exaggerations. Gentile readers probably were.

We see the use of exaggeration to convey the knowledge that this story is not to be read literally all over the Hebrew scriptures. In addition to Jonah, there is the narrative in Genesis 11, where human beings decide to build a tower so tall it would not only reach beyond the sky, but would bring them literally into the presence of God, who was assumed to live above the sky. Do you really suppose that ancient people believed this was possible? It was an exaggerated folktale, designed to communicate that the audience was to pay attention to the *meaning* of the story, not to its literal details. This particular story was designed to explain just why it was that there were so many different human languages.

I am convinced that the Exodus story of the Israelites crossing the Red Sea on dry land is another example of that Middle Eastern form of exaggeration. Wind does not push back the flow of water to create dry land in the midst of the sea so that hundreds of thousands of escaping slaves can make it to freedom. This too was a parable about God's infinite caring for the oppressed people of Israel.

Like these accounts, the book of Jonah is filled with exaggerated details. The destroyed city of Nineveh is resurrected and magnified. The book of Jonah describes Nineveh as "an exceedingly great city, three days' journey in breadth" (Jon. 3:3). At its height in history, this city probably had fewer than ten thousand people. In today's world, I could walk from the Hudson Tunnel entrance leading from one side of New York City to the other in less than three days, and New York has almost a thousand times more inhabitants than this biblical town. Clearly the size of Nineveh has been exaggerated.

The account continues with a great fish large enough to swallow a man whole and to have that man live within its belly for three days and three nights—again, signs of this same quality of exaggeration. Only Western Gentiles, locked, as so many of them still seem to be, inside a literal understanding of the Bible, would ever have read the Jonah story as an account of a literal event in history. The book of Jonah had a far more profound message to convey, and the Jews saw that message as a Yom Kippur message. Matthew, aware of that, pulls the book of Jonah into his Yom Kippur story in chapter 12.

Jonah's "sin," as noted above, was that he dared to limit God's definition of what is holy to his own definition of what is holy. He assumed that God had no ability to love beyond the boundaries of Jonah's love. He called "evil" what God had called "holy." That is the nature of human prejudice. If Jonah saw the people of Nineveh as having no worth, he assumed that God likewise saw them as worthless. Jonah, just like Jesus' critics in the Yom

Kippur chapter of Matthew's gospel, was calling "evil" what God had called "good."

Unable to embrace Jesus' vision, these critics responded by demanding that Jesus produce a validating sign proving that he really was in God's service. Jesus replied: "An evil and adulterous generation seeks a sign" (Matt. 12:38). Matthew filled his gospel in the Rosh Hashanah section with signs drawn from the prophet Isaiah (Isa. 35). The kingdom of God will be announced, Isaiah said, by the blind being able to see, the deaf to hear, the mute to sing, and the lame to leap. These signs are all around, said Matthew in that earlier section, but you do not see them because you call good evil and you call God Satan.

Matthew then expands his Yom Kippur message. The queen of the South (Sheba), he has Jesus say, will also condemn this generation. She came from the ends of the earth to hear the wisdom of a Jewish king named Solomon. You do not listen, Matthew has Jesus tell those seeking signs, though one greater than Solomon is present (Matt. 12:42).

In Yom Kippur, the status of being unclean fades before the divine presence. Yet if one cannot distinguish between God and Satan, if one calls evil good, if one's religion places limits on the love of God, if one claims that being God's chosen means that all others are God's rejected, then there can be no atonement, and Yom Kippur is a failure.

Chapter 12 is a powerful, cohesive Yom Kippur message. Matthew continues to relate Jesus to the liturgical calendar used in the synagogue, but Jesus always transcends that calendar's religious limits. When one enters the life of God, Matthew is saying, one can no longer call unclean anything that God has made, nor can one see any person who is loved by God as having no worth. We can no longer use religion to assert that those beyond the boundaries of our religion are somehow also beyond the boundaries of God's love. Prejudice dies in this moment and universalism is born. That is what atonement is all about. How badly organized religion, including Christianity, has misunderstood this! The love of God can never be bound by the limits of human love. That is the meaning of Yom Kippur.

How then did Christianity get to the point where atonement meant that God punished Jesus because of your and my sinfulness? Where did the Christian emphasis on "original sin" arise? Why have Christians called the cross the place where Jesus died for our sins? Why has Christianity become primarily a religion of guilt, rather than of grace; of divine punishment, more than divine love?

It all relates to a Gentile misunderstanding of the Jewish meaning of Yom Kippur. Matthew, properly understood, will lead us to uncover the fact that Gentile ignorance has turned Christianity into a religion based on atonement theology. That is a momentous message, because the dated distortion of atonement theology is killing Christianity in our generation.

CHAPTER 19

The Curse of
Atonement Theology

MODERN CHRISTIANITY, which was strongly influenced by St. Augustine in the fourth century of the Common Era, has been built on a sense of human alienation from God. It is thus a story of how salvation overcomes alienation. It portrays the Christ as a God-sent savior dispatched to bring about a new union between the human and the divine. That is the meaning of "atonement," as that term has come to be used in the church. Atonement theology reflects the idea of a fall from our original perfection into the status of brokenness. We were, according to this understanding, created to be at one with God, but that oneness has been destroyed by human disobedience. Atonement theology draws much of its meaning from Yom Kippur, which was always known as the Day of Atonement. I will suggest, however, that the idea of atonement in Yom Kippur and the development of atonement theology in Christian history have almost nothing to do with each other. So deep is this distortion that I have become convinced that we must put an end to atonement theology or there will be no future for the Christian faith. This confusion comes about because Gentile Christians have read a very different understanding into the Jewish Day of Atonement from the meaning the Jews contemplated on their own. We turn now to this story.

The "fathers" of the church, especially Augustine, the bishop of Hippo in North Africa, read the Bible as if it were one continuous book written presumably by God. That is why they called the Bible "the Word of God." They had no understanding, as we have come to learn in the last two hundred years, of the relationship between various parts of the biblical story to history or to one another. The book of Genesis, with which the Bible opens, is, we now know, the composite of at least four Jewish sources written over a period of up to six hundred years. It was not a single story in which one event followed another in sequential order. For example, the story of creation in seven days that forms the bulk of Genesis 1 comes from the pen or pens of the priestly writers who expanded the Hebrew scriptures dramatically during the Babylonian exile of the late sixth century BCE. This seven-day story was actually based on a Babylonian myth of creation. Its primary function was to ground the Jewish Sabbath day tradition in the act of creation. Observing the Sabbath was among the cultic rituals that were part of the priestly writers' attempt to keep the Jews separate from their oppressors, thus making the Jews different. In this late-developing creation story, two things are of particular note. First, creation, in this depiction, was the act of God, and therefore all created things, including human life, were perfect and complete. Second, God created the world ex nihilo, so that not only was creation good, but the material out of which creation was forged was also good. In this dramatic poem God first looked out on all that God had made and pronounced it good. Then God completed the creation and declared the Sabbath day to be a day of rest. The world had been made. Creation was complete, and God had called it good.

The second chapter of Genesis, or at least beginning at Genesis 2:4b, which is where we believe this second source originally started, tells a story written probably in the middle years of the tenth century BCE, or some four hundred–plus years before chapter 1. It obviously, therefore, did not follow on from chapter 1 of Genesis.

This chapter was an attempt to explain the presence of evil and to give some content to what appeared to be a universal human yearning for oneness with the divine. It presupposed a human sense of separation or alienation and it yearned to see that separation overcome. It called the goal of that yearning "atonement," the process of being made at-one with God. Augustine, who assumed that Genesis 1 was chapter 1 in a book that contained the literal words of God, and that Genesis 2 was the second chapter in the same book, put the two chapters together and read the latter as a sequel. Genesis 2, he assumed, described the fall from the perfection and original goodness of creation depicted in chapter 1. So almost inevitably the Christian scriptures from the fourth century on were interpreted against the background of this (mis)understanding.

The primary trouble with this theory was that by the fourth century of the Common Era there were no Jews to speak of left in the Christian movement, and therefore the only readers and interpreters of the ancient Hebrew myths were Gentiles, who had no idea what these stories originally meant. Consequently, they interpreted them as perfection established by God in chapter 1, followed by perfection ruined by human beings in chapter 2. Why was that a problem? Well I, for one, have never known a Jewish scripture scholar to treat the Garden of Eden story in the same way that Gentiles treat it. Jews tend to see this story not as a narrative about sin entering the world, but as a parable about the birth of self-consciousness. It is, for the Jews, not a fall into sin, but a step into humanity. It is the birth of a new relationship with God, changing from master-servant to interdependent cooperation. The forbidden fruit was not from an apple tree, as so many who don't bother to read the text seem to think. It was rather from "the tree of knowledge," and the primary thing that one gained from eating the fruit of the tree of knowledge was the ability to discern good from evil. Gaining that ability did not, in the minds of the Jewish readers of the book of Genesis, corrupt human nature. It simply made people take responsibility for their freely made decisions. A slave has no such freedom. The job of the slave is simply to obey, not to think. The job of the slave-master is to command. Thus the relationship of the master to the slave is a relationship of the strong to the weak, the parent to the child, the king to the serf, the boss to the worker. If human beings were meant to live in that kind of relationship with God, then humanity would have been kept in a perpetual state of irresponsible, childlike immaturity. Adam and Eve had to leave the Garden of Eden, not because they had disobeyed God's rules, but because, when self-consciousness was born, they could no longer live in childlike dependency. Adam and Eve discovered, as every child ultimately must discover, that maturity requires that the child leave his or her parents' home, just as every bird sooner or later must leave its nest and learn to fly on its own. To be forced out of the Garden of Eden was, therefore, not a punishment for sin, so much as it was a step into maturity.

By the end of the fourth century of the Common Era, Christianity had become a legal religion in the Roman Empire. The great majority of the world's Christians no longer understood or cared about the original Jewish worldview in which these Genesis stories had been created. They were Greek-speaking Gentiles, not Hebrew-speaking mythmakers. As Greeks, they saw the world not as a unity but as a duality. Good was separate from evil. God was separate from the world. Bodies and souls were antithetical concepts. Flesh and spirit were in a dualistic war waged within each one of us. That became the matrix in which what we now call "traditional Christianity" came to be understood.

The problem facing the church today is that this fourth-century understanding of Christianity is dying before our eyes. It no longer translates into anything that we know or understand about life. It no longer seems relevant to our minds. Because we know no alternatives to the ancient pattern, however, we watch Christianity being split today into two mutually exclusive halves, neither of which can tolerate the other. One half insists on literalizing the ancient Hebrew stories, making them mean something they were never intended to mean, while the other half dismisses everything that its adherents see as "religious content" as so much nonsense. Neither of these two sides would accept this definition of themselves, of course. Those who cling to the religious definitions of the past perfume their religious understandings, seeking to make them socially acceptable for a few more years. Those who dismiss religion as of no ultimate worth are not hostile or aggressive about its role in society and are willing to ignore religion until it begins to infringe upon their secular lives with religiously inspired prejudices or religiously inspired laws that they too must obey. Out of neither of these two sides in the contemporary religious debate is there any hope for building a Christian future.

Adherents of the first of these two sides are defined today as biblical or creedal fundamentalists. These are the ones who believe that the predictable pattern of understanding Christianity that they received from the fourth century, and which they think is what Christianity has always been, is an "unchanging, eternal truth." These fundamentalists come in both a Protestant and a Catholic variety.

On the Protestant side of Christianity, its adherents make a case for both the ultimacy and the adequacy of the Bible. If it is not the literal "Word of God," then it at least still has a powerful claim on truth that must be respected. So they quote it to justify their current prejudices, whether they be against the rise of equality for women or the full acceptance of gay and lesbian people. Before it became socially unacceptable to do so, they also quoted it to support slavery and segregation without embarrassment. On the Catholic side of Christianity, its adherents make the case for the infallibility of the pope, the unchanging nature of truth and the fact that the Catholic Church alone is both the defender of this truth and the articulator of this truth, and thus the only institution that properly professes it.

Neither the Protestant nor the Catholic form of fundamentalism, however, can exist with credibility inside the knowledge available in the modern world, which is so different from that which was available in the medieval world. Fundamentalist proclamations and public statements thus tend to hang in the public arena with a note of embarrassment attached to them, and politicians embarrass themselves by refusing to respond to such questions from reporters as: Do you accept evolution as true? They do not seem to realize that to waffle on that question when evolution is the assumed truth taught in every medical school in the developed world marks them as either profoundly ignorant or deviously manipulative.

Cardinal Joseph Ratzinger, later to become Pope Benedict XVI, said in an address to the College of Cardinals just before his papal election that "relativity" in truth must be vigorously opposed in order to maintain the power of the Catholic Church's claim that it possesses "saving and unchanging truth." That is the same mentality that allowed and encouraged the Catholic Church to put a man named Galileo on trial for heresy in the seventeenth century. Galileo had challenged "the eternal truth" as to the shape of the universe and how it operated. If Galileo were to turn out to be correct, then that church's claim to be able to explain reality in traditional terms would clearly be challenged. The earth *had* to remain the center of the three-tiered universe because all Christian thinking assumed that. In 1991 the Vatican announced that it now had come to the conclusion that Galileo was right. It was about time! Space travel had already begun. "Unchanging truth" has a way of changing constantly. Relativity is in every explanatory word that has ever been uttered.

Even more than that, how could the church continue to claim or even to pretend that God lived just beyond the sky, close enough to be able to see and to document in the record books of life all the deeds and misdeeds of a human being? If there were no ledgers containing the recordings of the deeds of human beings, there would be no basis upon which to assign a person to his or her ultimate destination in either heaven or hell. If there was no all-seeing supernatural being above the sky, then the whole guilt system by which the church sought to control behavior would be fatally compromised. Cardinal Ratzinger's fear was that if "relative truth" replaced "unchanging truth," the inevitable result would be a shift in the world's moral compass, which would place enormous pressure on all sources of traditional authority. The fact is that this shift has occurred whether anyone likes it or not.

Protestantism, especially in its evangelical form, has not been much different, though it was never as monolithic as the Catholic Church was in its response. I listened recently to a well-known television preacher who was speaking in a cavernous church that was filled to capacity with worshippers, all nodding their heads in approval and applauding regularly as he spoke.* This evangelist defended the literal accuracy of every verse of the Bible, which he regularly called the "Word of God." "If every word of this holy book is not true," he roared, "then *none* of it is true." "Only three books in all of humanity," he continued, "have ever claimed to be the 'Word of God': the Koran, the Book of Mormon and the Bible." He then proceeded to ridicule both the Koran and the Book of Mormon, calling each of them demonic in nature. Then, by a strange leap in logic, he said that left us only with the Bible.

Having claimed for the Bible alone literal authority, he then made the case that removing the Bible from the public schools of America had opened the door for the rise of "atheism, communism, feminism, cross-dressing, child abuse, divorce, alcoholism and homosexuality." He then railed against the U.S. Department of Education and the "bureaucrats who controlled the curriculum used to teach our children in public schools." He appeared to yearn for the "good old days," when the education of our children was in the hands of preachers, who taught the children in their

---

*This was an earlier recorded sermon by Jimmy Swaggart, taped before his fall from grace into sexual scandals.

churches with their only textbook being the King James Version of the Bible. He cited statistics about how many children today cannot read, spell or solve simple problems of arithmetic. This, he contended, was part of a deliberate attempt, carried out by the "liberal graduates of Harvard, Yale, and Princeton," to keep our children "so dumb that they will not resist turning America into a big government-type communist state."

He was quite sure that every event in the Bible was true, absolutely true. The world was not formed billions of years ago, he argued. Human life did not evolve from lower forms of life. The Red Sea actually did split in half so that God's people could escape slavery in Egypt by walking through that sea on dry land on their journey to freedom. The walls of Jericho did fall to allow Joshua's troops to enter. A star did travel through the sky so slowly that the wise men could keep up with it. The virgin birth was biology. The resurrection was the physical resuscitation of a dead body. Finally, in his greatest rhetorical flourish, he stated that not to believe each of these basic biblical truths was to "assign yourself to the eternal lake of fire spoken of in the book of Revelation."

Despite the animosity that cultic Catholic imperialists and Protestant fundamentalists have for each other, at their cores there is a remarkably similar understanding of truth. That is why in the United States, Catholics and evangelical Protestants tend to be consistent members of the religious coalition organized around the conservative principles of right-wing politics. Whether we are comfortable admitting it or not, this is also where the majority of America's traditional Christian population is.

Working against this traditional Christian mentality are proponents of a revolt against *all* things religious. Theirs is not an impotent attempt to shore up yesterday's truth so that it will endure forever, but rather a rejection of all religions based upon their supernatural assertions. The people who share this point of view form the core of a newly organized, growing and thoroughly secularized society. They see no place in their lives for yesterday's religious systems. Reflecting the educated ranks in our society today, they have come to embrace not just Galileo, but an understanding of the vastness of the universe that even Galileo could not have imagined. Since most of them have never heard of a God other than the supernatural deity who lives above the sky and who possesses miraculous power, they assume that there must not be any God at all. Their former image of God violates everything they know about how the world operates, and so the idea of God itself becomes an irrelevant idea for them.

In a world of emancipated women, who are no longer willing to be subservient to men and no longer willing to have their bodies controlled by men, the attitudes of the traditional Christian church are anathema. These women are today heading up Fortune 500 companies. They occupy seats on the United States Supreme Court. They serve as our representatives in Congress and in the Senate of the United States and in just about every other elected office in this nation. They are professors, clergy, doctors and lawyers. They are also bankers, stockbrokers, analysts and primetime anchors on major news and even business television channels. The White House is now clearly in their sights, and everyone, whether they like it or not, can now imagine a woman as the president of the United States. That hurdle of imagination has been passed. It is no longer inconceivable to anyone. Reality always follows closely behind the ability to imagine.

These members of the secular society also see a world in which people of color are entering every area of power from which they once were forbidden. An African-American has already now been twice elected to the White House. African-American governors have been elected in states as diverse as Virginia and Massachusetts. Familiar American corporations from American Express to Citigroup to McDonald's have had CEOs of color. The Black Caucus in the United States Congress is large enough now that it exercises enormous power. Black commentators cover the world's news from a black perspective. An openly gay man has chaired the U.S. House of Representatives committee on banking; the Dodd-Frank bill, by which big banks are regulated today, bears his name. The military no longer discriminates against homosexual persons. Professional athletes now include openly gay, lesbian and transgender participants. Equality of the sexes in the government's support of university athletic programs has now swept through our country, based on a ruling by the United States Supreme Court. The God of the past, who confined and maintained the ordered ranks of society, where people of color, women and gay and lesbian people "knew their place," has simply died. Yes, traditional religion remains strong and vibrant in the rural areas and in the small towns of this nation and in some of the less well educated nations of the world. When traditional religious leaders make pronouncements on public events today, they generally achieve nothing more than to provide lines for late-night comedians.

There is little doubt that despite the sound and fury of the political right, rooted most significantly in that same small-town and rural America, where traditional religion still undergirds both their values and their prejudices, these attitudes are dying. The birth and growth of a deeply secular, non-religious society is the primary evidence for this. The traditional forms of religion, which the secular society is today rejecting, were ultimately based on a security that they could never deliver. They also reflect an understanding of reality that is believed by fewer and fewer people.

How does this analysis of contemporary life fit into our discussion of atonement theology? The answer is simple. The version of Christianity that is dying today is rooted in the grossly misunderstood concept of atonement described above. Although that concept's roots lie in Jewish faith and worship, it has been corrupted over the centuries into an understanding that Jews observing Yom Kippur would never recognize. Gentile Christianity became a legal religion within the Roman Empire in the fourth century. That was when the councils, made up of Greek-thinking, Gentile leaders, adopted creeds, created doctrines and formulated "dogmas." Later centuries of Christians would adopt liturgies and write hymns to be used in worship, based on those creeds and dogmas.

It was in that transition movement in Christian history that Christians first co-opted and then corrupted the Jewish concept of atonement, turning it into something they called "substitutionary atonement." It was based on the ancient myth rooted in Augustine's misunderstanding and subsequently on the literalization of that misunderstanding. That transition period was when Christians began to talk about "the fall of man." This kind of thinking became so dominant that by the time Christianity achieved power in the Roman Empire, substitutionary atonement had become the cornerstone of all Christian theology, and would remain so throughout the centuries until this very day. This theology was captured best in the words that became the Christian mantra that I have previously identified: "Jesus died for my sins." This mantra was then incorporated into everything that was called Christian. Substitutionary atonement, which became the Christian view of salvation, presented us ultimately with a God who is a punishing monster, with a Christ who is God's eternal victim and with a humanity characterized by a debilitating guilt.

There is no way that this kind of Christianity can survive, but I suspect it will take another century to convince the last hangers-on of this fact. Those people we now designate as "millennials," adults who achieved maturity in the twenty-first century, announce it rather loudly. The way Christianity has generally been misunder-stood has no future. I make that announcement as one who is a deeply committed, practicing Christian. The place the Christian church went wrong was when we literalized a misconception of the doctrine of atonement, mistakenly drawn, as it was, out of the Jewish practice of Yom Kippur.

Atonement theology assumes that we were created in some kind of original perfection. We now know that life has emerged from a single cell that evolved into self-conscious complexity over billions of years. There *was* no original perfection. If there was no original perfection, then there could never have been a fall from perfection. If there was no fall, then there is no such thing as "original sin" and thus no need for the waters of baptism to wash our sins away.

If there was no fall into sin, then there is also no need to be rescued. How can one be rescued from a fall that never happened? How can one be restored to a status of perfection that he or she never possessed? So most of our Christology today is bankrupt. Many popular titles that we have applied to Jesus, such as "sav-ior," "redeemer," and "rescuer," no longer make sense, because they assume that state of original sin into which we had suppos-edly fallen and from which we must be saved. Those titles, too, will have to go. The atonement aspects of the way we have tradi-tionally told the Jesus story have become morally repugnant. The idea of a God who, in order to forgive, requires a human sacrifice and a blood offering is absurd. Why would anyone be eager to worship such a deity? If the father God has to kill the divine son on the cross, as atonement theology constantly implies, does that then not make God the ultimate child abuser?

Look also at what atonement theology has done to human life. It has turned the negative emotion of guilt into the ultimate coin of the Christian realm. Our hymns enhance our guilt: "Amazing grace, how sweet the sound that saved a *wretch* like me." We sing to God "How great thou art," but the cause of greatness turns out to be that God can stoop to rescue so worthless a sinner as you and me. Many of our Christian hymns, but especially our Lenten hymns, traffic in guilt. "Who was the guilty? Who brought this upon thee? Alas, my treason, Jesus, hath undone thee. 'Twas I, Lord Jesus, I it was denied thee. I crucified thee."* Another example of this kind of destructive, negative theology is found in the hymn "There Is a Green Hill Far Away." Among its words are: "He died that we might be forgiven, he died to make us good."** The assumption is clear: We are sinful, evil people by nature.

If one thinks our hymns are bad, one has only to look at traditional Christian liturgies for something even worse. The primary note struck in Christian worship today, whether Catholic or Protestant, is to denigrate human life as evil. Our humanity is regularly judged, insulted, and condemned in Christian liturgies. Worshippers have absorbed this negative content for so long that we are almost immune to its destructive power. Perhaps liturgy is

---

*From the hymn "Ah, Holy Jesus," written by Johann Heermann in 1630. It appears in the 1940 Episcopal Hymnal as Hymn 71.

**This hymn was written by Cecil Frances Alexander in 1848. It appears in the 1940 Episcopal Hymnal as Hymn 65.

something like "drip torture." Christian liturgy assumes the definition of human life as fallen. We were born in sin, we have said. We once taught that if babies died before they were baptized, they had died in the "sin of Adam" and were, therefore, bound for the fires of hell. That was, however, too harsh a sentence for people to accept without pain, so "limbo for children" was created. In this limbo, unbaptized children did not experience the presence of God through all eternity, but at least they did not have to endure the fires of hell. Theirs was a neutral eternal destiny. That was thought to be an "improvement." In traditional Christian liturgy, we are taught to kneel before God, who is defined as our master and judge. Is that not a strange concept? A slave might kneel before his or her master, a serf before the lord of the manor, or a beggar before the source of the next meal, but is that the proper posture for a child of God to assume before the God whose name is love? Yet churches still instruct, or if they wish to be less directive "invite," worshippers to kneel. It is for me a directive that violates everything I understand about who God is. We are told in worship that "there is no health in us," and that "we have done those things we ought not to have done and we have not done the things we ought to have done." No improvement appears to be possible, for we repeat these words every week. They constitute traditional Christianity's liturgical definition of the meaning of human life. In Christian worship the assault on the dignity of our humanity is relentless. We are told that we are not worthy to "gather the crumbs" from underneath the Lord's table. The constant prayer coming from the lips of these fallen sinners is the plea for mercy: "Kyrie eleison!" Lord have mercy; Christ have mercy; Lord have mercy. Over and over again we hear these words. We have threefold kyries and ninefold kyries. We even respond in our prayers with the plea for mercy: "Lord, in your mercy, hear our prayer." Is the prayer for mercy ever a worthy prayer for anyone? If you and I conceived of ourselves as children trembling before an abusive parent, then perhaps "Have mercy on me" might seem to be an appropriate prayer. If you and I were convicted felons awaiting judgment from a "hanging judge," then perhaps the prayer for mercy would be understandable. Is it, however, ever appropriate as the prayer of a child of God standing before the source of our life? I do not think so. This prayer, like the posture of kneeling in worship, comes directly out of a definition of human life as fallen from perfection, tainted by original sin and somehow worthless until redeemed.

Has any one of us ever known a human being to be helped by being told constantly how wretched and miserable he or she is? Would we, as parents, use this understanding of human life as the basis upon which to raise our children; can any of us imagine a good result coming out of that practice? If we are able to understand that truth as parents, then why are we not able to understand it as people of worship? If John's gospel is correct that Jesus' stated purpose is that we might "have life and have it abundantly" (John 10:10), will the practices present in our liturgies today ever produce that result?

The idea that our sins are the cause of the death of Jesus is nothing other than a gigantic guilt trip, and it constitutes barbaric theology. Jesus originally was seen as the sacrificial lamb of Yom Kippur; but the lamb of Yom Kippur was a symbol of the human yearning for perfection, not the victim who had to be killed to cover our sins. Jesus was seen as the scapegoat, the sin bearer, upon whose back our sins were loaded so that he could carry them away, but the scapegoat of Yom Kippur was a symbol of our desire to be free of our own distortions. It was a liturgical act designed to bring us to a new sense of wholeness, not to cause us to wallow in self-deprecation.

Does this mean that we are not to take seriously the reality of evil? Of course not. Evil is certainly not an illusion. One does not have to argue about its existence. We read about evil every day. A disturbed, armed man murders innocent children in a primary school in Connecticut. A vigilante on a self-appointed security patrol kills a black teenager in Florida, simply because in the mind of the vigilante, this teenager was in the wrong neighborhood. A young gay man is beaten into unconsciousness by a gang of homophobic attackers and hanged upon a fencepost in Wyoming's subfreezing weather to die. Politicians lie about the non-existent threat of weapons of mass destruction in Iraq, or about the firing of a Vietnamese gunboat on an American destroyer in the Gulf of Tonkin that we now know never happened, and then use these lies to launch this nation into military adventures that claim the lives of tens of thousands of our sons and daughters and hundreds of thousands of civilians. Manipulators of the financial markets distort these markets for personal gain at the cost of robbing millions of their life savings when this financial house of cards comes crashing down. Priests abuse children under the guise of being in God's service. Religious ideologues bomb embassies, the World Trade Center, family planning centers, or the Boston Marathon, killing and injuring countless numbers of people. They also behead their captives on live television or burn them alive in cages. One doesn't have to argue about the reality of evil, but does evil stem from a mythical fall from perfection? I do not think so. If my conclusion is correct, any theology that starts with this assumption is born in error, and the error is compounded a thousand-fold when we act theologically out of that definition.

The fact is that human life does not need to be saved, rescued or redeemed, because we have never fallen from a pristine state of perfection. "Original sin" is simply wrong. What we call evil comes from a very different source. Everything living, from plants to insects to animals to human beings, is born with a biological drive to survive. That drive is universally present. It inevitably expresses itself in the stance of subjugating everything and everyone in the service of our survival. That force is not conscious in plants or in insects, but it is operative nonetheless. We cannot judge how the levels of awareness to this survival drive operate in conscious animal life, but the observance of animal behavior confirms its presence. Yes, there are illustrations in animal life when one creature will sacrifice its life so that the pack can survive, but we suspect that that too is biologically driven, not voluntary. The survival instinct, however, *is* self-conscious in human beings; and when it consciously motivates our behavior, it defines us as radically self-centered creatures. Our self-centered drive to survive is a universal reality rooted in our biology. It was this aspect of our humanity that led our ancient religious mythmakers to try to describe its origins. "Original sin" was their answer to the question of the source of our universal human self-centeredness. No one understood that survival was an involuntary biological drive in life. Instead it was understood as the result of sinfulness and of disobedience. Atonement theology was born as a way to address this universal flaw in our understanding of human life.

What we need, however, is not to be rescued from this biological fact of our existence, but rather to discover the power to transcend survival as the primary goal in life. What we need is to discover a meaning in life that is so powerful that it enables us to give our lives away to others. We are not "fallen sinners," as our theology asserts;

we are rather "incomplete human beings." We need to be loved just as we are, and thus to be called beyond our boundaries into being all that we are capable of being, transcending survival as our primary motivator at every point.

Atonement theology is not the pathway to life. The ability to give ourselves away to others in love is. It is not the winners who achieve life's meaning; it is the givers. That is the basis upon which a new Christianity can be built for a new world. Atonement theology was born in Gentile ignorance of Jewish worship traditions. It was fed over the centuries by literalizing biblical narratives in ways that Jewish worshippers, who knew about storytelling, would never have understood. I say it again: Biblical literalism is nothing less than a Gentile heresy. Its results are now revealed in the fact that Christianity has been transformed into a religion of victimization. For centuries we have practiced our faith by building up ourselves as winners, survivors, the holders of ultimate truth, while we have denigrated the humanity of others. That is the source of evil. That is why Christianity has given birth to anti-Semitism. That is why the crusades were initiated to kill "infidels." That is why we gave our blessing to such things as the divine right of kings, slavery, segregation, and apartheid. That is why we defined women as sub-human, childlike, and dependent. That is why we became homophobic. That is why we became child abusers and ideological killers. What human life needs is not a theology of human denigration. That is what atonement theology gives us. What we need is a theology of human fulfillment.

Can we find that and encounter it anew hidden in the symbols of the Christian faith? I believe we can, but not unless and until we change our understanding of human life, our understanding of Christ and our impoverished theistic definition of God. Can we do that and still be recognizable as disciples of Jesus? Again I believe we can, but it will require a reformation one hundred times more powerful and more influential than that of the sixteenth century. I am not sure that institutional Christianity will ever see how distorted it has become, and thus it will not recognize how it could begin the process of reformation. I can only hope that our fears of changing the old formulas can be challenged successfully enough to enable the reformation to begin. That reformation will be painful for some, who will be sure that they are witnessing the death of Christianity. That pain, however, will be nothing other than the birth pangs and the hard labor required to bring something of enormous value into life, namely a Christian future and a Christian dream.

PART VI

From Sukkoth Onward:
The New Harvest

CHAPTER 20

The Symbols of Sukkoth and the Food That Satisfies Hunger

THE PATTERN IS NOW FAMILIAR. The liturgical calendar of the synagogue moves on toward its next major observance, and Matthew's gospel moves in harmony with it.

There is at this point in Matthew's gospel a mood shift that is quite discernible. That, too, can be explained by the change in the liturgical seasons. Yom Kippur was a somber day of penitence, while Sukkoth was marked by a spirit of celebration. Sukkoth, the final one of the three observances in the festive month of Tishri, was the most anticipated and joyous time of the Jewish year.

Sukkoth was called by at least two other names: Tabernacles and Booths. The meaning of these two terms will become clear as we explore this Jewish festival. We begin with the primary definition of Sukkoth. It was above all else a harvest celebration, the Jewish equivalent of Thanksgiving Day—except, for the Jews, the time of thanksgiving was extended for eight days.

People living in modern urban societies cannot really understand what the harvest meant to ancient people who lived in agricultural societies. The harvest was crucial to life itself and thus to the survival of their tribes. A poor harvest was the harbinger of death by starvation, so the worship associated with the season of the harvest was invested with deep emotions, gratitude being the most significant. Seasonal rains and abundant sunshine were realities over which human beings had no control. To have both sunshine and rain provided personally by God was, therefore, an occasion for deep thanksgiving. It is no surprise to discover that every agricultural society developed some kind of harvest festival to mark the conclusion of the growing season.

As the distance between the farm and the dinner table has grown in the modern world, we have lost that harvest connection. In secular America we do still observe Thanksgiving Day, but it tends to be marked more by eating orgies, athletic contests and shopping splurges than by worship.

For the Jews, however, the emotions of the harvest season had to be expressed as worship. To celebrate this holy day properly they had to journey to Jerusalem. The symbols employed in Sukkoth's observance make that Jerusalem setting abundantly clear. Matthew will use Sukkoth in his gospel in two ways. First, he will borrow some ideas and symbols from Sukkoth and use them to shape his entire Jesus story. We will look at these symbols in detail. Second, he will provide harvest-oriented material to relate Jesus to this particular synagogue celebration. As we consider Matthew's dual use of Sukkoth, the conclusion that Matthew in his gospel is following the liturgical year of the synagogue will once again be obvious.

The Jewish observance of Sukkoth began with the worshippers marching in solemn procession around the city of Jerusalem and into the Temple. It was a festive parade. These marchers carried in their right hands something called a "lulab" (pronounced "lulav"), a bundle of leafy willow, myrtle and palm branches tied together so that the people could wave them in the air as they processed. They carried in their left hands a box called an "ethrog" (pronounced "e-trog"), into which they tended to place the sweet-smelling flowers, leaves and even the zest of the fruit of the citron tree. As they marched through the city streets toward the Temple waving their lulabs and carrying their ethrogs, they would chant the words of Psalm 118, a psalm that was particularly identified with this celebration. Among its words are these: "Save us, we beseech thee, O Lord" (Ps. 118:25). In Hebrew, "Save us" would be written "Hosanna." This psalm went on to say: "Blessed is he [or the one] who enters [or comes] in the name of the Lord" (Ps. 118:26). This psalm then instructs the worshippers "to bind the festival procession with branches up to the horns of the altar" (Ps. 118:27).

These symbols are, or perhaps should be, quite familiar to Christians. We know them, however, not as the symbols of a fall harvest festival, but rather as part of the Palm Sunday story, which opens the final week in Jesus' life and thus begins what is called "the passion of Jesus." This means that a series of harvest symbols, born in Sukkoth, were, over the years, shifted into the observance of Passover, the Jewish festival that comes in the early spring of the year and is the context in which Matthew and the other gospel writers relate the story of the crucifixion. This suggests that originally the crucifixion might have occurred in the fall of the year, not in the spring. Perhaps the motivation for shifting it from the harvest season into the spring season of Passover was that early Christian leaders began to identify Jesus with the paschal lamb sacrificed at Passover to break the power of death. Paul appears to have begun that shift when he referred to Jesus as "our new paschal lamb who was sacrificed for us" (I Cor. 5:7). I will come back to this Sukkoth-Passover connection when we reach Matthew's story of the passion of Jesus, but I wanted to mention it here to show how deeply Jewish liturgical forms shaped the memory of Jesus in the years before the gospels were written.

To return to the Jewish liturgical practice of Sukkoth, we note that the original Torah direction for the observance of this fall festival is written in Leviticus (23:33–36), where this day is called the "feast of Booths." Building a booth adjacent to or at one's home was an important part of the Sukkoth celebration. This temporary shelter was to remind the Jewish people of that difficult part of their history when they were homeless nomads traveling between Egypt and what they believed was their promised "Holy Land." This booth was also called a "tabernacle," a term filled with meaning for the Jews, who saw the mobile tabernacle carried by the people during their wilderness years as a sign of God's presence in their midst. They even turned this noun into a verb and spoke of God "tabernacling" with them.

The booth/tabernacle used in the Sukkoth celebration was, as noted, a temporary structure, somewhat like a lean-to. One requirement of the Sukkoth liturgy was that the family must eat at least one ceremonial meal inside their booth/tabernacle on one of the eight days of this harvest celebration.

All of these Sukkoth symbols had a way of coming together liturgically. The leafy branches (the lulab) carried in the procession might be placed across the roof of the temporary booth to give it cover. The sweet-smelling fragrances of citron carried in the ethrog might serve to make the temporary shelter fragrant and thus more appealing while the symbolic meal was being shared in that setting.

Are there some other, less obvious connections between Sukkoth and the story of Jesus' passion? I think we should probe for them and speculate. Did the temporary shelter, the booth, evolve into being the tomb of Jesus, his temporary abode before the resurrection? Did the contents of the ethrog find expression in the spices carried by the women to the tomb of Jesus in the story of their visit to the tomb at dawn on the first Easter? Did the eucharistic meal shared by the risen Christ with Cleopas and his friend in Emmaus on the evening of the first Easter, a story that only Luke tells (Luke 24:13–34), reflect the symbolic meal that had to be eaten in the temporary booth or tabernacle? I think all of these things are deeply connected, but my purpose in raising these possibilities to our conscious minds is to point out again and again the significant connections between the way the Jesus story was written in the gospels and the worship traditions of the Jews. When these connections enter our consciousness, we become aware that the gospels are Jewish liturgical interpretations of the meaning of Jesus; they are not biographies or the chronicles of history. Jesus was presented in each of the gospels as the fulfillment of all things Jewish.

We move away now from the ways the Jesus story in general has been shaped by the traditions identified with Sukkoth and turn our attention to the specific ways in which Matthew correlated his story of Jesus with the liturgical celebration of the harvest season. That turns out to be easy to do: All one has to do is to read his text. Matthew tells his Sukkoth story in chapter 13. How do we know? We know because, as previously noted, in chapter 12 he was dealing with Yom Kippur. In the liturgical calendar of the synagogue, Sukkoth follows. So when we move with Matthew beyond Yom Kippur into chapter 13, we discover that he provides us with a series of harvest parables presumably spoken by Jesus. Two of them are explained in great detail. After all, Matthew knows that he has to provide Jesus material for an eight-day observance.

There is first the parable of the sower (Matt. 13:1–9). The sower sows the seed on four different kinds of soil and thus gathers in four different kinds of harvest. The disciples do not understand, so Jesus goes into a long explanation (Matt. 13:10–23). Next Jesus gives us the parable of the man who sowed good seed in his field only to have an enemy sow tares (weeds) amidst the good wheat (Matt. 13:24–30). The question this parable poses is: Should the workmen go through the fields and pull out the tares? No, is the conclusion. The wheat and the tares are growing together so closely that to remove one would be to kill the other. So let the wheat and the tares grow together until the harvest, and only then separate them. That will be when the good wheat is stored in barns, and the evil tares are burned. This parable is also then explained in detail (Matt. 13:36–43).

Still on the harvest theme, Matthew next has Jesus give us the parable of the mustard seed (Matt. 13:31–32), in which the tiny mustard seed grows until it becomes a tree capable of providing a place for the birds of the air to build nests in its branches.

Then, in a number of quick vignettes, the kingdom of heaven is likened to the leaven hidden in a measure of flour, which unknowingly proceeds to give to all the flour the power to rise (Matt. 13:33); then to a treasure that a man finds hidden in a field and acquires by selling all that he has to buy that field (Matt. 13:44); then to "a pearl of great value" that a merchant purchases, selling everything he owns to do so (Matt. 13:45–46); and finally to a net in the sea which gathers up fish of every kind (Matt. 13:47–50). When, in this last vignette, the moment of judgment comes, the net is drawn ashore; then the separation of the fish into the good, which are stored in vessels, and the bad, which are thrown away, occurs. This image of the finality of the last judgment is present in all of Matthew's harvest parables.

This long series of parables constitutes the third of Matthew's five extended teaching segments. The eight-day Sukkoth festival is thus fully covered.

Before leaving Matthew's treatment of the harvest festival, let me raise once again the question of literalism. Were these familiar parables of the sower, the wheat and the tares, the mustard seed and the "pearl of great value" ever delivered by the Jesus of history? The answer to that question should be quite obvious. No, Jesus of Nazareth was not the original source of those parables. How can we be so certain? We have only to look at their content.

First, Matthew has Jesus change the focus of this Sukkoth celebration from gratitude for the harvest that feeds one's body, to the idea of heavenly food that satisfies one's deepest hunger as one journeys to the messianic age. The harvest itself has been transformed into a symbol for the final judgment. The theme of these parables is not the meaning of Jesus, but the need for the expansion of the Christian movement. As such, these parables address the concerns of the early Christian church and thus must have originated in that period of history when the growth of the church was a primary concern. Since there is no evidence that the Jesus of history envisioned the establishment of a church, much less its growth and development, there is no way that these parables could have originated with Jesus.

The parable of the sower is about the need to plant the Christian message in the kind of soil that will bear fruit. The parable of the wheat and tares is about the compromises one must make with the world in order to accomplish the tasks of the church. Human life is always a mixture of good and evil; one cannot separate them from each other without destroying both. The parable of the mustard seed is a picture of the early church. It was at that time as small and as insignificant as a mustard seed, but was destined to grow, Matthew and his fellow adherents believed, to be so large that even the birds of the air could build their nests in its branches. The "birds of the air" was a reference to the Gentiles, who would ultimately make their homes in the Christian movement. The treasure in the field and the pearl of great price were symbols of the way early Christians valued their Christ message, believing that its success was worth any sacrifice. These are the concerns of the Christian community at the time Matthew's gospel was being written. They would have been totally foreign concerns to the Jesus of history.

So Jesus has now been related to the great fall festival of the harvest. The liturgical calendar of the synagogue is still revealed as the organizing principle behind the writing of Matthew and indeed of all the synoptic gospels. Literalism begins to die as a viable alternative for understanding the gospels and new possibilities begin to emerge. Claiming their Jewish background, reading these gospels with Jewish eyes opens to us vastly different ways of approaching, reading and engaging the Jewish scriptures. Think of the centuries wasted in trying to fit these words into a literal frame of reference. No wonder literalism becomes so strident and aggressive. Biblical fundamentalists are not unlike the preacher who wrote in the margins of his sermon notes: "Argument weak. Yell like Hell!" No wonder those who have never heard of any way to read the gospels except literally have given up on Christianity to take up citizenship in "the secular city."*

---

*This phrase is the title of Harvard theologian Harvey Cox's popular twentieth-century book. See bibliography for details.

CHAPTER 21

The Beheading
of John the Baptist

THERE ARE SOME SIX TO TEN SABBATHS between the fall harvest festival of Sukkoth and the midwinter celebration known as Dedication-Hanukkah. If Matthew is following the worship pattern of the synagogue in the telling of his Jesus story, then he must supply sufficient material to cover these transition Sabbaths. When we examine the material between the end of the harvest observance, which occurs in chapter 13, and the telling of the story of the transfiguration of Jesus, which starts in chapter 17, it then becomes clear that the material in chapters 14–16 is what he will offer on these six to ten Sabbaths.

Examining these chapters, we discover that this material breaks roughly into three units: First, the execution by beheading of John the Baptist; second, the two feeding of the multitude stories wrapped, as they are, around the narrative of Jesus walking on water; and third, the dramatic stories of two symbolic characters, the Canaanite woman and Simon Peter, and how they respond to who Jesus is. A closer look at each of these three units will reveal that this material is both symbolic and stretchable—that is, it can be used as the lessons in the synagogue on as few as six Sabbaths or expanded for use on as many as ten Sabbaths.* This, I contend, is not an accident. Over the next three chapters of this book I will examine these three units. Each is a compelling narrative, and each reveals that it is to be understood as anything but literal truth.

The story of the execution by beheading of John the Baptist is told first in Mark and then in Matthew. Luke and John both omit it. Is this story history? We have no corroborating data that suggests that it is; furthermore, the deeper one goes into this story, the more obvious it becomes that it is filled with symbolic, interpretive images based on the Hebrew scriptures. It does not, therefore, appear to have been intended to be read or understood as literal history. It is, however, a compelling story, one that has captivated the public's imagination far beyond the boundaries of the Christian religion. The story of the execution of John the Baptist has been expanded into the traditions of the secular world, so the first thing we need to do is to separate the non-biblical elements that have attached themselves to secular society's version of this biblical tale.

Nowhere in the Bible, for example, is the dancer who performed at King Herod's birthday party named Salome. There are only two references to that name in the entire New Testament. Both are in Mark, and they refer to the same person: Salome is one of the

---

*The difference between six and ten Sabbaths is determined by whether Passover comes early or late in that year.

women who watched the crucifixion from a distance (Mark 15:40), and she is also one of the women who went to the tomb of Jesus at dawn on the first day of the week (Mark 16:1). The fact that in no biblical source is the dancer who performed for King Herod named Salome would perhaps have come as a shock to the great German composer Richard Strauss, who turned this biblical story into an opera entitled *Salome*.*

The second mythological detail that has been added to this biblical story is that this dance was called "the dance of the seven veils." That was simply a later device to heighten the sexual aspect of this story and thus to increase its popularity by suggesting that it be given an X rating.

A third mythological element, the detail that King Herod was so pleased with this dance that he promised "with an oath" to grant the dancer any request she wanted, is grounded in the biblical story itself (Matt. 14:7). Such wish-granting oaths are familiar in mythology, but they are never literally true. Mark makes this mythological aspect even stronger by having the promise of the king include the phrase "even to half of my kingdom." That is such a familiar mythical line that it shouts out at us not to assume that this episode ever really happened.

So we take away from this biblical story those culturally added and mythological details before we begin our inquiry. Now we are down to the basics. What did the story mean when the Jewish author Matthew included it in his gospel, and how would it have been perceived by the original audience of Jewish people who heard it being read in their synagogue? To answer these questions

*Strauss's opera *Salome* premiered in Dresden, Germany, in 1905. It was regarded as both salacious and scandalous, but it survived on its musical genius.

we have to ask another: Who was John the Baptist to the early Jewish followers of Jesus?

The answer to this last question becomes clear if we are familiar with Jewish messianic thinking. As we saw in chapter 14, Jewish mythology had long suggested that Elijah must come before any messiah figure, to prepare the way. The idea of an Elijah-like figure who would prepare the way for the "day of the Lord" to dawn is found throughout the Hebrew scriptures. This forerunner is identified in II Isaiah simply as "a voice crying in the wilderness, prepare ye the way of the Lord." This voice, it was said, would "make straight in the desert a highway for our God" (Isa. 40:3), a highway on which the messiah would arrive. This theme is then picked up by the prophet we call Malachi, which I noted previously but will repeat in this new context.* The book of Malachi has God say: "Behold, I send my messenger to prepare the way before me, and the Lord whom you seek will suddenly come to his Temple" (Mal. 3:1). The prophet then concludes his book by naming that messenger: "Behold, I will send you Elijah, the prophet, before the great and terrible day of the Lord comes" (Mal. 4:5). The Jewish followers of Jesus, well versed in that tradition of messianic thinking, at some point came to the conclusion that the figure known as John the Baptist was to fill the Elijah role. The John the Baptist we meet in the gospels is the John the Baptist of Christian interpretation. Recall that John the Baptist did not enter the Christian tradition until Mark wrote his gospel in the early years of the eighth decade.

Does the New Testament portrait of John the Baptist have within it even a nugget of historical truth? In all probability Jesus

---

*This word "Malachi," unlike the labels by which other prophets in the Hebrew scriptures are known, is not a name. It is simply Hebrew for "my messenger," once again a reference to the forerunner.

was in history associated with the person of John the Baptist before emerging on the stage of history in his own right. Bruce Chilton, the brilliant chaplain and professor at Bard College in New York, in his book *Rabbi Jesus,* argues that Jesus had his professional beginning as an apprentice in the John the Baptist movement.*

Chilton suggests that a hint of this can be found in the Lucan story of Joseph and Mary taking the twelve-year-old Jesus to Jerusalem and leaving without him (Luke 2:41–51). They were taking him, Chilton argues, to apprentice him to John. They *intended* to leave him. It was not an accident. Whether that idea can be substantiated as a fact of history is far from universally agreed, but two things in the gospel tradition indicate a significant relationship between John the Baptist and Jesus, a relationship in which John was the older and Jesus the younger of the partners.

The first indicator is that the New Testament repeatedly asserts Jesus' superiority to John. Indeed, it is such a consistent theme as to appear to have been emotionally necessary to the Christians to have this fact both heard and established. In the service of that cause, the writer of the Fourth Gospel has John say about Jesus: "He must increase; I must decrease" (John 3:30). Mark has John say: "After me comes one who is mightier than I, the thong of whose sandals I am not worthy to stoop down and untie" (Mark 1:7). Luke goes so far in this direction that he actually has the fetus of John the Baptist, still in the womb of his mother Elizabeth, leap to salute the fetus of Jesus, still in the womb of his mother Mary, in order to portray John the Baptist as acknowledging the superiority of Jesus to John before either was born (Luke 1:39–45)! All of these references support the fact of history that John's "movement"

---

*See bibliography for details.

preceded Jesus' "movement" in time. They also suggest some rivalry: No one would have gone to such lengths to demonstrate the superiority and the primacy of Jesus over John unless that issue had been in dispute.

The second item in the gospels that appears to connect the two figures is that Jesus did not start his public ministry until John the Baptist had been arrested (Mark 1:14; Matt. 4:12–17). In that sense, Jesus actually succeeded John. That is why such a powerful effort was undertaken by the followers of Jesus to demonstrate that though Jesus had started as part of John's movement, he did in fact surpass John's primacy. This was done by turning the ministry of John into the role of the promised forerunner, who would herald the messiah's arrival. From this perspective, the claim could be made that the second was actually first and the first was actually second in importance.

So the gospels interpret John as the Elijah who was to come. That is why John the Baptist was said to have been clothed in the attire of Elijah, as we saw in the Rosh Hashanah discussion. He wore a camel's-hair garment with a leather girdle about his loins (compare I Kings 1:8 with Mark 1:6 and Matt. 3:4). The gospel writers also placed John in the wilderness, the location of Elijah (Matt. 3:1), and gave him the diet of the wilderness to eat, namely "locusts and honey" (Matt. 3:4). None of that is history. All of it is interpretive mythmaking: John was clearly being co-opted by the Jesus movement to serve as the Elijah figure who would "prepare the way" for the messiah's arrival.

When Matthew reaches the seventeenth chapter of his gospel, he has Jesus himself assert the identification between John the Baptist and Elijah, when Jesus tells his disciples that "Elijah has already come" (Matt. 17:10–13).

Now with that background in mind, we turn to look at the story of John's execution. When we do, we discover that this story was actually designed to cement the identification between Elijah and John the Baptist. To see this clearly, however, we must be familiar with one of the great stories in the career of Elijah, for the execution of John the Baptist is told in such a way as to serve as the final exclamation point in the identification between the two.

In I Kings 18:20–46, the story is told of a showdown between two rival religious claims on the loyalties of the people of Israel. King Ahab was the monarch of the Northern Kingdom. His foreign-born wife was named Jezebel (I Kings 16:3). She was a devotee of the cult of Baal, a fertility God, worshipped by the people of Canaan prior to the conquering of that land by the Hebrew people. Elijah, the prophet, thus stood between this queen and her imposition of Baal worship throughout the land of Israel. This showdown was to take place on the top of Mt. Carmel in Northern Israel. The test was designed to demonstrate whether Baal or Yahweh was the true God. The details of the test were these. The priests, or the representatives of each deity, would prepare an altar, laying on it the prepared sacrificial animal. Then those same representatives would pray to the deity they believed was God, asking their God to send fire from heaven to ignite the sacrifice. The deity who responded to these prayers would be declared to be the true God and all the people would thus worship this deity. The story was told in dramatic fashion. The people gathered. Baal was represented by four hundred priests. Yahweh was represented by Elijah alone. The priests of Baal went first. The bull was sacrificed and placed upon the altar. The priests entreated Baal to send fire from heaven to consume the sacrifice, but nothing happened.

Elijah, who must have been a "hair shirt" of a personality,

taunted them from the sidelines. "Pray louder," he suggested. "Perhaps Baal is asleep and needs to be wakened. Perhaps Baal is on a journey and cannot hear." So the prayers became more frantic and the voices of the priests of Baal became louder and louder. The movement of these priests began to resemble a ritualistic dance. They even, in their fervor, cut themselves with knives and lances, but still nothing happened; no fire from heaven fell.

After hours had passed it was finally Elijah's turn. With great dramatic flair he stepped forward and placed the carved pieces of his sacrificed bull on top of the wood on his altar. Next he dug a trench around his altar. Then, in a startling and calculated manner, he ordered four cisterns of water to be poured over the altar. He repeated that act a second time and then a third time, until not only were the sacrifice and the wood drenched, but the water also filled the newly dug trenches around the altar. Only then did Elijah invoke Yahweh to send fire from heaven to burn up the sacrifice. Fire fell immediately from the sky in devastating force, says the story. It ignited the sacrifice, sending the fragrance of roasted meat heavenward. The fire also lapped up the water in the trenches. The people observing fell back in wonder and awe and began to chant with one voice: "The Lord [Yahweh] is God; the Lord [Yahweh] is God" (I Kings 18:39).

Elijah, emboldened by his victory in this test and feeling the support of the people, then turned and ordered the priests of Baal to be seized. When these priests had been seized and bound, Elijah beheaded every one of them with his sword. When the last head of a Baal priest rolled onto the ground, Elijah and his God, Yahweh, stood supreme. It was not a good portrait of interfaith sensitivity!

When Ahab the king later reported the events of this day to Jezebel, his queen, she was filled with anger and sent a message to Elijah that included an oath and this solemn vow: "So may God do to me, and more also, if I do not make you [Elijah] like one of them [the priests of Baal] by this time tomorrow" (I Kings 19:2). Her vow was that Elijah's head would also roll.

Elijah, fearful for his life, went immediately into hiding. Thus Jezebel's vow was never carried out. Indeed Elijah was said to have escaped death altogether, for at the end of his life the story was told that he was transported into God's presence by a magical fiery chariot drawn by magical horses. When King Ahab died, Jezebel continued to exert influence as the queen mother until a revolutionary movement, led by a man named Jehu, gained power. It was then, under Jehu's reign and at his command, that Jezebel was hurled from an upper window of the palace onto the street to her death (II Kings 9:30–37).

The story of John the Baptist's execution by beheading at the request of Herodias, King Herod's wife (and Jezebel's successor as a foreign queen in the land of the Jews), thus carried out Jezebel's oath and thereby, in the minds of Matthew's Jewish audience, sealed John's identity as the new Elijah. That is what this story is all about. There is no historical meaning connected with the account at all. It only meets an apologetic and interpretive agenda. In order to claim the designation of messiah for Jesus, his followers had to create the role of Elijah for John the Baptist. John then had to die the death intended for Elijah. The "new Elijah" was beheaded at the initiative of the "new Jezebel," Queen Herodias.

Matthew reflected this position very well. He was not, however, writing history. He was interpreting John the Baptist in life and in death as the new Elijah who prepared the way for the messiah to come.

The first of Matthew's three units, designed to move his story through the Sabbaths from Sukkoth to Dedication-Hanukkah, is now complete. Things get more exciting, and more obviously non-literal, as Matthew moves next to the story of the miraculous feeding of the multitudes.

CHAPTER 22

Loaves and Fishes, Walking on Water: Moses Stories Expanded

THE SECOND CLEAR UNIT of Jesus stories that Matthew uses to fill the Sabbaths that move his worshipping community from Sukkoth to Dedication-Hanukkah is also quite familiar. Like the account of the beheading of John the Baptist, these stories have moved out of the domain of "religious knowledge" and into the realm of "general knowledge." Having become an assumed part of our cultural wisdom, they can be referred to in common speech with some degree of certainty that one's hearers will understand what one is saying. Included in this unit in Matthew's text are the two distinctively different and separate accounts of Jesus feeding a multitude of people with a limited supply of loaves and fish. Most people tend not to be aware that in Mark and Matthew, the first two gospels to be written, these two stories stand in close to identical form. Nor do people tend to be aware that in the later gospels of Luke and John these two feeding stories have been collapsed into a single narrative. Even among those who *are* aware of these things, most have never stopped to wonder why. We Christians seldom seem to ask "why" questions in the study of the gospels. So long as we read gospel accounts assuming that they are describing literal events that actually happened, then "why" questions, which seek a different level of meaning, will not be encouraged. It is also worth mentioning that, attached to these feeding of the multitude stories in every gospel, there is an account of Jesus walking on the water. Never in any of the gospels are these stories separated from each other. These are crucial things to note, because without them the meaning of these stories will never be unraveled.

Let me first isolate and then compare the two separate feeding of the multitude stories to fix these details in our minds; then I will look at the walking on water story. While I am aware that Matthew has taken much of this material from Mark, I will nonetheless focus on the unique ways in which Matthew uses it.

In the first feeding narrative in Matthew the text informs us that "five thousand men" are fed, "plus women and children" (Matt. 14:21). In the second of Matthew's feeding narratives we are told that "four thousand men" are fed, "besides women and children" (Matt. 15:38). In the first story the provisions available for this feast were said to be "five loaves and two fish" (Matt. 14:17). In the second story it was "seven [loaves], and a few small fish" (Matt. 15:34). In the first story, we are told that after all had eaten and "were satisfied," they took up "twelve baskets full of broken pieces, left over" (Matt. 14:20). In the second story, after they all had eaten "and were satisfied," they took up "seven baskets full of broken pieces left over" (Matt. 15:37). Keep these differences in mind.

Perhaps the most telling difference between the two stories has to do with their location. The account in which five thousand were fed occurred "in a lonely place" that was reached only by boat on the Sea of Galilee, but it was still in Jewish territory (Matt. 14:13). Matthew is quite specific in his text: It was in the tribal lands that had been assigned to Zebulon and Naphtali, two of the less well known sons of Jacob. These tribal lands were on the fringes of the Jewish province known in the first century as Galilee. In these remote, but still Jewish, areas the lines dividing Jews from Gentiles had begun to fade. Indeed these lands were sometimes called "Galilee of the Gentiles" (see Gen. 30).

In Matthew's second feeding story, however, Jesus appears to be in Gentile territory. It is fair to say that the first feeding story was located in the Jewish lands, but on the edges, and the second feeding story was located on the Gentile side of the lake. These distinctions become crucial when we begin to probe for the Jewish meaning of these feeding episodes. So we hold onto these locations for the time being.

There are also some similarities in these two feeding episodes that need to be noted. In both stories the crowd in the wilderness was far from any food supply (Matt. 14:13, 15:29). In both stories Jesus is said to have been moved by compassion (Matt. 14:14, 15:32). In neither story is the source of the loaves and fish identified. In both stories the same four verbs are used. Jesus "takes," "blesses," "breaks," and "gives" the bread (Matt. 14:19, 15:36). In both stories the people are told that they need not go away, but are ordered to sit down.

The first thing that should now become obvious is that neither of these narratives was written with the intention that the reader would treat these words literally. These are not descriptions of experiences that actually happened in time and history. Matthew surely knew that when he wrote these stories, and so did the Jewish audience for whom this gospel was originally intended.

So let me try to recover and to restate the way Jewish readers would have understood the implications of these two contrasting, and yet similar, apparently miraculous feeding stories.

First, note that in both instances the location is described as "the wilderness." Among knowledgeable Jews an account of a multitude being fed in a great wilderness would immediately have brought to mind the figure of Moses, since one of the major stories in the Hebrew scriptures is the account of how Moses fed the hungry people with "heavenly bread" as they traveled through the wilderness toward what they believed was their Promised Land (Exod. 16). Many magical features have been attached to that Exodus narrative. The bread, called manna, was said to have fallen from heaven each day along with the dew. The source of this heavenly bread was quite clearly the God who was believed literally to live above the sky. This bread fell, at least according to a later development of this story, on only six mornings a week (Exod. 16:22). Each person gathered only the bread one needed for a single day on the first five days of the week. Then on the sixth day one gathered as much as one would need for both Friday and Saturday, the Sabbath. This adaptation to the story meant that neither God in the act of sending the bread, nor the people in the act of gathering it, had to violate the Sabbath by working. It mattered not how much or how little anyone gathered on the first five days, for it was always enough. Those who gathered little were never hungry, and those who gathered much never had leftovers; and so the bread of God satisfied the hunger of God's people in the wilderness for a period of forty years. This was the story as recorded in the book of Exodus.

The second thing to note in both of Matthew's stories is the use of the four verbs that I mentioned previously: "take," "bless," "break" and "give." These verbs are used together in the Christian liturgy: "For in the night in which he was betrayed, he *took* bread, and when he had *given thanks* [that is, *blessed* it], he *broke* it and *gave* it to them." The words are familiar because they are still used in almost every Christian Eucharist. When Matthew later relates the story of the Last Supper, which in this gospel is the Passover meal, he will use those four verbs once more. "Now as they were eating, Jesus *took* bread and *blessed* and *broke* it and *gave* it to the disciples" (Matt. 26:26). On this occasion, however, at this Passover meal, Jesus is said to have identified the bread with his body. The fact that Jesus uses these same four verbs in both of his feeding stories seems to indicate that in Matthew's mind the feeding episodes represented a kind of symbolic eucharistic feast, rather than a literal happening.

That point of view is certainly made clear in the Fourth Gospel, written some fifteen years after Matthew. In that Johannine source the author does not relate a Last Supper in his gospel at all. He substitutes a foot-washing ritual that focuses on Peter (John 13). The Fourth Gospel does, however, attach all of its eucharistic teaching, which involves a symbolic eating of the flesh of Jesus and a symbolic drinking of the blood of Jesus, to the story of the feeding of the multitude (see John 6). In this gospel the author goes to even greater lengths to identify Jesus with the bread that fell from heaven in the Exodus story. John has Jesus say: "I am the living bread which came down from heaven" (John 6:51). He goes on to contrast the bread that he offers with the manna in the wilderness.

"The bread I give you," John's Jesus says, "is my flesh," and it will enable you to live forever (John 6:51). Certainly all of the clues available in the New Testament point to the conclusion that these feeding of the multitude stories are to be understood as symbolic eucharistic meals. With this idea in mind we now go back and explore more deeply the contrasting numbers that appear in Matthew's two feeding of the multitude stories.

In Jewish territory, Matthew says that it was *five thousand* men who were served with *five* loaves. This double use of the number five forces us to ask: "Does the number five have any specific identification that might be sacred, revered or even defining inside the Jewish experience? Answers begin to appear. Five was a familiar marker in Jewish worship. Jews referred constantly to the "five books of the Torah" and the "five books of Moses." Reading these five books organized the annual worship life of the synagogue. Is that a clue? Perhaps, at least I think it might be, but this is not yet a very convincing argument.

A stronger case for Jewish identification can, I believe, be made for the number twelve. Twelve for the Jews was the number of tribes that made up their nation. These tribes were thought to be the descendants of the twelve sons of Jacob, whose name had been changed by God to Israel.* So we note that in Matthew's first feeding of the multitude story, after all those on the Jewish side of the lake had eaten their fill, twelve baskets of fragments were gathered up.

So the number five in both the loaves and in the thousands of people, and the number twelve in the baskets of leftover fragments, appear to carry special Jewish meanings. Perhaps following these

---

*The number twelve seems to be more important than the *content* of that number. I have previously tried to explain how they actually got to the number twelve. See chapter 7 on Joseph.

clues, we can head more deeply into this narrative's original Jewish meaning.

On the Gentile side of the lake, and turning to the second feeding story, we note that while much about both stories appears to be identical, the numbers have in fact shifted dramatically. In this episode there are *four thousand* who are fed. So, probing for clues, we ask: Is four a significant number in the Jewish mind in regard to Gentiles? Perhaps, but once again it seems a stretch. Since that is all we have to go on at this moment, we take it and begin to probe the Hebrew scriptures in search of anything that might offer corroborating data. There, for what it is worth, we discover that when the Jews sought to speak of the entire world, they referred to the "four corners of the earth" (Isa. 11:12). That phrase is picked up and used by followers of Jesus (Rev. 7:1). Of course this vision reflected a flat earth, but it was nonetheless a Jewish way of describing the entirety of the planet, which included both the Jews and the Gentiles. So perhaps the number four thousand to the Jewish readers of this gospel was a more Gentile number than five thousand. Thus far, this is a weak argument, but it might still be a hidden clue.

The number seven, when referring to the Gentile world, offers stronger possibilities. We note first that the number seven appears twice in this second feeding story set on the Gentile side of the lake. There were *seven* loaves distributed and *seven* baskets of fragments gathered when all were satisfied. What might the number seven mean in this story to Jews in regard to their understanding of Gentiles?

The history of the Jewish nation had been lived under the domination of seven Gentile empires. Each of these empires was a significant factor in Jewish history. First there was Egypt. The Jewish people were born as a nation out of slavery in Egypt. Second, the

Northern Kingdom, called Israel, was destroyed by the Empire of the Assyrians. Third, the Southern Kingdom, called Judah, was destroyed by the Babylonian Empire. Fourth, the Jewish captivity in Babylon was ended by the rising of the Persian Empire. Fifth, the Persians, in turn, were conquered by the Macedonians, who then ruled the world. Sixth, following the death of the Macedonian leader, Alexander the Great, the Jews fell under the power of the Syrian Empire, ruled by the Seleucid dynasty. Seventh, when Matthew's gospel was written, the Roman Empire was ruling the world. Perhaps the number seven represented in the Jewish mind the entirety of the Gentile nations of the world.

So we play with these numbers. At the very least we are driven to acknowledge that the feeding stories are filled with symbols. It is clear from our survey that these stories were not originally meant to be read literally. If they were not literal stories, could they be parables? Was the purpose of these parables to describe the sufficiency of the Christ to satisfy the deepest hunger found in all people, both Jews and Gentiles? These stories appear to be saying that the bread of the Christian Eucharist is a symbol of the human yearning for eternal life. I think that something like this was what both Matthew and Mark were trying to communicate in these feeding stories to their Jewish audiences. That is also what the original Jewish readers of these gospels would have understood when they first encountered these stories.

It is of interest to note that though Luke, like Matthew, has taken these stories from Mark, his more cosmopolitan congregation, made up not just of Jews of the diaspora, but also of Gentile proselytes, would not have had the same need to show inclusiveness, so perhaps that is why Luke dropped from his gospel the second feeding story describing the four thousand who were fed on the Gentile side of the lake. The Fourth Gospel, though also deeply Jewish, did the same thing. This author, however, was struggling to redefine the Christian movement in more universal ways following the expulsion of his community of Jewish disciples of Jesus from the synagogue.

So the two stories of the feeding of the multitude in Matthew appear to be symbolic eucharistic stories designed to tie Jesus once again to the memory of Moses. That is a long way from treating them as literal miracle stories. Developing Jewish eyes with which to read the New Testament does open up a remarkably new way to hear the gospel message.

To strengthen this case I now turn to the story of Jesus walking on the water, which supplements Matthew's two feeding episodes. This particular juxtaposition makes it clear that the early Christians, who were overwhelmingly Jewish, saw these stories as connected. Their symbolic character is far too obvious and too apparent. The walking on water story is simply another Moses story. Moses demonstrated power over water by splitting the Red Sea. Jesus will demonstrate power over water by walking on it without sinking.

The story of Jesus walking on water has been so literalized through the centuries in our art that the picture is burned into our awareness. This story has also entered our jokes, especially our golf jokes, in which the ability to walk on water is equated with divinity.

Moses was known in the Jewish tradition primarily for two things. One was feeding the multitude in the wilderness, and the other was crossing the Red Sea* by cutting a pathway of dry land

---

*I have previously suggested that Red Sea is an inaccurate translation of *Yam Suph*, which means "Sea of Reeds."

in the midst of a body of water. If the feeding of the multitude by Jesus was a version of the manna story starring Moses, then is it possible that the walking on water story was a version of the Red Sea story? I think it is.

In Matthew's narrative, when the five thousand have been fed and the twelve baskets of fragments have been gathered, the hunger of the Jews has been satisfied by "the bread of life." Then, before his story moves to the feeding of the Gentiles, Matthew has Jesus send the disciples across the lake before him while he dismisses the crowds. Next, Matthew says that Jesus went up the mountain alone to pray. By this time the boat was "many furlongs distant from the land" (Matt. 14:24). That boat was also being beaten by the waves, since the wind was against it. So "in the fourth watch of the night [that would have been between 3:00 A.M. and 6:00 A.M.], he came to them walking on the water" (Matt. 14:25). The disciples, seeing him, thought they were seeing a ghost and were terrified. Jesus spoke, identifying himself and telling them to have no fear. In Matthew's version of this story, that was not enough for Peter, who is always portrayed as the one who struggles, the one who is constantly wavering between faith and doubt, between commitment and denial. Peter said: "Lord, if it is you"—Matthew suggests that Peter is clearly not convinced—"bid me come to you on the water." That would be, he thought, a good test of identification. Jesus bade him to come. So Peter, too, walked on the water. The power of Jesus could be the power of the disciples. As soon as Peter saw the wind, however, he became afraid and cried out: "Lord, save me!" Jesus, says Matthew, extended his hand and said: "O man of little faith, why did you doubt?" When they got into the boat, the wind ceased, and Matthew added that those in the boat now "worshipped him" and confessed him as "the son of God" (Matt. 14:33).

Once again this is clearly not a literal story. Moses was believed to have had power over water. The new Moses must have the same power. When this boat finally arrived on shore, Matthew suggests, Jesus' divinity was so apparent that the people sought to touch the hem of his garment to be made whole. Matthew is describing the faith that was slowly evolving in the disciples. It seemed present until the storms of life appeared, and then that faith disappeared. The disciples were not ready to make it without him.

The story moves on and the Pharisees and scribes, having descended to a new level of religious trivia, approached Jesus. They were worried about why Jesus' disciples did not keep the religious traditions. They charged that the disciples did not wash their hands before eating and did not honor their elders. To the Pharisees and scribes, Jesus and his disciples were making void the literal "Word of God" (Matt. 15:1–3).

Jesus called them hypocrites. He talked about the difference between external religion and internal faith. Judgment cannot be made on externals, he said. Religious rules mean nothing, Matthew's Jesus was saying, because it is the inner heart that must be changed.

With that affirmation the second unit in this segment that carries Matthew's gospel from the festival of the harvest in the fall to the festival of Dedication-Hanukkah in the darkness of winter is now complete. There is nothing literal about the stories in this segment, yet the truth they capture is profound.

We turn now to the third unit in this transition section of Matthew. It too will be revealed as symbolic and yet true, because it too never happened in the realm of either time or space. There is a better way to read the gospels, we are learning, than to pretend that their words are literal history.

CHAPTER 23

Two Characters, Two Insights

T HE THIRD UNIT of Jesus stories that Matthew used to
complete his journey through the Sabbaths between the
fall harvest festival of Sukkoth and the midwinter celebration of Dedication-Hanukkah involves two characters.
One may well be Matthew's literary creation, though she appears
to be based on a character in the gospel of Mark. The other appears
to be a person of history, but one who in every gospel is a figure of
inner turmoil, whose wrestling with the Jesus experience reflects the
journey of the disciples into the Christian faith. In this chapter we
will examine both of these characters in detail.

It is certainly fair to say that when it comes to the task of creating memorable characters to populate the gospel tradition,
Matthew simply does not have the same level of expertise that is
revealed by the author of the Fourth Gospel. That gospel writer,
known as John, confronted his readers, time after time, with beautifully drawn literary characters, who to this day still lodge in our

minds in unforgettable ways. One thinks of such figures as Nicodemus, the Samaritan woman by the well, the man born blind, the "disciple whom Jesus loved" and Lazarus raised from the dead, none of whom appears in any other gospel.

There is in Matthew's gospel, however, one uniquely drawn and memorable character. She makes only a brief cameo appearance, materializing in one unique story and then disappearing forever. At least in the way that Matthew describes and names her, she is mentioned nowhere else in the New Testament. Matthew portrays her as very confrontational. She seems to be for him a symbol, perhaps an icon. Matthew first places her before Jesus and then before his followers throughout history, but her message is always the same. She is one who stands on the outside, demanding to be heard, asking to be embraced and to be incorporated into the life of the community of believers. She is not named, but is always referred to simply as "the Canaanite woman."

Matthew has borrowed some aspects of this woman's story from the gospel of Mark, but there she is identified as a "Syrophoenician woman (Mark 7:25–30)." Matthew has deliberately changed her designation so that in his gospel she becomes a "Canaanite woman." Why was that change important to him?

A look into Jewish history provides a clue. The word "Canaanite" elicited from the Jewish population a far more negative reaction than did the word "Syrophoenician." Both designations among the Jews marked this woman as a Gentile and therefore as unclean. She was thus by definition rejectable. The Syrophoenician people, however, were regarded by the Jews as respectable competition, while the Canaanite people were regarded as worthy of nothing but oppression. The word "Canaanite" harkened back in Jewish history to the time of Joshua and his conquest of the land of Canaan. The Canaanites were primarily tillers of the soil. As such, they worshipped Baal and Astarte, both of whom were fertility deities. In the book of Joshua, it was said of the Canaanites that they were worthy only of being "hewers of wood and drawers of water" (Josh. 9:24). They were for the Jews capable of no higher calling than that of manual labor and, therefore, occupied the bottom rung on the socio-economic ladder. All of that was in the background of Matthew's story and was the reason, I believe, that he changed the woman's identification.

Matthew introduced this Canaanite woman by informing us that she was a mother, whose daughter was "severely possessed by a demon" (Matt. 15:22). In biblical times, that diagnosis could have meant almost any malady from epilepsy to various forms of mental and even physical illness. She came to Jesus laden with this burden, a mother crying out in pain for her daughter, whose life appeared to be in a hopeless condition. Matthew's portrait of this woman was deliberately designed to humanize her in a way that would challenge the stereotype that Jews held of Canaanites. Her portrayal is thus similar to the characterization of a "caring Samaritan," which Luke alone recorded in the parable we call "the good Samaritan." The fact that the adjective "good" was attached to this story of a caring Samaritan indicated that it too was challenging a stereotype that undergirded a prejudice that had not yet been challenged. Until the basis of a stereotype is publicly challenged, even the most obscene prejudice can still be thought of as proper and even virtuous.

So Matthew presented this Canaanite woman as a caring mother, crying out to Jesus, beseeching him to listen to her and to bring healing to her afflicted daughter. She also appeared to acknowledge Jesus as one who was superior, one who had power that she did not have. She was made to address him using a familiar messianic title: "Son of David," she demanded: Heal my daughter (Matt. 15:22)!

The response of Jesus to her cry was a startling one, quite out of character. He, too, appeared to have defined this woman as unworthy of help. She was to him apparently an outcast possessing no value. Jesus, through his response, seemed to suggest that the way she had been defined was not only accurate, but legitimate. Matthew informed his readers that Jesus "did not answer her a word" (Matt. 15:23).

The disciples, presumably following their teacher's lead, joined in this act of rejection. "Send her away," they urged, for "she is crying after us" (Matt. 15:23). This reaction is not surprising: Most people do not want to see, much less encounter, the victims of their prejudices.

This scene grew even darker. Jesus finally broke his silence and responded to the woman's constant and pitiful pleas. His tone was harsh and his attitude exclusive. "I am sent," he said, "only to the lost sheep of the house of Israel" (Matt. 15:24). This woman apparently did not qualify. At the very least, however, this text suggests that Jesus had now noticed her. Grasping this tiny shred of hope, the Canaanite woman entered his physical space, falling at his feet and daring to challenge the tribal lines that Jesus had just drawn, lines that excluded her. Having gotten his attention, she now implored him: "Lord, help me" (Matt. 15:25).

Jesus' next response sounded harsher still, violating deeply the image that most of us have of him: "It is not fair to take the children's bread and throw it to the dogs" (Matt. 15:26), he said. These words are rude, insulting and even cruel. If "the children" were "the lost sheep of Israel," as this text implies, then "the dogs" must be the Gentiles in general and the Canaanites in particular. It is tribal bigotry at its worst! One feels the pain of this rejection. The Canaanite woman, however, accepted his attention as positive; she even appeared to accept his definition of her as accurate and hurled his own words back at him in her defense: "Yes, Lord," she says, "but even the dogs eat the crumbs that fall from the master's table" (Matt. 15:27). It is a strong response, an unexpected way to confront rejection and prejudice. She accepted it, and by doing so she turned this conversation in a dramatically new direction.

How can one continue to reject a person who has accepted and absorbed the insults of prejudice and who nonetheless continues to stand before you, still acknowledging your ability to be of great help? It is not easy. Insults hurled back at the insulter usually generate only more insults, more justification for yet more insults. Absorbing the pain of the insult and not retreating, not insulting in return, is not a popular response, but it is an effective way to transform prejudice.

So Jesus responded to this Canaanite: "O woman, great is your faith. Be it done for you as you desire" (Matt. 15:28). Matthew then concluded this memorable encounter with the words: "And her daughter was healed instantly."

We are shocked by this narrative and cannot help but wonder why Matthew included it. Is it just one more miracle story that Matthew wanted to tell depicting Jesus' power to heal? If that is the case, then its strangeness is offensive. That, however, would be to view this story literally. That, as we are learning, is not the way to read Jewish sacred stories. The gospel of Matthew is a narrative written by a Jewish scribe for a Jewish audience. We must learn to read it through Jewish lenses and seek to discover its Jewish meaning.

We begin by noting that this is not the first time in Matthew's gospel that he has denigrated a Gentile woman. The four ancestral "mothers" that Matthew placed into the genealogy with which he opened his gospel were all, as we noted earlier, both Gentiles and sexually tainted (and thus rejectable) women.* I suggest, therefore, that this tactic of denigrating Gentile women is a familiar device to this author.

This Canaanite woman, in common with all Gentiles, lived outside the covenant between God and Israel. So the question Matthew was posing in this episode is, How far will the love of God stretch? How universal is the Christ story? Will it cover the Canaanite woman, who is made to reflect the depths of Jewish prejudice? Can community ever be formed between "chosen people" and those the "chosen people" call "dogs"?

The disciples wanted to send her away. That is one way of dealing with a burdensome reality. People exert political pressure to remove the poor and the homeless from the streets of our cities. We put them in shelters or workhouses where we do not have to see them. Every nation in Europe at one time or another in history sought to expel the Jews from its borders. When that tactic failed, they forced the Jews to live in ghettoes where they would become invisible. Rather than deal with the social problems that slavery and segregation created in the United States for African-Americans, some people proposed sending them back to Africa. When that proved to be impossible, the solution was to build more jails and fill them with

---

*I hasten to say that the concept of these women being "sexually tainted" would be the moral judgment of that time in which this story appeared. From another perspective these women might also be viewed as survivors, who used the only power granted to them in that patriarchal time, namely the power of their bodies, to achieve their goals. I do not want to participate in that practice of moral pronouncements by which males have justified their treatment of females historically.

these people of color. "Out of sight" means "out of mind." During the second Iraq war, President George W. Bush refused to allow photographs of caskets bearing the mortal remains of American soldiers killed in battle to be shown on television. Why? One is not horrified by the results of war if one is not allowed to see those results.

The Canaanite woman forced Jesus to *see* her. He did not succumb to the tactic of pretending that a prejudice will disappear when the victims of that prejudice become invisible. Perhaps that is why the rhetoric of this story is made to sound so harsh. Matthew designed it carefully, so that it expresses the depths of the feeling that the Jews held toward the Canaanites. Keeping themselves separate had been for the Jewish people a tactic of survival. They had erected fixed boundaries to guarantee their continued Jewish existence. They had adopted certain customs that made them different and therefore not absorbable, so that they could always be survivors. The universal claim to the love of God, which Jesus acknowledged, ran counter to those survival techniques, learned and fashioned over many centuries. The collision between survival themes and universalism was deep among the Jews, and Matthew suggested that the collision between the two *in the life of Jesus* was at the heart of what Jesus meant. The Canaanite woman thus became a powerful symbol in Matthew's understanding of the Christ story. Can the love of God embrace those who are the most eminently rejectable? Can any limit whatsoever be placed on the availability of the love of God?

That theme had echoed before in the Jewish prophets. Jesus did not invent it. Is the love of God great enough to embrace the people of Nineveh? That was the question the prophet Jonah addressed (Jon. 1:2). "Have we not all one father? Has not one God created us?" (Mal. 2:10). Those were questions raised by the prophet Malachi. "*Every* valley shall be lifted up and *every* mountain and hill shall be made low" (Isa. 40:4). Those were the universal images of the prophet we call II Isaiah.

Matthew, a Jewish scribe, confronted his Jewish audience with a vision of universalism. This Canaanite woman was to be the icon, which he hoped would stand before the exclusive claims that religious systems always seem to create. Paul certainly shared this view of Jesus when, writing to the Galatians, he said: "In Christ, there is neither Jew nor Greek. There is neither slave nor free. There is neither male nor female; for you are all one in Christ Jesus" (Gal. 3:28).

The first battle that divided the Christian church was whether Gentiles could come to the worship of Jesus just as they were, or whether they had to come through the already established gate called Judaism. Paul championed immediate access. Peter championed the traditional Jewish doorway. The battle was intense until, at least according to the book of Acts, Peter had a vision and heard the words: "What God has cleansed, you must not call common [or unclean]" (Acts 10:15). Then these words were placed on Peter's lips: "Truly, I perceive that God shows no partiality" (Acts 10:34).

Matthew, in his narrative of the Canaanite woman, is continuing this theme of universalism. The love of God includes the one whom you have defined as the most despicable of all humankind, the most unclean, the most unworthy. That is Matthew's meaning in the story of the Canaanite woman, and a powerful story it is.

I referred in the opening chapter of this book to the history of victimization of human beings on the part of the body of Christ in its institutional forms. It is there for all the world to see. This means that the Canaanite woman has assumed many forms throughout Christian history. She has been the Jews, scorned, hated, and persecuted by the Christians from the writings of the church fathers in the second century, who described the Jews as "vermin, unfit to live"; to the sixteenth-century Reformation, in which its leader, Martin Luther, called for the burning of synagogues; to the Holocaust of the twentieth century, watched by Christian leaders, including Pope Pious XII, with, at best, "benign neglect."

The Canaanite woman has also been the Muslims, called "infidels" during the church-inspired crusades of the eleventh, twelfth and thirteenth centuries. The intention of the crusades was to free Christian holy places from the control of the infidels, all of whom were Muslims, and in the process to destroy as many infidels as possible. If one wants to understand the killing hatred in Islam toward Christians and toward the ostensibly Christian nations of the West in the twenty-first century, one needs only to read the history of the crusades. One always reaps what one sows.

The Canaanite woman has also been the Africans, kidnapped, transported to a new world and sold into slavery. She has been the women in Western civilization who were defined by the leaders of the church as sub-human, meek, dependent and incapable of participating in the affairs of society. Like the Canaanite woman in Matthew's gospel, women today stand before all the closed structures of society—religious, educational, political and cultural—whose guardians and members act as if the privilege of defining a human being rightly belonged to those still-male-controlled structures.

The Canaanite woman is also present among those members of the gay, lesbian, bisexual, and transgender community who stand in the integrity of their humanity before the community of faith, as well as before the aforementioned political and social structures, historically informed by that community of faith. The question is still the same: How far does the love of God stretch? The nature of human prejudice has nothing to do with objective values and traditional definitions. It arises in the human heart, which convinces many that the love of God must be limited to those that *we* are able to love.

The Canaanite woman is, therefore, not a person of history, but an eternal symbol, always standing before the human conscience, challenging its limits, demanding to be heard; and she will not go away until she is embraced. If we reduce this Matthean character to a literal person, we can deal with her once and for all and then move on. If she is a symbol, an icon, her challenge will be eternal; her face will change throughout history, but her demands will remain, constantly challenging our security and eroding our barriers. Jewish readers of Matthew's gospel knew that she was a symbol. Gentile readers, later, would assume that she was a literal figure and that they had dealt with her once they had brought themselves to accept Canaanites. Perhaps we need to confront the possibility that Christianity has not failed, as our critics constantly assert; the reality, I believe, is that Christianity has never been understood and thus has never really been tried.

Matthew next moves to his second character in what will be his last episode before he relates Jesus to the festival of Dedication-Hanukkah, the next great feast of the Jews. This character's name is Peter. He is a person of history, but he is so much more. In the narrative of Peter's confession of faith, which Matthew locates in a place called Caesarea Philippi, Peter uses all the correct words. Of Jesus he says: "You are the Christ, the son of the living God" (Matt. 16:16). For this confession, he is said to have received the affirmation of Jesus. "Flesh and blood alone could not have revealed that to you, Peter," says Jesus (Matt. 16:17). You have become capable of receiving this knowledge only as the gift from God. It has come to you because you finally understand, says Jesus. Now you will be given the keys of the kingdom (Matt. 16:19).

Armed with Peter's remarkable confession, Matthew then has Jesus begin to reveal what it meant to be "the Christ." Living "in Christ" did not mean the accumulation of power, but the willingness to embrace weakness. To be "the Christ" meant allowing others to do their worst. It meant the willingness to lose all, to endure arrest and suffering, and even to be put to death. Peter was not ready to live out what his own confession meant. He did not understand the revolutionary nature of the kingdom. He did not understand that following Jesus meant a cross, not glory, that life was found only by giving it away, that meaning was found not in possessions, but in the freedom to live without possessions. Peter could say the words, but he could not live the message. That same pattern of behavior would also plague the church through the centuries. The call to universalism has long been countered by our inability to live that message out.

Matthew has forced these insights into his readers' minds in his stories of the Canaanite woman and Peter at Caesarea Philippi. Now he is ready to take us deeper into the Christ story than we have yet imagined. We move to the festival of Dedication-Hanukkah and what it means for the light of God to be seen in Jesus.

Part VII

Dedication-Hanukkah and Transfiguration: The Light of God Reinterpreted

CHAPTER 24

Dedication: The Return of the Light of God

THE LITURGICAL CALENDAR of the synagogue has now arrived at the winter festival called Dedication. As noted earlier, in the Hebrew language the word for "Dedication" is "Hanukkah," so in time this festival came to be known by that name.* In this discussion, though, I will call the festival Dedication, because that word is essential to its history.

The observance of Dedication comes at the time of the winter solstice in the month of Kislev, which corresponds roughly with our month of December. Dedication is not a Torah festival, since it did not enter the Jewish calendar until the second century BCE at

---

*There are many variations in the way that Hanukkah is spelled, because this word is simply transliterated from the Hebrew, and all of the Hebrew letters do not translate easily into English letters. So you will see this word written Chanukah, Hanukkah, Hanukah and Hanuka. While none of them is wrong, I will use Hanukkah as the spelling that seems to reflect a consensus.

the time of the Maccabees. Its roots, however, stretch back deeply into human history, and its meaning comes close to reflecting a universal human anxiety and a universal experience.

Almost every group of people in the world, regardless of their stated religious connections, has developed a liturgical event to mark that time of the year when the sun seems to stop its relentless journey into darkness and begins to return to light. Today we refer to that moment, rather mundanely, as the shortest day of the year. So this natural phenomenon has historically been thought of as a proper time for a liturgical celebration.*

The early Jews, however, had a very difficult time adopting this practice, for to them it reeked of paganism and sun worship, concepts repugnant to the idea of a universal God called Yahweh. Then, in the second century BCE, their outlook changed. The Jewish people were living through a particularly difficult time, oppressed and persecuted by their Syrian conquerors. In response to their persecution, a group of rebel Jews known in history as the Maccabees managed to turn the darkness of that experience into a great moment of victory. Only then were the Jews finally able to fill this winter festival with distinctively Jewish, non-pagan content and thus to incorporate this celebration of the return of light in the darkness of winter into a part of their liturgical practice, naming it the "festival of Dedication." By the time the gospels were written, this festival was not only observed in the synagogue, but it had become one of the most popular holidays of the year. We turn first to the story of how this day was born, and then to how the narrative of Jesus being transfigured on top of a mountain, where he

---

*I am aware that in the Southern Hemisphere the shortest day of the year comes in the heat of summer, not the cold of winter. I am writing from a Northern Hemisphere perspective.

talked with Moses and Elijah, became the story that the followers of Jesus attached to this Jewish observance.

First the history: Following the death of Alexander the Great in 323 BCE the Macedonian Empire was divided up among his generals. The land of the Jews ultimately came under the control of a royal family known as the Seleucids, who governed Syria. About the year 175 BCE, a man named Antiochus IV became the new Seleucid king of the Syrian Empire. He adopted the nickname Epiphanes, a not altogether humble title, for it meant that he thought of himself as "the revelation of God."

In the land of Judah this king cultivated the support of those Jewish citizens who might have called themselves "secular Jews," or "non-religious, non-practicing Jews." Armed with that support he began to suppress the traditional religious practices of the Jewish people. First, Antiochus authorized Gentile worship forms to be practiced in the land, breaking the exclusive Jewish norms. Next he built himself a Greek gymnasium in Jerusalem, in which the human body was displayed in a way contrary to Jewish practice. The appeal of these changes was strong, and more and more Jews began to abandon the "faith of their fathers and mothers" and to participate in these "modern trends." The cultural practices that marked Judaism as a separate and distinct people, such as circumcision, kosher dietary laws and Sabbath day observances, began to fall into disuse. These defections from among the people of the covenant were, to the faithful Jews, cruel signs of their oppression.

Encouraged, however, by the wide acceptance of these secularizing moves, Antiochus Epiphanes pressed this campaign, which he believed would ultimately break the will of the people in this normally rebellious vassal state of Judah. In his boldest act yet, Antiochus next moved to desecrate the Jewish Temple. First, he removed from its walls and holy places all of the familiar symbols of Judaism. Next, in an act thought by the Jews to be the most dastardly and egregious yet, he installed in the most sacred space in the Temple, the space known to the Jews as the Holy of Holies, an offensive pagan symbol. Some believe that what he did was to place the head of a pig, an unclean animal to the Jews, on the "mercy seat" of God, which you may recall was believed by the Jews to be God's earthly throne. Faithful Jews referred to this act as "the abomination of desolation." It was to the oppressed Jews a visible and ever-present reminder of their powerlessness, of their status as a conquered and, of necessity, subservient people.

With the Jews subdued for the moment, Antiochus Epiphanes then turned on Egypt and forced the Egyptian Pharaoh Ptolemy to flee before him. With the defeat of Egypt, his campaign against all things Jewish was intensified. Those Jews who persisted in Jewish worship were subject to execution. There was no effective way to stand up to Antiochus Epiphanes' power directly, so the Jewish people did what oppressed people always do: They began to use guerrilla tactics as the focus of their resistance.

A descendant of a priestly family, Mattathias, became the leader of the nascent guerrilla movement. He had five sons. Together they planned a strategy of resistance. These plans received a great impetus when Mattathias watched a Jew, who in obedience to the command of Antiochus, offered a pagan sacrifice on a Jewish altar in a public place. Infuriated by this act, he broke onto the scene and killed one of Antiochus' military officers, before proceeding to tear down the now-desecrated altar. He then issued a call to all those who were "zealous for the law" and who supported "the covenant" (I Macc. 2:27) to join him in his resistance movement. He and his new recruits fled, in the classic style of guerrilla activity, into the hills, where they organized themselves into a movement with a clear focus. When Mattathias died, the leadership of the movement fell to his son Judas. So successful was this Judas in dealing hit-and-run blows to the army of Antiochus that he achieved the nickname "the hammer." In Aramaic the word for hammer was "maccabeus." So Judas "the hammer" was called Judas Maccabeus, and his name became the name for this movement; in Jewish history this period was known as "the age of the Maccabees."

Judas Maccabeus was clearly a brilliant military strategist. In a series of calculated, stunning victories on terrain that favored the smaller, more mobile guerrilla forces against a massive standing army, he won victory after victory, until finally Antiochus had to retreat from Jerusalem itself. Judas and his ragtag army of fighters then entered the holy city in triumph. All of this occurred in the month of Kislev,* in the dead of winter.

Now in charge of Jerusalem, the Maccabees began a systematic cleanup of their traditional holy places. Their stated purpose was to restore "true worship" to the Temple. They removed the "abomination of desolation" from the Holy of Holies. They restored Jewish symbols that had been torn down. They reconstituted the Jewish sacred vessels used in worship and returned the Jewish hangings to their "proper places." The book of Maccabees states that "the reproach of the Gentiles" was taken away (I Macc. 4:58).

Then they called the people to worship, to "dedicate" anew their restored Temple. The tradition says that the liberators and the citizens of Jerusalem celebrated together for eight days. They lit candles in the Temple. An eight-pronged candelabra, called a menorah, was said to have burned miraculously for all of those

---

*Sometimes spelled Chislev.

eight days and nights without ever needing to have its oil replenished, while the people celebrated with singing, dancing and worship. The light of God, they shouted, has been returned to the Temple.

When these eight festival days were over, Judas Maccabeus enjoined on the people henceforth to observe this period each year as a holy time. So every year from that day forward the Jewish people have in the darkness of winter observed this "festival of light," celebrating the moment when the light of God came back to the Temple. That is how the festival of Dedication, or Hanukkah, was born in the liturgical life of the Jewish people. It was, like Sukkoth, established to be an eight-day celebration.

In typical Jewish style, once the worship festival was established, religious leaders began to search the Hebrew scriptures for material that could be used in liturgy. This was not the first time, they said, that the light of God had come to the Temple. These earlier stories out of Jewish history, stories about the light of God coming in various ways to God's people, were then lifted into the Dedication-Hanukkah liturgy. In this way, the celebration was rooted deeper and deeper into Jewish history and came to be viewed not just as a recent addition to their worship life, but as a time in which many details of their past found new focus. With eight days to celebrate, they needed a good number of lessons regarding how light and God were connected. We will review some of these stories briefly so that we can understand how Dedication-Hanukkah looked to the followers of Jesus when the gospels were being written.

There was the story of the building of the second Temple that followed the destruction of Jerusalem at the hands of the Babylonians in the sixth century BCE. That building was not completed until the time of Ezra, the priest, and Nehemiah, the governor, in the fifth century BCE. When that Temple was consecrated, it was said that the light of God, the "shekinah," had once again been restored to the Temple. So it was that this celebration was also incorporated into Dedication-Hanukkah.

Walking further backward in Jewish history, they noted next that when Solomon, who carried out the plans developed by his father, David, built the first Temple in Jerusalem, he dedicated it in a sacred assembly with prayer (I Kings 8). On that occasion, it was likewise said, the light of God, the "shekinah," descended upon the Temple as their worship was begun. So restoring the light of God to the Temple was deep in the tradition of the Jews.

As they kept walking ever backward into their history, they discovered that this tradition stretched back even before there was a Temple. In Hebrew history God had been portrayed as present in the tabernacle that these nomadic people carried with them through their years in the wilderness between Egypt and the land of Canaan. This tabernacle was also a sign that the light of God was present with the people. A pillar of cloud by day and a pillar of fire by night connected the tabernacle directly to the God who reigned from above the sky. God, they said, had "tabernacled" among them. God's light, God's "shekinah," always connected the people to their God. God was never too far away from the Jews. Light was thus the symbol of the divine presence.

Other stories about light were also brought into the Dedication-Hanukkah orbit. The first one had to do with Moses. In this particular narrative, one that we have referred to several times previously, Moses was negotiating the covenant between God and the people. In that capacity he was said to have journeyed up to the top of Mt. Sinai (sometimes called Mt. Horeb) to confer with God and to receive from God the law of which the Ten Commandments were a part. When Moses returned and found God's people worshipping a golden calf, he smashed the tablets, which necessitated a second trip up the mountain to talk with God again. When Moses returned from this second trip, the Torah notes, the light of God on Moses made his face shine with a luminous brightness. This brightness remained on him when he returned to the people. It was indeed so bright that he was required to put a veil on his face lest the people's eyes be burned by Moses' translucent skin (Exod. 34: 29–35).

Next there was a story found in the book of the prophet Zechariah (chapter 3). It was about a priest named Joshua. There are only two people named Joshua in the entire Old Testament. The first was the well-known successor to Moses, who was the hero of the conquest at Canaan. The other was this little known priest, who is mentioned in only two books of the Bible, once in this Zechariah story and again in a book called Haggai (Hag. 1:1).

The names Jesus and Joshua are identical in Aramaic, Jesus being only the Greek spelling of Joshua. So both of the Joshuas in the Old Testament would have been read as having the same name as Jesus in the first century. To those "Jesus" texts the followers of Jesus would have paid special attention.

This second Joshua, the priest, we are told rebuked Satan (Zech. 3), and for this he was rewarded by having his filthy garments removed from him; he was then "re-clothed" with luminous new apparel. Both the account of Moses' skin shining with the light of God and of Joshua's clothing being transfigured were brought into the Dedication-Hanukkah celebration.

Two other stories from the Hebrew scriptures need to be mentioned, because they too informed the content that Matthew would apply to his Dedication-Hanukkah story. They were the accounts of the deaths of Israel's "twin towers," Moses and Elijah. I will treat these stories in more depth when I get to Matthew's Easter story and look at the Jewish understanding of resurrection. For now, suffice it to say that the stories of Moses' death and Elijah's departure from life were shrouded in mystery in the biblical texts, making it easy to bring both characters back into Matthew's account.

All of this material out of the Hebrew scriptures was gathered around Dedication-Hanukkah over the years after its original establishment, and by the first century most of them had become deeply associated with this winter festival. When Matthew arrived at his Jesus narrative at Dedication-Hanukkah, he followed the lead of Mark and told a Jesus story appropriate to the synagogue observance of that day. We know that story as the transfiguration of Jesus. Every Jewish reader of Matthew's day, familiar with their Jewish past, would have known that he never intended this narrative to be understood as a literal event that actually happened. It was designed, rather, to incorporate Jesus into the ongoing pattern of synagogue worship. We analyze the story of the transfiguration next, for this Jewish perspective.

CHAPTER 25

The Transfiguration:
A Dedication-Hanukkah Story

How could the light of God be restored to the Temple in Jewish worship life after 70 CE? That was the year the Temple was destroyed by the invading Roman army. Its destruction was the climactic moment of a disastrous war that had been initiated in Galilee in the year 66 CE by a group of Jewish guerrilla fighters known as "the zealots." The hills of Galilee offered these hit-and-run fighters a perfect cover. They chose their targets carefully, swooping down on isolated groups of Roman soldiers when they held numerical superiority, killing them quickly and then retreating back into the hills of Galilee, just as the Maccabees had done in an earlier time. These tactics served the guerrilla warriors well, but eventually Rome became unwilling to absorb these attacks any longer. Believing that one does not defeat one's enemy militarily by fighting on the fringes of that enemy's land, the Romans decided they needed to strike at the heart of this rebellious nation. So the Roman army gathered outside the city of Jerusalem and began a siege that would last for five months before Jerusalem's protective walls were finally breached, allowing the Roman legions to pour into the "holy city." This army went through Jerusalem like the Russian army went through Berlin in 1945. Everything standing was struck down, including the Temple, which was reduced to rubble. The Jewish people now had to worship without a Temple. Thus began a very difficult time in Jewish history. The survival of the religion of the Jews hung by a single thread.

At that time there was considerable rivalry between the followers of Jesus and the Orthodox party that had once controlled the Temple. Both of these groups were Jewish. The followers of Jesus did not yet call themselves Christians; they were known as "followers of the way." The Temple authorities called them "revisionist Jews," while calling themselves "Orthodox Jews." (The term "orthodox" is frequently used by proponents of a stated norm to define the opposition: Anyone disagreeing with that norm—anyone not "orthodox"—is thus "deviant," "irregular" or "heretical.") The authorities who controlled the Temple had been supportive of this unwise war that brought with it the destruction of everything they held sacred. The Jewish followers of Jesus were not above rubbing salt into the wounds of this Orthodox party by suggesting that the fall of Jerusalem and the destruction of the Temple were in fact expressions of God's wrath against the Temple leaders for their unwillingness to see in Jesus the expected messiah. From the year 70 CE on religious hostility was clearly rising between these two groups. The Orthodox party had to adjust to the absence of a Temple to give order to their common life, while the Jewish followers of Jesus wanted to offer Jesus as the new Temple, designed to stand in place of the destroyed Temple. The story of the transfiguration of Jesus was created in this context. It was and is a deeply Jewish story.

If one reads the story of Jesus' transfiguration literally, it is nonsensical. No faithful Jew would ever have been tempted to do that. This narrative says that "after six days" Jesus, together with his inner core of disciples, Peter, James, and John, went up to a "high mountain," where they were alone. There Jesus was "transfigured" before his disciples—that is, "his face shone like the sun," and his garments became an unearthly "white," whiter than any bleach could ever have made them (Matt. 17:1–2). It was a luminous whiteness, as if he had been illumined by an external light. Suddenly, the story suggests, there were two figures with him. One was Moses, who had been dead now for about twelve hundred years; the other was Elijah, who had been dead for about eight hundred years (Matt. 17:3). Both appeared to be talking with Jesus, though the details of their conversation were not related. Here, however, were "the father of the law" and "the father of the prophets," speaking out of heaven. Since the faith of the Hebrew people was built on "the law and the prophets," this story was describing the foundation of that faith. The response of the disciples of Jesus to this event was interesting, almost amusing. Peter was the spokesman and was portrayed, as he is regularly, as speaking off the cuff, struggling to understand. "Lord," he said, "it is well that we are here." Then, as if offering a proposal to commemorate this rather historical gathering, he continued: "If you wish, I will make three tabernacles [or booths], one for you, one for Moses, and one for Elijah" (Matt. 17:4). It was meant to be high praise. No one had at this time thought to couple Jesus with Moses and Elijah as equals.

As Peter spoke, however, the author of Matthew informs us, "a bright cloud overshadowed them." Then a voice spoke out of that cloud designating Jesus as something quite different, set apart even from Moses and Elijah. "This is my beloved son, in whom I am well pleased; listen to him" (Matt. 17:5). The words of this heavenly voice had been heard before in this gospel. At the baptism of Jesus in the Jordan River by John the Baptist, the heavenly voice had proclaimed: "This is my beloved son, in whom I am well pleased" (Matt. 3:17). Elijah, in Matthew's narrative, was also present at the baptism of Jesus, but in the person of John the Baptist. By this time Elijah had become, as we have previously noted, not the eighth-century prophet but the mythological forerunner of the messiah.

Moses had also been deeply present earlier in this Matthean narrative. We have already traced that connection by showing how the baptism of Jesus echoed the Red Sea experience. Matthew here simply added a new dimension to that theme: He used the transfiguration story to make both of Israel's most important symbols point to Jesus and to find themselves fulfilled in him.

Matthew suggested that, when the heavenly voice was heard, a new dimension of reality was born in Peter, James and John. "They fell on their faces and were filled with awe" (Matt. 17:6). It was not dissimilar to the response of the disciples when they saw Jesus walking on the water (Matt. 14:26). Matthew then said of the disciples that when this illumined vision was complete, they lifted up their eyes and saw no one, but Jesus only (Matt. 17:8). The story of the transfiguration was over.

Note the similarity to other aspects of the Jewish tradition. As we have seen, the face of Moses also shone with an unearthly light when he entered into the presence of God. The high priest in Zechariah, who bore Jesus' name (Joshua), had his earthly rags transformed into exquisite splendor in a vision in Zechariah. Most important of all, however, is that in this Hanukkah story in Matthew's gospel the light of God, which the festival of Dedication celebrated returning to the Temple, was now being portrayed as descending on Jesus. The Temple, thought of in the Jewish tradition as the dwelling place of God, the place where God and human life came together, was no more. So Matthew had the light of God fall on Jesus, thought of by his followers now as the new Temple, the new dwelling place of God in human life, the new meeting place between the human and the divine. Matthew was making theological claims, not historical claims. It was a Jewish portrait, painted by a Jewish artist to describe in a way that Jews would surely understand the experience, first articulated by Paul, that the holy God was perceived to be present in Jesus (II Cor. 5:19).

One other thing becomes obvious when reading the transfiguration account. No one would be telling the story of how the light of God came on Jesus instead of the Temple unless there was no longer a Temple. This helps us date the earliest gospel, Mark, since it too reflects in its transfiguration story the destruction of the Temple. Since we know the date of the destruction of the Temple by the Romans, we must date Mark *after* 70 CE; and since Matthew copied and expanded Mark, we must date Matthew even later.

The idea that Jesus has replaced the Temple grows as the New Testament is written. That identification becomes fixed by the time the Fourth Gospel is composed. John's gospel first moves the story of Jesus cleansing the Temple of the money changers from a point near the end of Jesus' life, where it is located in the first three gospels, to a point near the beginning of Jesus' public ministry. The Fourth Gospel then has Jesus defend his action by claiming that he has replaced the Temple. "Destroy this Temple," this gospel has Jesus say, "and I will rebuild it in three days." That extravagant claim created great consternation among those who heard it, so the author of the Fourth Gospel explains to his readers that Jesus was speaking about his body (John 2:13–22).

So Matthew is quite within the developing tradition in following Mark's lead and telling, as the Jesus story for the festival of Dedication-Hanukkah, the account of how the light of God transformed Jesus on the Mount of Transfiguration, since there was no longer a Temple in existence on which the light of God, the "shekinah," could fall. Matthew's gospel clearly continues to follow the outline of the synagogue's liturgical calendar.

In this episode we also find the fourth of Matthew's five sections of Jesus' teachings. In every case these long teaching collections have been associated with the celebration of a major holy day. So in this practice we see again the truth of the thesis that Matthew's gospel is organized liturgically rather than historically.

Since the festival of Dedication-Hanukkah is an eight-day celebration, Matthew has to provide his readers with eight Jesus stories. That in fact is exactly what he does. He follows the story of Jesus' transfiguration, which is day one, with the story of the epileptic boy, whom Jesus' disciples could not cure, and he then gives us a word from Jesus on the power of faith (Matt. 17:14–21).

For the third day Matthew has Jesus direct the disciples in Galilee to prepare to begin the fateful journey into Jerusalem. We also have in this segment the second prediction of Jesus' passion, followed by a strange story about whether or not the followers of Jesus should pay taxes to the Roman authorities. The relationship of Matthew's congregation to their oppressors is always an issue (Matt. 17:22–27).

The fourth day features Jesus' teaching on the meaning of the kingdom, which was about to dawn. Jesus uses a child to focus his teaching and discusses to the degree to which one should allow oneself to be burdened by temptation (Matt. 18:1–10).

On the fifth day, Matthew has Jesus tell the parable of the lost sheep and stress the value to God of the single individual (Matt. 18:10–14).

On the sixth day, Jesus discusses how internal disputes among his followers are to be managed. In this narrative the assurance is given that where two or three are gathered in Jesus' name, he is present in their midst (Matt. 18:15–20).

On the seventh day Jesus is made to give us his teaching on forgiveness, borrowing his text from the book of Genesis, where the punishment for Cain's sins was said to be sevenfold but the punishment for Lamech's sins was to be seventy times sevenfold. So seven times to forgive is not enough, Jesus says; he calls for a capacity to forgive that will reach seventy times seven, or unto infinity (Matt. 18:21–22).

Finally on day eight Matthew has Jesus see the kingdom of heaven as like unto the final accounting, in which forgiveness is our only hope. Forgiving another allows forgiveness to pass to the forgiving one. It is an ever-flowing stream. If one stops the flow of forgiveness, then one can no longer receive it (Matt. 18:23–35).

The eight-day celebration of Dedication-Hanukkah is now complete. Matthew adds the line that has come to mark all of the five long teaching segments (see 7:28, 11:1, 13:53, 26:1): "Now when Jesus had finished these sayings, he went away from Galilee and entered the region of Judea" (Matt. 19:1). It is time for the final journey. The cross slowly comes into full view. Matthew drives his story toward Passover.

PART VIII

Journey Toward Passover: Apocalypse and Judgment

CHAPTER 26

Introducing the Journey Section of Matthew's Gospel

EFORE WE REACH THE CLIMAX of our story, I need to take a brief time-out to speak to the problems of why it has been so difficult in Christian history to bring the gospel accounts together against the format of the liturgical year of the synagogue. The things that have hidden this connection for so long are not irreconcilable problems, so much as they are inconvenient dislocations. I have alluded to some of these things before; but now they impact the narrative, and so I feel the need to refresh my readers' memories.

The first difficulty has to do with timing. The end of the gospels' story, the cross and resurrection of Jesus, comes not at the end of the Jewish year, but in its first month of the calendar that the gospel writers are following. The crucifixion, the final event in Jesus' life, is told against the story of Passover, the first celebration of this Jewish year. The crucifixion, therefore, comes in the Jewish calendar between the second and third Sabbaths of the first month of the New Year.

Add to that the Christian liturgical practice of devoting two Sabbaths after the crucifixion to the telling of the Easter story, and you have a situation in which the Christian story will always begin, not at the beginning of the new Jewish year, but on the fifth Sabbath of that year.

The second difficulty is that the Jews at this time followed a lunar calendar based on twelve moons. That will never give us the 365.25 days that it takes the planet earth to make its elliptical journey around the sun, a fact that ancient people had not yet discovered. They did know, however, that if they did not make a periodic adjustment to their lunar calendar, it would not be long before the seasons of the liturgical year no longer correlated with the seasons of the natural year. The harvest season of Sukkoth, for example, becomes ineffective and irrelevant if it does not come at the end of the agricultural cycle. The midwinter festival called Dedication-Hanukkah, which celebrates the return of light to the Temple, makes no sense if it does not come at the darkest time of the winter solstice.

So to keep the liturgy of the synagogue in touch with the seasons of the year, which that liturgy was designed to reflect, the Jews added to the calendar a "leap month" in seven out of every nineteen years. Since the last month of the Jewish year was called Adar, this "leap month" was simply called Adar II.

A third calendar problem at this time in history is that the date of Passover was not fixed.* Because it was related to the cycles of the moon, it floated in the Jewish calendar. Most of us are aware

---

*Coming between the second and third Sabbaths of the month, Passover could be as early as the eighth day of the month and as late as the fifteenth day of the month. In a lunar calendar that was always losing time it would never fall on the same day of the year. Finally, when Adar II is added to the year to catch up with the lunar schedule the place where Passover falls could vary up to a month.

that Easter, because it was originally attached to Passover, also floats, coming in some years as early as near the end of March and in others as late as near the end of April. The lunar rule was that Easter was the first Sunday after the first full moon after the twenty-first day of March.

Because Shavuot or Pentecost was fixed at "fifty days," or seven weeks and one day, after Passover, it too floats, depending on where Passover is celebrated, coming in some years in late May and in others in early to mid-June.

It is necessary for us to embrace all of these non-fixed features about the Jewish calendar before we can demonstrate just how closely the synoptic gospels related to that calendar. These abnormalities served for centuries to hide from the eyes of a mostly Gentile Christian church the close connection between the order followed by the gospels in telling the Jesus story and the great celebrations of the Jewish liturgical year.

These "abnormalities" of the Jewish calendar will now intrude upon our consciousness. We have completed the celebration of Dedication-Hanukkah, which was fixed at or near the winter solstice. We are ready to begin our journey, not only toward the end of the Jewish year, but also toward the floating observance of Passover. In some years the interval of time between Dedication-Hanukkah and Passover would be as few as thirteen Sabbaths, while in other years it would be as many as eighteen Sabbaths.

It is into that accordion-like span of time that Matthew, following Mark's example, will have Jesus set out on his long, final journey from Galilee to Jerusalem. In this period of time the major agenda of the synoptic gospel writers is to add significantly to what they call "the teaching" of Jesus. In doing this, the synoptic authors are also following a Jewish pattern that becomes crucial to our understanding of gospel formation.

As we saw in chapter 3, it was the pattern in traditional Jewish circles to read the entire Torah in synagogue worship on the Sabbaths of a single year. That being so, in the calendar born in the Exile, faithful Jews would begin their Torah reading on the first Sabbath of Nisan, the first month of that Jewish year, with Genesis, the first book of the Torah. Since the Torah was read in sequence, on the last number of Sabbaths of the Jewish year the readings would be from the last book of the Torah, Deuteronomy. This meant that the book of Deuteronomy would be the primary part of the Torah read on most of the Sabbaths between Dedication-Hanukkah and the end of Adar I or Adar II.

The title of the book of Deuteronomy means, literally, "the second [*deutero*] giving of the law [*nomas*]." This book was designed to be the document in which the final teachings of Moses, the founder of the Hebrew nation, would be given to his people just prior to his death. The death of Moses is actually described in the last chapter of the book of Deuteronomy. So this book reads something like the "last will and testament," or the final words, of the founder of Israel.

By attaching the major part of the teaching of Jesus to the journey section of the gospels, the gospel writers were deliberately emulating the pattern of Deuteronomy, in that the journey section of these gospels is made up of the final teachings of Jesus to his disciples prior to his death. The death of Jesus would come, therefore, as it did with Moses in Deuteronomy, with the conclusion of his "last will and testament." So this teaching journey section of the synoptic gospels was deliberately designed to emulate Deuteronomy and thus to follow, yet again, the pattern of the synagogue.

There is one further background piece of information that we must clarify before we can begin to look at the teaching material contained in the journey section. Once again it is something that the early Gentile community would not have been able to grasp.

In the years before Christianity emerged out of Judaism, Judaism itself had, interestingly enough, become something of a missionary religion. That is, the synagogues had begun to have a significant number of Gentile converts to Judaism. The reasons for this were complex. In the Mediterranean world, the "gods of the Olympus" had fallen into disrepute. The mystery cults, which would flourish as competitors with Christianity years later, were not yet well known. There was a vacuum in the space that a living faith tradition had once occupied. Judaism, with its emphasis on the oneness of God and the demands of this God for an ethical response on the part of God's people, appealed to many non-Jewish people, leading some of them to frequent the synagogues. Most of the attracted ones were not drawn to the cultic practices of Judaism, which had been developed specifically to keep Jews separate from Gentiles— Sabbath day requirements, the kosher dietary laws and the rite of circumcision, for example. To embrace these cultic practices was for most Gentiles too large a step. There were some, however, who were not put off by cultic requirements, and so Gentile converts to Judaism were not unknown. Indeed they comprised a sufficiently large number of people that the synagogue leaders had to make some provisions for the proper preparation of these converts, as well as for the development of a liturgy of incorporation.

The incorporation plans that were developed had several elements. First, there was a need to provide some instruction as to what it meant to be a Jew. People needed to know just what it was to which they were going to commit themselves. The obvious choice for catechetical material on the nature of Judaism was the book of Deuteronomy. This book not only incorporated the meaning of Judaism and the law, condensing it into a manageable portion, but it also purported to contain Moses' final instructions.

Second, the induction of converts needed to be worked into the life of the community. A consensus developed that Passover, the meal of the Jewish people, was the proper time to induct these new converts. At the Passover celebration the history of the Hebrew people was retold. That appeared to be the appropriate time for new converts to make this history their own. With Deuteronomy as the teaching material and Passover as the time of new-member incorporation, synagogue leaders slotted their preparation and instruction, their "confirmation classes," if you will, into that segment of the Jewish liturgical year bounded on one side by the readings of Deuteronomy and on the other by Passover. So new prospective converts began their preparation for membership during the last twelve or so Sabbaths of this Jewish calendar year, the same weeks in which Deuteronomy, the last book of the Torah, was being read in the synagogue.

When this preparation was complete, the male converts would undergo circumcision, in which the mark of Judaism would be placed on their physical bodies. If that rite was administered at the end of the Deuteronomy readings, and thus at the end of this Jewish calendar year, converts still had time for healing to occur before they were inducted, since Passover came two weeks into this Jewish New Year. When healing was complete, the converts were given "the ceremonial bath," designed to cleanse them from any impurity or uncleanness in their past. After that they were welcomed to the Passover meal as Jews, now grafted by adoption into being part of the covenant people.

When Christianity was born as a movement separate from Judaism, it quickly became a missionary religion, effectively dry-ing up the growing missionary appeal of Judaism. Large numbers of converts began to knock on the doors of the Christian churches. This meant that Christian leaders also had to develop an appropriate process of incorporation. Not surprisingly, they adopted and adapted the pattern that the Jews had developed.

They agreed, first, that it was necessary for new converts to be given instruction on what it meant to be a Christian. That being so, they had to develop a resource on which this instruction would be based. While the book of Deuteronomy was judged not to be the proper text for this purpose, they felt that perhaps the *form* of Deuteronomy was. Since Deuteronomy purported to be the final teaching of Moses to his people prior to his death, why not create a set of final instructions from Jesus to his people, the church? Perhaps Jesus could be portrayed as delivering these instructions to his disciples just prior to his death. That would certainly invest those teachings with great authority. It was a winning idea, and so the journey section of the synoptic gospels was born. One might even say that the journey section of each of the synoptic gospels began as the first set of baptism or confirmation instructions.

Since baptism and incorporation of new converts were set at the time of the Easter Eucharist, the instruction presented in preparation had to come on the Sabbaths leading up to Easter. So the journey section of the gospels was reminiscent of the last will and testament of Jesus, just as Deuteronomy was seen as the last will and testament of Moses. Would it surprise anyone to discover that this was how the season of Lent was born? Lent started as a time of preparation for baptism, a time to instruct new converts and a time for the renewal of the faith by the whole community of believers.

Even though the source from which the Christians adopted this pattern is clear, we need to note that they did not adopt every aspect of the Jewish plan for incorporation. The rite of circumcision, for example, was simply dropped from Christian practice. The ceremonial bath of the Jews, however, was turned into the act of holy baptism, and the Passover meal became the Eucharist. The patterns of incorporation were in fact very similar.

When we turn next to the journey section of Matthew's gospel, we need to be aware that it got its shape from the way the teaching of Jesus was being used at the time that Matthew's gospel was being written, which was some two generations after the first Easter. The gospel writers, including Matthew, were trying to relate the teachings of the Jesus of history to the issues being faced by those coming into the Christian community in their own time, and they were trying to discern "the mind of Christ" in regard to those issues. These post-Jesus "teachings" are, therefore, attempts on the part of the followers of Jesus to have him speak to the problems they were facing in the ninth decade of the Christian movement.

What this means is that we cannot and should not relate to these teachings as if they represented the literal words of Jesus. Only those who were not familiar with the Jewish practices out of which this teaching section arose would ever have made that mistake. That is why biblical literalism is, in the last analysis, a Gentile heresy.

With that introduction now in our minds, we turn to the journey section of the gospel of Matthew and we listen to the "teachings of Jesus" being given through the church to the second and third generation of those who described themselves as followers of Jesus. It will be a different perspective on this part of the gospels from the one to which most of us were introduced earlier in our lives, but it will get us closer to the meaning of the original gospel formation.

CHAPTER 27

The Heart of the Journey

WHAT WERE THE ISSUES that concerned the disciples of Jesus in the ninth decade of the Common Era? We will discover the answer to that question when we enter into the journey section of Matthew's gospel. The answers might surprise us, for they are not the issues that the Christian church would spend most of the years of its institutional life debating.

No one, for example, at this time in Christian history seemed to be debating theology. That concern did not come into the life of the church as a major issue until the fourth century, when Christianity became an established part of the religious life of the Roman Empire. In Matthew's generation there were no creedal minutiae to debate. If the Christians in Matthew's day had a creed at all, it was made up of only three words: "Jesus is messiah." That sounds more like an affirmation than a creed. When this affirmation "Jesus is messiah" was first spoken, it was among followers of Jesus, who

were Jews and for whom the word "messiah" had a long and interesting history. When the Jewish word *maschiach,* which literally
meant "the anointed one" and which was later translated "messiah," first came into Hebrew history, it was simply the title of the
king. Recall that the prophet Samuel anointed both Saul and later
David to be the kings of Israel. When the Davidic line of kings
disappeared in the Jewish world during the Babylonian exile in
the sixth century BCE, the title "the anointed one" entered into the
developing mythology of the Jewish people. There its meaning was
stretched to include not just the one who would restore the throne
of David, but also the "son of man" who would usher in the kingdom of God at the end of time. It was always a distinctly Jewish
word understood in a distinctly Jewish way.

As Christianity moved into an increasingly Gentile world,
however, "messiah" became a meaningless, almost untranslatable
word, so Gentile Christians decided to change their primary affirmation about Jesus from "Jesus is messiah" to "Jesus is Lord," with
the Greek word *kurios* replacing the Hebrew word *maschiach.* The
shift seemed small, but it was in fact gargantuan. Calling Jesus
"Lord" opened the doors to creedal development, because the
word "lord" had all sorts of divine and supernatural connotations
associated with it. That was the path that Christianity followed,
which led finally to the debate between Arius and Athanasius at
the Council of Nicea. When Athanasius, who held that the word
"lord," when applied to Jesus, meant that Jesus was of identical
substance with God, won that debate, doctrines such as the incar-
nation and the holy Trinity followed soon thereafter. In the wake
of the definition of Christian "orthodoxy" came religious wars,
religious persecution, heresy trials and the burning of heretics at
the stake. When any human group decides that they can define

God, the outcome is always predictable. The "true faith," once defined, must then be defended against all critics, and it must also then be forced upon all people—"for their own good, lest their souls be in jeopardy."

It is interesting to note that in Matthew's time, when the followers of Jesus wanted to depict him giving to his disciples his final teaching on the great issues before that community, none of these later theological topics was in their minds. What the community wanted at that time was some insight into "the mind of Christ" on how their behavior would distinguish the followers of Jesus from the rest of the world. That is what we find in the journey section of Matthew's gospel. It was not the nature of God, the issues of Christology or even the meaning of the Holy Spirit that Jesus was made to address on his final journey to Jerusalem.

It was also not liturgical matters. Jesus was never made to address such things as the number of sacraments, the meaning of baptism or the essence of the Eucharist. At the time in which Matthew was recording the teachings of Jesus, the followers of Jesus were still members of the synagogue; thus the liturgical patterns of the synagogue were simply assumed, they were not debated. In the synagogues the Jews, which still included the followers of Jesus, listened to the readings of the Torah and to the insights of the prophets, and they sang their psalms of praise to God. They did not question the forms being used in the liturgy. So Matthew's interpretation of "the mind of Christ" addressed neither theology nor liturgy, but rather what Jesus' followers *were* concerned about, which was practical problems that had arisen in their community of believers.

The fact that theological debates and liturgical conflicts over the proper forms of worship were *not* the concerns of Matthew's period of Christian history raises for us a question: Is it possible that if those matters have become *our* primary concerns, we may have lost contact with the essence of Christianity? That is an idea that needs to be at least considered in the life of the church in the twenty-first century.

What then were the issues about which a word from the Lord was deemed to be so important? We turn to the journey section, chapters 19–25 in Matthew's gospel, to find out. It divides neatly into two segments. First, chapters 19–23, with that segment's ethical concerns, and then chapters 24–25, with their "end of the world" concerns.

Chapter 19 begins with Jesus' teaching on divorce (vv. 1–12). Can a Christian man divorce his wife for cause? It had not yet occurred to that deeply patriarchal age to think that a Christian woman might want to divorce her husband for cause.

Jesus responded, quoting the Torah. There it was written that a man shall leave his father and mother and cleave to his wife, and they shall become "one flesh" (Gen. 2:24). Jesus then drew the proper conclusion. If marriage is the will of God, breaking the bond of marriage is wrong, so Jesus was made to amplify the Torah: "What God has joined together, let no man put asunder" (Matt. 19:5). It was a good rabbinic answer. The ideal was stated in the Torah, but no one of us lives in an ideal world, and so the ideal is always tempered by the reality of existence. Out of the complexities of existence his critics responded, quoting the Torah right back to Jesus (Deut. 24:1–4). If marriage is so indissoluble, they said, why did Moses command that when a man divorces his wife he must give her a bill of divorcement?

Jesus then entered into the debate about the relationship between the ideal and the existential. The bill of divorcement, he stated, was necessary to protect the woman so that the man who had divorced her could no longer control her choices. The ideal must be tempered by the just.

Then Matthew added a bit of commentary designed to make a man divorcing his wife see that step as difficult and not desirable. There is only one cause that rises to the level of being serious enough to justify divorce, he said, and that is "unchastity." If a man divorces his wife for any other reason and marries another, he becomes guilty himself of adultery. Casuistry and situational ethics clearly entered the Christian church shortly after the life of Jesus had come to an end.

It is of interest to note that the issues around marriage and divorce still plague the Christian church. The church still operates on the battle line between the ideal—that is, the ultimate principle—and the practical—that is, the existential circumstances. We still have segments of the Christian church that, at least in theory if not always in practice, oppose divorce in all circumstances. That position is held, however, primarily in churches that remain overwhelmingly patriarchal in their values and in their structures. The rising sense of equality among the sexes has rendered the autocratic rules of the patriarchal past no longer operative, whether these bodies recognize it or not.

Yes, marriage is still a vow made "till death us do part," and that is still the ideal. It is not, however, the reality in the life of our society. So what does the mind of Christ say to us today? That has to be worked out. Such interpretation is always in the process of taking place, but it is always done beneath the rules. The operative principle, however, is that the Christian church must always act in such a way as to enhance the life and the humanity of both husbands and wives, even when tensions make a breach inevitable. Jesus, it appears, validated this procedure in his comments, once he had quoted the ideal in the Torah.

The next topic to be addressed in this journey section had to do with the way children were to be treated in the life of the church (Matt. 19:13–16). In this vignette children were brought to Jesus that he might lay hands on them in blessing. The disciples, more concerned about human convenience than about human beings, rebuked those bringing the children. Jesus, however, rebuked the disciples and received the children. The "Word of the Lord" to the church, when Matthew wrote, was that the body of Christ must receive the children, no matter how inconvenient they might be at any given moment in time. Children are not to be blamed for the shortcomings of their parents. There is no such thing as an illegitimate baby. There is only inadequate behavior on the part of the parents.

Children are to be loved into the fullness of their potential. They are never to be rejected to satisfy adult sensitivities. They are never to be used as objects of gratification. They are never to be abused or misled. Children are to be numbered among those that Jesus called "the least of these our brothers and sisters."

I shall never forget the example of an elderly woman who sought to comfort a distressed mother whose baby cried constantly during a worship service at church. "Don't be upset, my dear," she said to this mother. "If you let the children's noises be heard in church, someday the church's noises might be heard in those children." Jesus said: "Let the children come to me, and do not hinder them, for to such belongs the kingdom" (Matt. 19:13).

Then the subject turns to how one is to achieve eternal life (Matt. 19:16–22). This section starts with a question from a man who is Matthew's version of the character we call "the rich young ruler." Other versions of this same story are found in Mark 10:17–31 and Luke 18:18–30.

"What must I do to inherit eternal life," this young man asked. Jesus responded again with a Torah answer: "Obey the commandments." The questioner responded: "Which one?" The Jews would know that there were 613 laws in the Torah. Could those laws be reduced to a single, most important one? Could the Ten Commandments be squeezed down to one? There was clearly some reductionism operating here.

Jesus replied by referencing some of the Ten Commandments as found in the book of Exodus (20:1–17). His questioner replied: "All of these I have observed; what do I still lack?" Jesus' response was startling. "If you would be perfect, go, sell what you possess and give to the poor and you will have treasure in heaven; and come, follow me" (Matt 19:21–22). It was a hard teaching, one that could not be received by the questioner; Matthew tells us that the young man "went away sorrowful, for he had great possessions." That conversation then precipitated Jesus' teaching on wealth (Matt. 19:23–30).

I always find it interesting to see where biblical literalists cease to be literal. This is one of those places. Far from listening to the demands of Jesus, we have rather developed a Christianity of affluence, in which the poor are judged and blamed for being poor. In the United States the political party that claims to represent the "religious" or the "Christian" vote constantly seeks to cut programs aimed at assisting the poor, and to do away with health coverage for any who cannot afford it. Yes, they would deny this charge, but every time they propose another way to accomplish health care without subsidizing the poor, their proposal passes no test that measures capability. Rhetoric never can be a stand-in for performance. The teachings of the Bible in regard to our responsibility for the poor are found on almost every page. The condemnation of homosexual people is found in only nine passages in the Bible, only one of which (Rom. 1:26–27) appears to mean what the homophobic "scripture quoters" of our fundamentalist churches claim that it means, yet fighting homosexuality has dominated a whole generation of biblical literalists. Meanwhile, their concern for the poor has been reduced to a footnote in those same churches' corporate attention. Perhaps this is why few people in our secular society pay much attention to the public teaching of the fundamentalist churches. Biblical literalism has little integrity left. Perhaps the time has come when those churches should have little power left either.

In Matthew's chapter the disciples of Jesus were themselves distressed about this teaching on wealth. What Jesus appeared to be suggesting was that in the kingdom of heaven the priorities that govern the world would be reversed: "Many that are first will be last, and the last first" (Matt. 19:30).

Then, as if to make that point very clear, Jesus is made to tell a story (Matt. 20:1–16). It is about a householder who hired workers at various hours of the workday, from sunup to sundown. He paid those who were hired at dawn what he and they had agreed to before they went into his fields. When the day was over, however, he paid *all* his workers, even those who had worked but a single hour, the same wages. "Not fair," shouted those who had borne the burden and the heat of the full day's work. Jesus responded: "Can the owner [God] not do what God wills with God's own?" Must God, or the followers of Jesus, be bound by the values of the old order, the values that were passing away? This issue was left unsettled, and the journey section resumed.

Then Jesus told the disciples what he would face in Jerusalem (Matt. 20:17–19). They were clearly not ready to hear about mocking and scourging and crucifixion. This lack of readiness was symbolized by the request from the sons of Zebedee to occupy positions of power and influence in the coming kingdom. In Matthew's version, to save the reputations of James and John, this request was put into the mouth of their mother (Matt. 20:20–28).

This was followed by a plea from the world of human pain. Two blind men cried out to Jesus, asking for their sight (Matt. 20:29–34). Needy people, like weak children, drew the rebuke of the crowd and, I suspect, of the Christians for whom Matthew was writing his gospel. The message they heard was that need is to be responded to with pity, compassion, healing and grace. This is "the Word of the Lord" to that situation.

The journey continued to provide the background to the teaching. In chapter 21, Jesus and his disciples are said to have reached the Mount of Olives, and there the preparation for the disciples to eat the final Passover with Jesus was made. Then the journey from the Mount of Olives to Jerusalem, what we today call the Palm Sunday procession, is described. Matthew based it, as Mark and Luke did also, on the image drawn from the book of Zechariah, in which a shepherd king approaches the "holy city" not as a conquering hero, but humbly riding on the back of a donkey as the crowds shouted "Hosanna!" and waved palm branches, both symbols drawn from Psalm 118.

Once in Jerusalem, Jesus went first to the Temple, where he drove out the money changers. "My house shall be called a house of prayer," he said, "but you have made it a den of thieves" (Matt. 21:12–13). To this Temple now came the blind and the lame, and Jesus healed them, we are told (Matt. 21:14). The wrath of the religious establishment became obvious, tensions mounted and Jesus retired to Bethany for the night (Matt. 21:15–17).

Back to the Temple the next day he went, still reclaiming it. The religious establishment challenged him. "By what authority?" they asked (Matt. 21:23). That is a favorite game of all religious hierarchies. We are the ones who represent God, we say. God operates only through legitimate and institutionally validated religious lives. Who are you? Is that not still the message of literal Christianity when we say: "The pope has spoken," "The Bible says" or "The church teaches"? Jesus said: My movement is not like that. We do not live within those rules.

A parable about two sons follows. This is Matthew's version of Luke's parable of the prodigal son. From where does life come? Is its source, Jesus asked, found among those who say yes but who do nothing, or is it found among those who say no and then do everything (Matt. 21:28–32)?

Still another parable illustrates the same theme: the parable of the householder who let his vineyard out to tenants (Matt. 21:33–46). These tenants, however, used it to enhance their wealth. They even killed the householder's son and heir when he came to collect his portion of the harvest. The kingdom of God, Jesus concluded, will be given to those who produce fruits for the kingdom, not for themselves. Jesus had become a prophet, but a very inconvenient prophet, one who had to be destroyed. That is always the fate of true prophets.

More proactive parables flowed from Jesus to inform his teaching. There was the parable of the wedding feast to which the proper guests were invited, but these guests all had excuses as to why they could not be present. So the initial wedding list was expanded to include *all*—the good and the bad, the clean and the unclean (Matt. 22:1–10). The kingdom of God will be open to the deaf, the lame, the halt and the blind. There will be no outcasts. There is a caveat, however: Even the outcasts must be wearing a proper wedding garment (Matt. 22:11–14).

Next the religious authorities tried to entrap Jesus. "Do we pay taxes to Caesar or not?" (Matt. 22:15–22). "How will one's marriage be recognized in heaven if one has remarried after one's spouse dies?" (Matt. 22:23–33). "Which is the greatest commandment?" (Matt. 22:36). All of these concerns can be addressed, Jesus responded, in the commandment to love God and to love your neighbor as yourself (Matt. 22:37–40). The traps failed. The tensions were reaching a fever pitch.

In chapter 23, Jesus was made to take on the Pharisees. There is some reason to believe that Matthew saw the Judaism represented by Jesus and the Judaism represented by the Pharisees as being in a battle for the soul and the future of Judaism itself. In this chapter he had Jesus spell out the differences in a great, almost warlike fashion. The Jesus movement, Matthew argued, was not about extending religious rules but about changing human hearts.

The first segment of the journey section is now complete. Jesus will now be made to move on in the strange and apocalyptic chapter 24, to talk about the signs that will accompany the end of the world.

CHAPTER 28

Apocalypse Now:
The Final Judgment

I BEGIN THIS CHAPTER WITH AN ASSUMPTION, perhaps an educated guess. I have the distinct feeling that the version of the annual Jewish liturgical year, which Matthew has been following, has come to an end. I see the final verses of Matthew 23 to be his conclusion of Jesus' journey to Jerusalem, undertaken after the transfiguration. The words Matthew has Jesus speak there provide a great summary of that journey thus far, and yet those words still look forward to the ultimate revelation, which Matthew has yet to describe, the events we call "the passion of Jesus." Listen to his words with that assumption in mind: "For I tell you, you will not see me again until you say: 'Blessed is he [the one] who comes in the name of the Lord'" (Matt. 23:39).

Matthew used very similar words in his story of Jesus' entry into Jerusalem, in what we call the Palm Sunday procession (Matt. 21:9). So this "coming again" has to refer to one of two things—

either the coming of Jesus in resurrected glory, which Matthew will soon describe, or the final coming of the messiah, which Matthew anticipates and which, according to Jewish mythology, would be marked first by the end of the world and then by the dawning of the kingdom of God on earth. These two comings are, in the mind of the author of this gospel, closely related.

Matthew, following the lead of Mark, will tell us the story of Jesus' death and resurrection as the way of giving the Passover observance of the synagogue some Jesus content. The Passover liturgy tells the story of the birth of Judaism. Matthew will transform it into the liturgy of the Christian Eucharist, which acts out the birth of Christianity.

It is clear to me that the story of Passover begins in Matthew 26:1, in which Jesus is made to turn toward his preparation for that event. So if the liturgical year Matthew is following ended with the last verse of chapter 23, and his climactic passion story is to be told as his Passover narrative beginning at chapter 26:1, then chapters 24 and 25 must have been designed for use on those two Sabbaths that come in the New Year, but before Passover, which falls on Nisan 15. On those first two Sabbaths of the New Year the Torah readings would start anew with the book of Genesis. To get through the entire Torah on the Sabbaths of a single year meant that each Sabbath reading had to be quite long, as we have seen; some five to six chapters of our present text would be the norm. The first twelve or so chapters of Genesis, then, would be read on these first two Sabbaths of the year. We need to remember, however, that chapters and verses were not imposed on biblical texts until the Middle Ages. So the length of a passage was always approximate, never fixed.

Knowing that this was the organizing scheme, we can now look for Genesis references to appear in Matthew's chapters 24 and 25. The dominant theme of that part of Genesis, those first twelve chapters, was the story of Noah and the flood. Noah is introduced in Genesis 5, and his story culminates in Genesis 11. The Noah story is preceded in the book of Genesis by stories that describe the increasing alienation from God on the part of the people—the banishment of the human family from the Garden of Eden, the murder of Abel by his brother Cain, and other narratives depicting human evil. This increasing wickedness, according to the biblical narrative, caused God to despair of the human enterprise and to decide to bring it to an end. It thus became God's plan to destroy the world, saving only Noah and his family, with whom the whole human race would be restarted. Noah would in effect become the "new Adam." The theme of the Noah story was that God would bring the world, at least as people knew it, to an end.

It is, therefore, not a surprise when, in reading Matthew's chapter 24, we discover a story of God bringing the world to an end. We call this chapter "The Little Apocalypse," to distinguish it from the more extensive apocalyptic text of the book of Revelation. This is one of those passages in the Bible upon which those who regularly predict the end of the world rely. The images of ultimate destruction in Matthew 24 are graphic: "Not one stone will be left on another." "The Temple will be thrown down." "You will hear of wars and rumors of wars." "Nation will rise up against nation and kingdom against kingdom." "There will be famines and earthquakes." These would be the signs that the end was near. Then Matthew described the pain that the followers of Jesus would have to endure: "They will deliver you up to tribulation and put you to death." "You will be hated by all nations for my name's sake." "Many will fall away and hate one another." "False prophets will arise." "Most men's love will grow cold." But all this concluded with a promise: "He who endures to the end will be saved." It was a grim description of the end of the world, which Matthew proclaimed was drawing near.

Then, in what I take to be a telling reference, Matthew had Jesus say: "As were the days of Noah, so will be the coming of the son of man. For as in those days before the flood they were eating and drinking, marrying and giving in marriage until the day when Noah entered the ark, and they did not know until the flood came and swept them away, so will be the coming of the son of man" (Matt. 24:37–39). The story of Noah and the flood was clearly Matthew's text for that first Sabbath of the New Year. He was still following the liturgical format of the synagogue!

Much of Matthew's content in this episode appears to have been drawn from the most cataclysmic event in both Jewish and Christian history in the memory of his readers. He was quite obviously describing the pain experienced in the recent war with Rome, which climaxed in the devastating destruction of Jerusalem. First the city's walls fell. Next the buildings, including the Temple, were leveled. Then, after the citizens fled, the Jewish nation disappeared from the maps of human history and would not reappear until 1948, when the provisions of the Balfour Agreement of 1917 were finally implemented and the modern state of Israel was born. I will not go into the political ramifications of that "restoration," which remain tense and difficult to this day. I only want to note that it was from this tragedy that Matthew got many of the images with which he described the "end of the world." He combined the Noah story with the memory of the fall of Jerusalem to create the pathos of the final days of human history. So he wrote: "Those who are in Judea must flee to the mountains; those driven for safety to their housetops must not come down to take what is in the house, but they are to flee immediately into the country. Those who are in the fields are not to turn back to take their mantle; those who are pregnant or nursing can only hope that this tribulation does not come in the cold of winter, for there will be no protection" (Matt. 24:16–20).

The fall of Jerusalem seemed to that generation of Jewish people to be the literal end of the world; indeed it was the end of the world that they had once known. Great persecution of the Jews by the Romans followed the war. This persecution fell both on Orthodox Jews and on the Jewish followers of Jesus alike. Rome made no distinction—a Jew was a Jew. The followers of Jesus now began to see their Jewish identity as a liability so severe that it might cost them their lives. This was what began the separation of the followers of Jesus from their Jewish identity. I do not believe we can overemphasize this event in shaping the history of both Christianity and Judaism. I am also convinced that this is the birthplace of anti-Semitism among the followers of Jesus, even the Jewish followers of Jesus. Recognizing its import, Matthew drew on this trauma to describe the apocalyptic end of the world. For him it would bring judgment on anything that had gone before; at the same time it was a prelude to the birth of the kingdom of God that would finally come when the destruction of the world was complete.

I say it again: When this dating system is embraced, the idea that the gospels are eyewitness accounts of history or biographical narratives about Jesus becomes impossible to maintain. It is on this rock that biblical fundamentalism finally breaks apart, and the possibility of reading the gospels in a new way begins to dawn. That is the possibility that I have sought to develop in this book.

Matthew was still clearly following the liturgical pattern of the synagogue when he penned this apocalypse chapter, since it corresponded to the reading of the flood story on the first Sabbaths of Nisan. The end of the world had a second phase, however, that was called the judgment; and that theme would also need to be addressed on those first two Sabbaths of the year. So, we conclude, chapter 25 in Matthew must have been constructed to complete the end of the world theme.

Matthew filled chapter 25 with three parables about the "day of judgment," which would follow the end of the world. First came the parable of the wise and foolish maidens, who had to be ready if they were to greet "the bridegroom." This parable stressed the need for watchful, prepared waiting for the second coming of the messiah (Matt. 25:1–13). Second was the parable of the servants who were called upon to give an accounting of their stewardship of the householder's "talents" when he returned (Matt. 25:14–30). The theme here was that the "talents" over which we have control must be invested, not protected, and allowed to grow. The third parable—probably Matthew's most familiar, and one told in no other place in the gospel tradition—was the parable of the final judgment, when the sheep and the goats were separated (Matt. 25:31–46). The sheep entered into the joy of their master, while the goats were cast into outer darkness. The theme here was that the basis upon which life is judged has nothing to do with religious involvement, pious deeds or even creedal belief—despite the extent to which these three things have been used to condemn those judged unworthy by the church over the centuries. In this parable the basis of the ultimate judgment was how able one was to see the presence of God in the faces of the poor, the hungry, the strangers, the sick and the imprisoned. If one does not see God in the lives of the least of God's people, then one is a liar to claim that he or she has seen the face of God. It is a scathing parable. Both the sheep and the goats were surprised at the judgment, for neither of them understood that the holy is always found in the mundane, the life of God is always encountered in the life of the human. Matthew has thus provided wonderfully for the two Sabbaths that came after the old year was over, but before the Passover observance had begun.

Seeing this portion of the gospel, too, as written in dialogue with the liturgical year of the synagogue furthers our effort to lift scripture out of the prison of literalism. It is a pity that it has taken the Christian world so long to discover this incredible doorway into meaning that has for centuries hidden the truth of Matthew and the other gospels from us.

Matthew now has reached both the climax of his story and the events that he regards as the climax of Jesus' life. We will now begin to walk with him on what Christians have long called "the way of the cross."

PART IX

Passover and Passion: The Climax

CHAPTER 29

The Climactic Events
of the Passion Narrative

NEXT TO THE STORIES OF JESUS' BIRTH, the narratives of the final days of Jesus' life are probably the most familiar parts of the gospel tradition. They are the climactic chapters in each of the synoptic gospels. There is, first of all, a common tradition that frames the narrative. That tradition was developed by Mark; his is the earliest story of the cross that we possess. Then there are the expansions and adaptations on that tradition written first by Matthew and later by Luke. The gospel of John is significantly different, and beyond the scope of this volume.* Through a non-discriminating blending process, however, most Christians have simply homogenized all of the passion stories in the New Testament into a single, undif-

---

*For those interested in John's treatment of the cross, I refer you to my 2013 book *The Fourth Gospel: Tales of a Jewish Mystic*. See bibliography for details.

ferentiated narrative. Our first task in this chapter, therefore, will be to focus on the original material. I will use Matthew's text for this, but I will be careful to show what he has copied from his earlier source, Mark, and how he has expanded and changed the earlier narrative.

The passion narrative begins in Matthew with the preparation for the Passover meal and then moves into the description of the content of that meal, which we are told was held in an "upper room." Jesus is said to have broken bread at the meal's beginning and to have proclaimed it to be "my body broken for you." At the end of this meal, he is said to have taken the cup and to have identified it with his blood, which he suggested sealed the covenant. He is said to have used that meal to announce that "one of you [the twelve] will betray me." The meal is then said to have ended, like all Passover meals, with the singing of a hymn, after which the participants went out into the darkness of night (Matt. 26:1–30).

The second scene in the passion drama is located in a garden called Gethsemane. We are told that Jesus took three of his disciples with him—Peter and the sons of Zebedee, James and John—and went deeper into the garden, leaving the others behind. Next, we see Jesus leaving even his chosen three to stand watch as he goes alone still deeper into the garden. There he wrestled, we are told, with his fate: "Let this cup pass from me," he prayed; but he is portrayed as ultimately becoming resigned to the fact that it would not pass unless he drank from that cup. He is said to have repeated this ritual prayer three times, and following each period of prayer, he returned to find his three disciples asleep. "Could you not watch with me?" he asked, not even one hour? Or two hours? Or three? On his return from the third prayer experience, he is portrayed as saying: "Are you still sleeping?" They were. Then Jesus is made to announce to his three disciples that they must rise and depart the garden, "for my betrayer is at hand" (Matt. 26:36–46).

Then the story of the betrayal is told. Judas Iscariot appeared, accompanied by a large contingent of followers from the chief priests and elders, who arrived with swords and clubs. The kiss of the traitor is next described, after which Jesus was seized by those who accompanied Judas. A brief skirmish followed as the disciples sought to defend him, but Jesus ordered them to put their weapons away. The kingdom he sought to bring, Jesus said, would not be ushered in through armed conflict (Matt. 26:47–56).

Jesus was then taken to Caiaphas and the council of the scribes and elders. There was a trial of sorts before the Sanhedrin. It focused on his claim to be the messiah, and the charge that he claimed to possess the power to rebuild the destroyed Temple in just three days. To understand his claim we need to recall that when the three synoptic gospels were written the destruction of the Temple by the Romans was vividly in their minds. Before this gathered council of Jewish leaders, Jesus, Matthew says, was judged to be guilty of blasphemy and thus to be deserving of death (Matt. 26:57–68).

The next scene involves Peter, presumably alone in the courtyard of the high priest, being accosted by a maid and accused of being a co-conspirator. "You were also with Jesus, the Galilean," she said. Peter then uttered the first of three ringing denials, the last one being the most sweeping: "I do not even know the man, Jesus," he is made to say. This scene ends with Peter broken and weeping bitterly. In Matthew's account this is the last we will see of Peter. There is no rehabilitation of him in this gospel (Matt. 26:69–75).

In Mark's original account, the trial before Pilate is described next. At this point, though, Matthew stuck into the drama one of his unique additions: the account of Judas repenting of his deed. Why would Matthew have added it? Perhaps he felt the need to add something to cover the time it would take Jesus to be delivered to Pilate. In any event, Matthew, who alone had stated that Judas received thirty pieces of silver for his act of treachery, now had him try to undo the deed by returning the money. Most people can tell you that the price of betrayal was thirty pieces of silver. Most, however, do not know that this detail is in no other gospel besides Matthew. Now, in this brief inserted interlude, Matthew had Judas say: "I have sinned in that I have betrayed innocent blood." The chief priests and elders were not responsive to his pleas. They stated, "That is your problem," though not in those modern words. So Judas threw the silver onto the floor of the Temple and then, said Matthew, he went out and hanged himself. The hanging of Judas in an act of suicide is a widely known part of the passion story, but few people know that it, too, is an addition to the story that appears in no other place than the gospel of Matthew (Matt. 27:1–10).

By now Jesus had arrived at the palace of Pilate, the procurator and representative of the Roman Empire. Pilate first listened to the charges brought against Jesus by his accusers, after which he interrogated his prisoner. To these charges, however, Jesus remained silent. The governor wondered about him in some amazement, we are told (Matt. 27:11–14). Matthew then added another of his unique embellishments. Pilate's wife, he said, sent a message to her husband warning him, as she herself had been warned in a dream, to "have nothing to do with this just man" (Matt. 27:19).

Pilate is then portrayed as seeking to find a means to release Jesus. He tried to free him through what he said was an ancient custom, namely that the Romans freed a prisoner at the Passover feast as a gesture of goodwill. But when he offered to free Jesus, the crowd called for the release of an alternative candidate. That is how the name Barabbas, which we looked at in chapter 17, entered the passion story. "What then shall I do with Jesus?" Pilate asked. The crowd responded with one voice: "Let him be crucified." Pilate squirmed: "Why, what evil has he done?" The crowd shouted even more vehemently: "Let him be crucified!" Pilate gave in, but before turning Jesus over to his soldiers for crucifixion, he symbolically washed his hands in a staged public ceremony and proclaimed himself "innocent of this man's blood." Then, in another unique Matthean addition, Matthew had the crowd respond with the words: "His blood be upon us and on our children." Those words, quoted again and again in justification of anti-Semitic violence over the centuries, are probably the source of more suffering and death than any other words in the entire Bible. Christians have consistently used them to justify abusive behavior against Jewish people, saying that "the Jews asked for it." I still shudder when this passage of Matthew's gospel is read in church and the reader concludes this lesson with the pious phrase, "This is the Word of the Lord." Not so, I want to scream. This phase of the story then ended and Jesus was delivered to be crucified (Matt. 27:15–26).

Next in this passion drama came the scourging, the mocking and the abuse of the prisoner. Jesus was charged with claiming to be "the king of the Jews," so the soldiers, Matthew tells us, expressed their disdain for the Jews by mocking one who would claim to be their king. A king must have a crown. So for this "Jewish king" they made a crown of thorns and pressed it on his head. A king must have a royal robe. So onto Jesus' back they draped a tattered purple or scarlet robe, a robe fitting, they said, for a

"Jewish king." A king must carry a royal scepter in his hand, a symbol of his power. So they placed into his hand a reed drooping, as reeds inevitably do. A fitting scepter, they said, for a "Jewish king." Then they bowed before him, spat upon him and struck him with his own scepter (Matt. 27:27–31). Prejudice tends to be a corporate game we human beings play. It is no fun to act out one's prejudicial hatred alone.

Finally, the fun and the games were over and Jesus was led to a place called Golgotha, there to be put to death. On the way, a man named Simon of Cyrene comes into the story. We know nothing about him before this moment and we learn nothing of him after this moment, but in this story he carried Jesus' cross (Matt. 27:32). We can only wonder about Matthew's purpose in adding this detail.

Jesus was then crucified, nailed to a cross and left to die. His garments were distributed among the soldiers by casting of lots. A sign was placed on the cross: "This is Jesus, the king of the Jews." Two robbers, new to the story, were crucified with him, one on each side (Matt. 27:33–38). They were, in Mark, only part of the scenery. In Matthew, they both actively reviled Jesus. In Luke, one of them became penitent and requested that Jesus "remember" him when Jesus would "come into his kingdom." The details of the story do grow over the passing years!

Mark was quite specific in telling us that the crucifixion occurred "at the third hour"—that is, at 9:00 A.M. Matthew omitted that detail, though in his narrative he appeared to assume it. That is a detail to which we shall return. It will be a significant clue.

Time then passed while the onlooking crowd at the foot of the cross continued to taunt Jesus. Matthew said: "They derided him, wagging their heads" at him. They urged him to show his power, to demonstrate that he enjoyed God's favor. They claimed that Jesus' reputation was one of "saving others"; now "Save yourself!" they shouted. You depended on God, now let God deliver you. When nothing happened, they concluded that God cared not at all for this Jesus (Matt. 27:39–44).

It was now, Matthew stated, the sixth hour—that is, 12:00 noon. At that moment, Matthew said, darkness covered the land. It remained until the ninth hour—that is, until 3:00 P.M. Then Matthew said Jesus cried out in a loud voice. It was a cry in Aramaic, Matthew said: "*Eli, Eli, lama sabach thani?*" Matthew translated it for his Greek-speaking readers: "My God, my God, why have you forsaken me?" In Aramaic, it sounded to some like a cry for Elijah to come to his aid, but again nothing happened. Then, Matthew reported, Jesus cried again, with a loud voice, but Matthew did not record what his words might have been. Perhaps it was a wordless cry. Then Matthew said Jesus "yielded up his spirit," an interesting way to say that he died (Matt. 27:45–50).

At this point in the narrative, Matthew repeated Mark's words about the veil in the Temple splitting from top to bottom (Matt. 27:51). Jewish people would have known that this veil separated "the holy place" in the Temple, to which observant, prepared Jews could enter, from "the Holy of Holies" in the Temple, which was thought to be the earthly dwelling place of God.

Matthew then added to Mark's narrative a number of other dramatic, perhaps supernatural, signs. This death of Jesus was accompanied by the earth shaking. Was that an earthquake? Its timing was certainly exquisite. The rocks were split, perhaps as a result of the earthquake. This in turn, Matthew said, caused the graves to be opened and many bodies from those graves were raised. Matthew then said that these resurrected bodies went into Jerusalem following Jesus' resurrection, and were "seen by many." Following that diversion, Matthew returned to Mark's text and concluded his narrative with a proclamation of faith placed on the lips of a centurion, a Roman, Gentile soldier: "Surely this man was the son of God" (Matt. 27:51b–54).*

It was now 3:00 P.M., and Matthew brought the women into the story. They were Mary Magdalene, Mary the mother of James and Joseph, and the mother of the sons of Zebedee, James and John. They were silent witnesses "looking on from afar," says the text. They were to observe the place of his burial (Matt. 27:55–56).

Finally Matthew, once more following Mark's lead, introduced Joseph of Arimathea. Mark called him "a respected member of the council, who was also longing for the kingdom of God." Matthew would add the words "a rich man" to his line of identification, and Matthew also made him "a disciple of Jesus." This Joseph then gained from Pilate access to the deceased body of Jesus. He proceeded to wrap it in a clean linen shroud and to place this now-prepared body in "his own tomb." He then was said to have rolled a great stone to the door of the tomb and finally to have departed (Matt. 27:57–59).

Matthew then added his final unique note to this drama. The chief priests and the Pharisees, he said, went to Pilate to request that a detail of Roman soldiers be assigned to guard the tomb for at least three days. They were fearful, Matthew said, that the disciples would come and steal the body from this tomb and then put out the fiction that Jesus had been raised from the dead. It was a clear piece of later apologetic writing. Pilate responded, we are told, by remind-

---

*Some ancient texts say "*a* son," not "*the* son."

ing them that they had their own Temple guards, and he instructed them to use their own. They did. So the tomb was sealed and a guard was placed around the tomb (Matt. 27:62–66).

That is the story of the passion of Jesus originally written by the author of Mark's gospel, but with Matthew's changes and additions highlighted. How are we to read it, to understand it? Was this narrative the product of eyewitness reporting? If so, who were the eyewitnesses? Are these episodes meant to describe events that really happened? Or is there some other way that the readers of these gospels were meant to view this narrative? Would the Jewish followers of Jesus, who would have been the first to read these words about the crucifixion, have understood it differently? Have the details of this narrative been shaped by the Hebrew scriptures? Do they reveal a later apologetic purpose by being presented as "the fulfillment of the prophets"? Have they been formulated by liturgical considerations? These are the questions to which we must now turn.

CHAPTER 30

Probing the Passion Narrative
for Interpretive Clues

W HEN WE SURVEY THE STORY of Jesus' passion, powerful and dramatic as it is, a number of questions
force their way into our awareness. This narrative
reveals some rather intimate details. It tells us, for
example, the content of Jesus' private prayers in the Garden of
Gethsemane. From where did that information come? It tells us
of the charges and responses that flowed between Jesus and the
chief priests, scribes and elders of the council. Who reported those
conversations? No one was with Jesus except the members of the
council. The account could hardly have come from Jesus, since
he is portrayed as having no time with any of his followers after
that confrontation in which to relay its content to them. Are we to
imagine that this information came from his accusers?

Jesus was then, according to this narrative, conveyed directly to the palace of Pilate, the Roman governor. The narrative purportedly contains the actual dialogue between Jesus and Pilate. How did that conversation become public? Who carried these private details to the one who first wrote the story of Jesus' crucifixion? Did Pilate have a post-crucifixion interview with some of Jesus' followers in which these details, to which only he and Jesus were privy, were shared?

The source of the dialogue is not the only question that this portion of the narrative raises. Are we to suppose that this official representative of the Roman Empire actually engaged the angry crowd, allowing them to shape his decision? Would this lofty representative have been involved with an individual prisoner in this manner under any set of circumstances? What would a subjected people have made of the story of Pilate washing his hands and proclaiming himself innocent? Would this not have conveyed an unacceptable political weakness?

We are also told what the soldiers said and did to Jesus just prior to his crucifixion: the purple robe, the crown of thorns, the limp reed. Who was the source of those details? We are then told what the crowd said to Jesus, what Jesus said to the crowd and what the thieves crucified on each side of him said. We are also told the exact words that Jesus spoke from the cross as he died, and then the words about him spoken by the centurion after Jesus died. How were these words recorded or remembered? None of his disciples is said to have been present in the synoptic accounts. Matthew does record that some women were present, but he states clearly that they looked on from afar. They were not within hearing distance. So if we seek to view this story as history, we need to ask: How did these words travel from hostile sources to find their way into the narrative of the crucifixion?

Then we look at the span of time between the events being described and when Matthew wrote his gospel, some fifty-five years after the crucifixion. If in the first century a generation was considered to be about twenty years, Matthew's writing would be close to three generations after the fact. How accurate is any version of any conversation that is said to have occurred almost three generations earlier? Granted, Matthew leaned heavily on the author of Mark's gospel, but that moves us only as close as forty-two years away from the events being described. The problems of historicity are not small, nor are they insignificant. What are we to make of them?

Next we have to engage the problem of translation. There are no Aramaic originals that lie behind the gospels. Mark, the author of the earliest story of the passion ever created, wrote in Greek, a language that neither Jesus nor his disciples spoke. So if we want to assert historical accuracy for the details of the crucifixion story, then we must postulate not only an original eyewitness present in scenes where none is mentioned, but also a perfect translation. There is, however, no such thing as a perfect translation. No language consists of just words, since language is also shaped by history, culture, values, perceptions of reality and many other things. So the case for historicity becomes an increasingly impossible case to make.

Ironically, one significant detail in the passion story that does seem to be historical supports the overall argument *against* historicity. We are told in both Mark and Matthew that, when Jesus was arrested, "all the disciples forsook him and fled" (Mark 14:50; Matt. 26:56). Is that a detail that would have been made up? By the time the gospels were written, the disciples were thought of as heroic figures. Following the human tendency to whitewash and thus to remove the embarrassing moments in a hero's earlier life, the gospels provided apostolic exonerations for this desertion on the part of the twelve, saying that it was done only to fulfill the scriptures. The gospel writers even developed a proof-text to support this version of reality, quoting Zechariah—"Strike the shepherd that the sheep may be scattered" (Zech. 13:7)—as justification for their desertion. Both Mark (14:27) and Matthew (26:31) employed this defense. Would that much effort have been exerted to transform into acceptability an event that did not happen? Because the abandonment of Jesus by his disciples at the time of his arrest seems to be a memory with historical roots, the overwhelming probability is that Jesus died alone. There would thus have been no eyewitnesses from among Jesus' followers to report on the events of Jesus' passion, because there were no such eyewitnesses to this crucifixion!

It is of interest to note that Paul, the earliest writer of material that in time came to be included in the New Testament, describes the crucifixion in one sentence: "Christ died for our sins in accordance with the scriptures" (I Cor. 15:3). These words were written about the year 54 CE, or some eighteen years before Mark's gospel appeared. Paul gives us no narrative details, no Judas, no Garden of Gethsemane, no Pilate, no Barabbas, no thieves, no words from the cross. Was that because he did not know these details or was that because these details had not yet been written? Of the burial of Jesus, Paul writes only: "He was buried" (I Cor. 15:4). There is no narrative of Joseph of Arimathea or of a tomb in a garden. Was that because the burial tradition involving Joseph had not yet been developed?

When Paul comes to describe the Easter experience, he is again sparse in details: "On the third day he was raised in accordance with the scriptures" (I Cor. 15:4). Paul gives no narrative details, but he does provide a list of those to whom Jesus "appeared" (I Cor. 15:5). The list is intriguing. Cephas—that is, Peter—is first, then the twelve, followed by "five hundred brethren" at once. Then he continues with what seems to be a parallel list: "Then he appeared to James, then to all the apostles" and finally, Paul says, "he appeared to me" (I Cor. 15:7–8). There are several things to note here. First, the phrase "the twelve." That seems to suggest that the twelve disciples are still intact as a group. Although Paul says that this appearance was on the third day after the crucifixion, he seems to be implying that Judas was still among them! Second, "the twelve" and "the apostles" appear to be two different groups. Third, Paul is claiming that the appearance of the raised Jesus to him (Paul) was no different from the appearances to any of the others on his list, except that his was last. Since Paul's conversion is dated anywhere from one to six years after the crucifixion, it is obvious that the resurrection to Paul was more in the category of some kind of visionary experience than it was that of a resuscitated body returning to the life of this world. Paul never speaks of the details of his conversion, however. The closest thing we have to Paul discussing that experience is when he couches it in terms of some kind of mystical, transcendent perception (II Cor. 12:2). So while Paul is not himself an eyewitness to the narrative of the passion story, he is the first to give us anything in writing; and what he writes includes no references to the narrative that first appears in the gospel of Mark.

One final note from Paul to which we need to pay attention is recorded earlier in this same epistle to the Corinthians (I Cor. 11:23–26), where we have the first mention of the institution of the Christian Eucharist. Paul dates this experience with the words "on the night when he was betrayed." There is nothing in this text to suggest that this event was related to Passover or even to the possibility that one of the twelve participated in the act of betrayal. These bits of the record from Paul lead me to conclude that no earlier and independent source affirms that the developed story line, purporting to describe the events from the Last Supper, the crucifixion and burial of Jesus, and the resurrection itself, might be remembered history. If this crucial part of our faith tradition is not to be understood literally, then how is it to be understood? Did the death of Jesus not happen the way we have been told for centuries? Is the Christian story based on a fantasy or on a developed mythology? If this part of the Jesus story is not trustworthy as objective truth, then is any part of the gospel story trustworthy?

Those are existential, anxiety-producing questions. I do not want to trample on holy ground, but I also do not want to fail to embrace the conclusions to which my search for truth points me. The heart will never be drawn in worship to that which the mind rejects. So we are driven to look at other possibilities. Faith can never rest on perceptions that are intellectually unbelievable.

Is it possible that the familiar narrative of the crucifixion originated, not in an attempt to describe what actually happened, but in an effort to assert that in his life and in his death, Jesus fulfilled the messianic expectations of the Hebrew scriptures? Could this passion narrative have been originally composed as an interpretive portrait, based on scriptural images? Are we the ones who have for so long misread this crucial climactic story about the life of Jesus? If, as I have suggested throughout the book, such other items as the narrative of Joseph the earthly father of Jesus describe a symbol, not a person; if the account of the Sermon on the Mount is not history, but a Moses story being retold about Jesus; if the account of

Jesus walking on the water is not the description of an event that happened, but a story designed to suggest that Jesus, like Moses, had power over water; if the accounts of Jesus giving sight to the blind, hearing to the deaf, the capacity to leap to the lame and the ability to sing to the mute were never intended to be miracle stories, but were rather the signs of the kingdom of God breaking into human history as described by Isaiah (35), but now being wrapped around Jesus—then is it not possible that the story of the passion is similarly an account, not of history, but of messianic fulfillment told about Jesus? If that is so, then the problem is not the lack of historicity associated with this story, but the profound misunderstanding in the way we have treated this narrative through the centuries.

Armed with these possibilities, we are now in a position to turn back to the familiar narrative of the passion and death of Jesus outlined in the previous chapter and to search within it for interpretive clues that might open the passion story to truth that is not historical truth, but just might turn out to be profound truth. Perhaps truth need not be literal to be true. Have we been blind to the clues present in the story, because over the centuries, in what I have called "the Gentile captivity of Christianity," we have forgotten that we cannot read our own foundational gospels unless we learn to read them with eyes informed by the Jewish worldview that wrote them? Would they become clear if we looked at them through Jewish lenses? The future of the Christian faith may well rest on our ability to recover the original Jewish understandings of our faith story. In light of that possibility, let us probe these texts for hidden clues.

The first available clue that we find hidden in the text of the passion narrative is the initial saying attributed to Jesus on the cross.

Both Mark and Matthew say that Jesus from the cross spoke these words: "My God, my God, why have you forsaken me?" Have we ever confronted these words before in the Hebrew scriptures? Before addressing that question, it is worth noting that this so-called cry of dereliction disappears from the text of the two later gospels. If this were an authentic word spoken by the dying Jesus from the cross, would Luke and John have dared to omit it?

With very little effort we discover that this saying has been lifted quite literally out of the first verse of Psalm 22. That psalm appears to be directly related to the portrait of "the Servant" or "the Suffering Servant" first painted by the prophet we call II Isaiah (Isa. 40–55). That portrait, as we saw in an earlier context, originally was intended to suggest a way the Jewish people could still live out their messianic calling as a nation, even when they were in the despair of defeat, weakness and hopelessness. It was drawn in the period of Jewish history that followed the Babylonian exile, a period in which this nation was reduced to powerlessness. This situation raised for the Jews the question of how they could ever live out their God-given vocation, to be the nation through which all other nations of the world would be blessed. Could a defeated, exiled, powerless people still accomplish that defining role in history? To answer that question, the unknown prophet II Isaiah drew a portrait of one called "the Servant," who found a way to do just that. "The Servant" was defeated, abused and incapable of defending himself. He had "no form" that caused people to want to "look at him." He had no "beauty" that anyone "should desire him." He was "despised, rejected—a man of sorrows and acquainted with grief." He was one from whom people hid their faces, "for we esteemed him not" (Isa. 53:1–3). This figure, II Isaiah says, can, even through weakness and defeat, still be a blessing to the nations of the world. It is from this figure that the psalmist articulates the words: "My God, my God, why have you forsaken me?" There is no doubt that II Isaiah's portrait of "the Servant" was the means by which the death of Jesus came to be interpreted by his followers.

After that cry, which Mark and Matthew borrowed from Psalm 22 to close out the earthly life of Jesus in their gospels, we return to this psalm in search of other clues. If the cry of dereliction was borrowed from this psalm, was anything else borrowed? When we pursue that search, we are shocked to discover, if we were not familiar with this psalm before, a number of verses containing deeply familiar material. We listen to its words: "In thee our fathers trusted"; its words say, "They trusted and thou didst deliver them" (Ps. 22:4). Now listen to the voices in the crowd beneath the cross in Matthew: "He trusted in God; let God deliver him now" (Matt. 27:43). Does that not sound similar? The psalm goes on to say: "All who see me mock at me; they make mouths at me and they wag their heads. He committed his cause to the Lord; let God deliver him, let God rescue him if God delights in him" (Ps. 22:7–8). Now listen to Matthew's description of the crowd at the cross: "And those who passed by derided him, wagging their heads and saying, . . . 'He trusted in God; let God deliver him now, if God desires him'" (Matt. 27:39–43). Surely Psalm 22 is shaping Matthew's (and Mark's) narrative of the passion. Psalm 22 goes on to say: "They have pierced my hands and feet; . . . they divide my garments among them and for my clothes they cast lots" (Ps. 22:16–18). Now listen to Matthew's text: "And when they had crucified him, they divided his garments among them by casting lots" (Matt. 27:35–36). What are we to make of this?

Next we turn to the Isaiah portrait to which Psalm 22 is clearly related. Here we find these words: "Surely, he has borne our griefs and covered our sorrows; we esteemed him stricken, smitten by God and afflicted. But he was wounded for our transgressions, he was bruised for our iniquities; upon him was the chastisement that made us whole; . . . the Lord has laid upon him the iniquity of us all" (Isa. 53:4–6). Is this not the way the cross and the death of Jesus came to be understood? Jesus was being portrayed in the passion narrative as the fulfillment of the prophet. Isaiah goes on to say that it was "the Servant" who "poured out his soul to death and was numbered with the transgressors" (Isa. 53:12). Was not the story of the two robbers crucified on each side of Jesus a narrative developed to show that even in this detail he was fulfilling the prophets? Finally, Isaiah says "the Servant" was "with a rich man in his death" (Isa. 53:9). Was not the story of the burial by "a ruler of the Jews" described in Matthew as "a rich man" created out of this text to show that in his death he fulfilled the messianic expectations drawn by II Isaiah?

We return to the essential question of this chapter: Was the passion narrative that was first created by Mark and then substantially copied by Matthew ever intended by those Jewish authors to be read literally? Is there any possibility, as biblical literalists have long tried to maintain, that the confluence of words and ideas we just surveyed exists because the Hebrew scriptures miraculously contained hidden clues and literal predictions that Jesus would someday live out? I think not. It is now obvious that the memory of Jesus was written with the books of the prophets open so that Jesus could be made to fulfill those prophetic messianic expectations. Those who read the gospels with Jewish eyes and with Jewish understanding will quickly reach that conclusion, as did the Jewish audiences for which the gospels were originally written. These early readers would have been familiar with the biblical portrait of the Servant, who, though innocent, nonetheless in his weakness allowed the hostility and rejection of the world to be absorbed and transformed into love. Did not this broken, defeated people, symbolized in Isaiah's Servant, find a new way to bless the nations of the world by draining them of their poisonous hostility and leaving them whole? This was the messianic role that his followers believed that Jesus fulfilled. The story of the passion of Jesus is an interpretive painting of the role of messiah. What do these images mean for us? Does the passion cease to be true if it is not literal, if it did not literally happen? Were the gospel writers not describing what they had experienced as the meaning of the Christ? Are we not the ones who have failed to understand and who have proceeded then to impose a life-strangling literalism on this magnificent portrait?

One thing remains to be done to complete our understanding of the meaning of the story of Jesus' passion and his death. That is to see, not just the meaning of the content of this story, as the gospel writers understood it, but also to discover the way it entered the minds, hearts, and consciousness of the worshipping community of the followers of Jesus. The early Christians never read the passion narrative as history; they rather engaged it as liturgy.

CHAPTER 31

The Passion Narrative
as Liturgy

THE WORD "WATCH" is heard frequently in Matthew's gospel as the passion narrative unfolds. Matthew introduces this narrative with three parables about being prepared for the end of the world and the final judgment. These teachings, which we looked at in our earlier discussion of the apocalypse, are the parable of the wise and foolish maidens (Matt. 25:1–13), the parable of the householder who entrusted his servant with his property but demanded an accounting when he returned (Matt. 25:14–30), and the parable of the final judgment (Matt. 25:31–46). He ends the first of these parables with this admonition: "Watch, therefore, for you know neither the day nor the hour" when the bridegroom will appear (Matt. 25:13).

In Mark's version of this same judgment parable, another meaning of the word "watch" is introduced. Mark has Jesus say not just, "Watch, for you know not when the master of the house will come," but he also has Jesus list some of the "watches" of the day to be considered as possibilities for the master's return. He might come, Mark suggests, "in the evening, or at midnight, or at cockcrow, or in the morning" (Mark 13:35). The division of the day into eight three-hour "watches" is not a familiar concept in our clock-driven, Greenwich mean time–related world. It was, however, a quite familiar concept in the world of first-century Judaism. The psalmist refers to "the watches of the night" (Ps. 63:8). Lamentations makes reference to "the beginning of the watches" (2:9). Matthew says that it was during "the fourth watch of the night" that Jesus came to his disciples "walking on the water" (Matt. 14:25). Even Luke in another parable has Jesus say: "Blessed are those servants whom the master will find awake when he comes; whether it is in the second watch of the night or the third" (Luke 12:38).

The watches of the day and the night, with the former beginning at 6 A.M. and the latter at 6 P.M., were the standard at sea; sailors were assigned duty during particular watches. These watches also received attention when the synagogue observed a twenty-four-hour vigil ceremony. I referred previously to the Sermon on the Mount as having been designed as a liturgy lasting twenty-four hours, to celebrate the giving of the Torah by God to Moses on Mt. Sinai, and then through Moses to the people of Israel. I noted in our discussion that this sermon opens with eight beatitudes that are followed by eight commentaries on those beatitudes in reverse order. This enabled the twenty-four-hour vigil observance to be broken into eight three-hour segments, one for each of the eight divisions or watches of the twenty-four-hour day.

I go into all of these numbers because it is obvious to me that the followers of Jesus took the three-hour Jewish observance of Passover and stretched it into a twenty-four-hour vigil with eight distinct segments. Matthew's passion narrative was then purpose-written for that vigil. What we have in the passion narrative, then, is a scripture lesson, designed to be read at each of the eight segments of a twenty-four-hour vigil liturgy, allowing the followers of Jesus to "watch" with their Lord during the final twenty-four hours of his life. If I am correct in this assumption, and I believe that I am, we should be able to see in the outline of the passion narrative the eight divisions of the three-hour segments of the twenty-four-hour vigil.

We do know that early in Christian history, perhaps as early as the second century, a pattern of worship developed to enable the followers of Jesus to watch with him during the last day of his earthly life. The question is, When did this twenty-four-hour tradition begin? The internal evidence from both Mark and Matthew, the first two gospels to be written, indicates to me that this was the practice in the Christian community by the time these gospels were written. This would also mean that the original story of the cross was written as liturgy, not as history. If that is so, then we have been misreading these narratives for hundreds of years, assuming that they were eyewitness, not liturgical portrayals.

When we look closely at the Holy Week liturgy, still carried out today by the more liturgically oriented churches in the more traditional branches of Christianity, we can see the vestiges of this ancient pattern of a twenty-four-hour vigil. The Maundy Thursday liturgy begins at sundown. It is normally focused on the Last Supper that Jesus shared with his disciples. In the accounts of Mark, Matthew and Luke, this meal was assumed to be a Passover observance. In many churches the Maundy Thursday service concludes with "the stripping of the altar," during which time the altar is laid bare, giving it a tomb-like appearance. Then, with the

334 BIBLICAL LITERALISM: A GENTILE HERESY

church in total darkness, the people exit in silence into the night. Not all the worshippers leave, however, since in many congregations a "watch" is observed after the service for some who stay "to watch and pray." Others sign up to be present for later periods throughout the night so that the church is never empty. Someone is present to watch, not just for one or two hours, but throughout the watches of the twenty-four-hour period.

When morning comes, worshippers may come to receive the Eucharist, but there is no "celebration" of that Eucharist, in which the bread and wine are newly consecrated. This day is too somber for anything called a "celebration" to occur. So they receive the Eucharist from what is called "the mass of the pre-sanctified host"; that is, the elements are distributed from the reserved sacrament consecrated at an earlier time. That Eucharist then completed, the watch goes on until 12:00 noon. That is when the faithful gather for prayer and meditations on the cross in what is often called "the Good Friday three-hour service." As the name implies, this service lasts from noon until three o'clock, the hours during which the gospel tradition tells us there was "darkness over the whole land." Finally, there is a solemn wait from 3:00 P.M. until sundown—that is, 6:00 P.M. on Friday—when the season of Lent officially ends, and with it the twenty-four-hour vigil. Saturday is then observed as a quiet day until the darkness of Saturday night is broken with the lighting of the sacred fire and the singing of the "Exultet" serves to welcome the first Eucharist of Easter. No, the original liturgy is not followed in the same exact form in any church today, but if one looks closely one can see the remnants of what was once a twenty-four-hour vigil still operating.

I am suggesting that the passion narrative of the synoptic gospels was originally written not to inform the worshippers about what actually happened on the last day of Jesus' life, but rather to enable the worshippers to meditate upon the meaning of the life of this Jesus, whose earthly existence had come to an end on that day. It was, therefore, not ever designed to be objective history, but rather to be liturgical interpretation. If that was its original purpose, then we today must discover how to read the story of the passion as liturgy, not as history. History records; liturgy interprets.

Possessing that clue, let me now draw back into our attention the passion story as Matthew tells it, including his unique additions, and the even earlier Marcan passion narrative, from which Matthew has borrowed so freely. We will search in the corpus of these passion accounts for signs that reveal that the story itself was written to serve as a liturgical, twenty-four-hour vigil, a time of worship and remembrance. We will look for the three-hour time markers that separated the watches in the twenty-four-hour day. They are certainly present, when we know what it is for which we are looking.

Matthew, like Mark before him, has moved the story of the crucifixion into the season of Passover. That helped the followers of Jesus to identify him with the paschal lamb. When one reads the story of the first Passover in the book of Exodus (Exod. 12), one understands that it was the blood of the lamb of God sprinkled on the door posts of Jewish homes that banished death from those homes. Now, under the power of Christian preaching, the cross came to be understood as "the door post of the world." The blood of the new paschal lamb was placed upon that new door post, and the result was that death would be banished for those who came to God through the blood of Jesus, the new paschal lamb. The liturgy written for this Christian observance of Passover was then stretched into a twenty-four-hour format, with eight watches becoming visible. Trace them with me.

Matthew begins the vigil with these words: "When it was evening, he [Jesus] sat at table with the twelve disciples" (Matt. 26:20). "When it was evening" means that it was now 6:00 P.M. Sundown was when evening came in that non-electrified world. In this, the first segment of the vigil, the Passover meal was observed and interpreted. The traitor was present and was identified, but as we shall see, he could not finally join in the meal. The destiny of Jesus and his purpose was established: His body would be broken. His blood would be spilled. A new covenant between God and God's people would be written in this blood.

The Passover meal of the Jews normally lasted three hours, concluding with the singing of a hymn, usually a psalm. Matthew mentions that hymn right on cue (Matt. 26:30). The people attending then exited the house into the darkness. It was thus now 9:00 P.M. The first three-hour watch of the night was complete.

Jesus also exited with his disciples. They went to a garden named Gethsemane, as we saw in the previous chapter. Jesus then, we are told, took three of them with him deeper into the garden. Leaving this core group of three "to watch with me while I pray," Jesus went even deeper into the garden to be alone in prayer as he struggled about whether he must "drink this cup." At one-hour intervals, we are told, he checked with his waiting disciples. They had gone to sleep. He asked: "Could you not watch with me one hour [or two hours or three hours]?" After the third hour, Jesus is made to accept his fate: "Rise, let us be going," he says; "See, my betrayer is at hand." The second watch of the twenty-four-hour vigil was over. It was now 12:00 midnight.

It is certainly a dramatic liturgical touch to have the event that the authors of the three synoptic gospels believed to be the darkest deed in human history—the betrayal of Jesus—occur at midnight, presumably the darkest hour of the night. Drama, however, is not history. This liturgy then tells the story of the traitor, the kiss, the seizing of Jesus and even the resistance of the disciples. These details are followed by Jesus' admonition: You do not bring wholeness to the world by relying on weapons. The role of II Isaiah's "Servant" figure is operative behind Jesus' words and actions. Wholeness comes rather, we see through Jesus, from draining the hurt and anger from the lives of others, absorbing it and returning it only as love. Jesus is clearly living out the vocation of "the Servant."

Matthew's midnight portrayal of Judas acting as the traitor further pushes us to the conclusion that Judas himself is a symbol, not a person of history. I first began to suspect the historicity of Judas when I noted that, in Paul's reference to Jesus being betrayed or handed over, there was nothing suggesting that the betrayal was at the hands of one of the twelve (I Cor. 11:23–32). Then four chapters later in the same epistle, Paul indicated that the risen Christ had "appeared" three days after the crucifixion to "the twelve" (I Cor. 15:5). Clearly Judas was still among their number. This suggested to me that the Judas story was part of a tradition born after Paul's death, but before the gospels were written. This would also mean that the story of betrayal by one of the twelve was not part of the earliest Christian tradition.

Next I began to look at all the biographical details that gathered around the story of Judas. Every one of them, I discovered, had precedent in the Hebrew scriptures. First I noticed the similarities between Ahithophel betraying King David (II Sam. 15:12–17:23) and Judas betraying Jesus. Ahithophel in this text was said to have betrayed "the Lord's anointed," which was one of the royal titles that the king bore. Every Jewish reader would have known that the words "the Lord's anointed" was also a direct translation of the word *maschiach,* a word that was also translated "messiah." So it was said of Ahithophel, that he, an intimate associate of "the Lord's anointed," one so close that he shared "table fellowship," had done this particularly heinous act. This entire narrative seems to me to have been taken bodily and written into the Judas story.

Every gospel portrays Judas as part of the final meal. Indeed he is identified as the traitor in the Fourth Gospel by the morsel of bread dipped and given to Judas at the Last Supper (John 13:26). The connections between Ahithophel and Judas do not stop there. After Ahithophel's treachery failed, we are told, he went out, put his affairs in order and hanged himself (II Sam. 17:23). That story was also applied to Judas, but only in Matthew's gospel.

We move on to other details in the Judas biography. He received for his betrayal, again according to Matthew alone, thirty pieces of silver. In the book of Zechariah, the price of getting rid of the "shepherd king of Israel" was said to be thirty pieces of silver (Zech. 11:12). That silver was subsequently thrown back into the Temple treasury (Zech. 11:13). Both of these details have been placed into Matthew's story of Judas (Matt. 26:14–16 and 27:3–5). I do not think that is coincidental.

The "kiss of the traitor" appears to have been lifted out of yet another Old Testament traitor story, once again from the cycle of stories around King David. In this narrative David's captain Joab was replaced by a man named Amasa. Joab, not pleased, sought out Amasa under the guise of wishing to congratulate him. When he finally found him, he drew the face of Amasa to his own by grasping Amasa's beard with his right hand. His publicly stated purpose was to give him "the kiss of friendship." As he did so, however, he disemboweled him with a dagger held in his left hand.

Outside the gospels, there is one additional reference to Judas.

Found in Acts, in a sermon attributed to Peter, it also purports to tell the story of Judas' death (1:17–20). Here the account says he did not hang himself. He went, rather, to inspect a field he had purchased with the money given him to betray Jesus. While inspecting this field, the text suggests, he fell down and all his bowels gushed out. Could this be an additional reference to the fate of Amasa in the kiss of the traitor story? I believe it is.

My study of Judas has led me to the conclusion that he was a literary creation, a composite of various traitor stories of the Old Testament. If even the story of Judas Iscariot, a central fixture of the passion narrative, was not historical, why would we assume that the other details of the crucifixion were? The entire passion story was clearly an interpretive portrait designed for use in liturgy and written to present Jesus as the fulfillment of the Jewish scriptures.

The betrayal at midnight began as an individual deed at the hands of one who bore the name of the country of Judah, but it was soon joined by the leaders and rulers of that country. The passion narrative suggests that in the three-hour period between midnight and 3:00 A.M., Jesus was taken by those who came with Judas to Caiaphas, the high priest, and to the Council of the Jews, known as the Sanhedrin. Both the individual Judas and the ruling Council of the Jews would betray him. He was pronounced to be "worthy of death." It was now 3:00 A.M. The vigil was right on schedule.

The watch of the night between 3:00 A.M. and 6:00 A.M. was called "cockcrow." In this segment of the twenty-four-hour vigil Peter is the principal actor, denying Jesus three times, once for each hour of the watch, all before the crowing of the cock welcomes the dawn. Then, broken and weeping bitterly, Peter disappears from Matthew's text.

It was now 6:00 A.M. and Matthew, aware of how relentlessly time moves in a vigil, announces right on cue: "When morning came . . ." (Matt. 23:1). Morning means sunrise, or 6:00 A.M. In the first century's non-electrified world, one went to sleep after sundown; one rose at dawn. In this segment of the vigil the drama being described is the trial before Pilate. Barabbas is introduced. We have looked at his possible meaning earlier. The liturgy of the synagogue is, I believe, still shaping the passion narrative. Pilate is painted sympathetically, while Judas is painted in the darkest of shades. The blame for the death of Jesus is surely being staged. Some agenda is pushing the followers of Jesus to shift the blame for the death of Jesus from the Romans, who are clearly responsible, to the Jews. It is a shift that would cause the Jews to suffer untold hardship during the years of Christian history.

When the trial before Pilate was complete, Pilate delivered his prisoner to the soldiers for crucifixion. Matthew does not give us the time for this, but Mark does. It was "the third hour of the day," Mark says, "when they crucified him." That meant that it was 9:00 A.M. The fifth of the eight watches in the twenty-four-hour vigil was about to begin.

In this segment the mocking of Jesus by the soldiers is recounted. He would be executed on the political charge of calling himself the "king of the Jews." When their taunts had run their course, the soldiers crucified him.

During Jesus' first three hours on the cross, Matthew portrays the thieves, crucified on each side of Jesus, as joining in the mocking voices that included those who passed by. The sixth watch of the twenty-four-hour vigil was now complete.

Twelve noon had arrived. The seventh watch of the vigil was at hand. Matthew, following Mark's lead, announces that "from the sixth hour" (that is, 12:00 noon) until "the ninth hour" (that is, 3:00 P.M.), there was "darkness over all the land" (Matt. 27:40). The light of the world was being extinguished in the death of Jesus. Then, as this seventh watch of the day concluded, Matthew has Jesus cry out: "My God, my God, why have you forsaken me?" Then crying out again "with a loud voice," Jesus, Matthew says, "yielded up his spirit." Death had come to him.

The last three hours of the vigil, from 3:00 P.M. to 6:00 P.M., gave the gospel writers the opportunity to describe how Jesus was taken from the cross and buried by Joseph of Arimathea. The work of removing the body from the cross and burying it would have violated Sabbath day laws if not done by sunset, when the Sabbath began; so all of that was accomplished before 6:00 P.M. Matthew alone then tells the story of how the chief priests went to Pilate, asking that he secure the grave with soldiers. Pilate declined, but suggested that, if this was a concern to them, they secure it with some of the Temple guards. They did. The burial was accomplished and sundown having arrived, the twenty-four-hour vigil was complete.

The evidence continues to mount: It is becoming increasingly clear that the story of the passion of Jesus was written to serve as liturgy, not to describe what actually happened. It was not history. It was interpretive portrait painting.

Yes, the death of Jesus by crucifixion at the hands of the Romans was history, an event that actually happened. The narrative of the crucifixion, however, was not. It was, rather, developed liturgy. The reason it took us so long to see this narrative for what it is lies in the fact that the primary readers and interpreters of the passion story through most of the years of Christian history were Gentiles, not Jews. As Gentiles they did not have the background

to see the Jewish symbols being employed in the story of the cross.
When we discover these symbols, literalism dies, but the interpretive power of the story remains. The story of Easter is ultimately
the interpretation of the crucifixion. We turn next to that story as
the gospel of Matthew nears its end.

PART X

Matthew's Easter Story: A New Perspective

CHAPTER 32

Easter Dawns:
Myth or Reality?

E HAVE ARRIVED NOW at Matthew's final chapter. Here he will give us his understanding of the resurrection of Jesus, or what I have called "The Easter Moment."* For Matthew the Easter experience will be the climax of his story, the time of God's ultimate revelation. Does Matthew understand his Easter narrative as being the account of an event that took place in time and space? Does he, at the end of his gospel, shift his gears so dramatically that the Easter story stands in jolting counterpoint to everything he has written thus far? Does he, in the final scenes of this narrative, cease being an interpretive portrait painter and become an objective historian? I do not think so. Does his story then wind up being little

---

*This is the title of my first book on the Resurrection. See bibliography for details.

more than an expression of the mythological yearnings of a human being? Before drawing any conclusions regarding these questions, let me lay the groundwork for a different understanding by placing Matthew's Easter story into the context of all the Easter stories of the Bible, for the conclusions we draw about Matthew will surely affect the conclusions we draw about the entire Christian story.

First, before we look at the divergences and outright contradictions in the various accounts of the resurrection in the gospels, I think it would be helpful to list the significant areas where there is agreement. The writers of these accounts all, for example, set the event on the first day of the week. They all assert that the Easter experience forced them to see Jesus in a new way with a radically new understanding. They all assert their conviction that something happened following the crucifixion of Jesus that forced them to entertain the possibility that the ultimate barrier that faces human life, our finitude and mortality, had somehow been breached. It is also evident that whatever Easter was, or is, and whether or not it was an objective event that interrupted time and space, its effects on lives that live in time and space were not only real, but measurable. The category of objectivity may not be applicable to the Easter event itself, but it can be applied to the effects of whatever the Easter moment was. Let me amplify that statement.

First, following whatever the Easter experience was, the behavior of the disciples appears to have been altered. Those who at the moment of Jesus' arrest had forsaken him and fled were suddenly reconstituted with a conviction that manifested itself in a rare kind of courage. They displayed a willingness to go anywhere and to do anything that would support the reality which they were quite convinced that they had come to know.

Second, following the Easter experience, however it is defined, the disciples found themselves forced to alter their understanding of God. The concept of the oneness of God, so central to the heart of Judaism, had to be stretched to the place where Jesus could be included in that God definition. Paul articulated this reality first when he proclaimed that somehow the reality of God had been met and engaged in the life of this Jesus (II Cor. 5:19). Then voices, including the voice of Paul, began to try to explain just how the divine and the human had come into such proximity—that is, just how it had happened that "God was in Christ." Paul's first explanation appears to be that, in whatever Easter was, God had somehow brought Jesus into the very meaning of God (Rom. 1:1–4). Mark next weighed in with the suggestion that at Jesus' baptism, the external God had somehow infused the human Jesus with the divine presence and the divine reality. Then Matthew first, and Luke second, suggested that God had entered Jesus at the moment of his conception (Matt. 1, 2 and Luke 1, 2). Finally, the Fourth Gospel suggested that there never was a moment in time or in history when Jesus was not part of the reality that we call God. The New Testament, while disagreeing on the method of divine-human unity, appears to be very clear about the nature of the Christ experience as some kind of God experience, or an experience of transcendence. The question we then must ask is: Can an experience be real if the explanations of that experience are inconsistent and divergent? I think it can be. My reasoning is that every experience has to be explained to be shared; and whenever human language is used, objectivity is inevitably compromised. There is no such thing as an "objective language" or a "God language." All of us must talk about our experiences of God in a human language. Human language can never be literal. Every word human beings speak is finally nothing more than a subjectively understood symbol. So while there is unanimity in the New Testament about the reality of the Easter experience, there is a wide divergence in the explanations of what that reality was.

Two explanations of the resurrection included in what came to be called the New Testament were written before Matthew wrote his gospel. They were the accounts penned first by Paul (51–64 CE) and later by Mark (ca. 72). An additional two New Testament explanations of the resurrection came *after* Matthew wrote. They were penned by people we call Luke (ca. 89–93) and John (ca. 95–100). In total, then, the New Testament provides us with five stories that purport to put the Easter experience into words. When we examine them, we find little that is consistent, little about which they agree.

Paul, for example, knows nothing about the burial tradition that focuses on a character called Joseph of Arimathea. This Joseph is not introduced into the tradition until Mark writes. Mark calls him "a ruler of the Jews" (Mark 15:43). This Joseph is then modified by Matthew, who calls him "a rich man" (Matt. 27:57). Luke portrays him as "a good and righteous man" who was "looking for the kingdom of God" (Luke 23:51). John calls him "a disciple of Jesus, but secretly" and has him joined by Nicodemus to make the burial enormously elaborate, suggesting that they used "about a hundred pounds" of "myrrh and aloes" (John 17:38–40).

Since Paul has no story of a tomb, he has no one to visit the tomb and thus no one to find it empty. While the narrative of the women coming to the tomb of Jesus at dawn on the first day of the week enters the tradition in Mark, we discover that by the time all four gospels have been written, there is no agreement as to the identity of these women. They all agree on Mary Magdalene, but otherwise the cast of characters is always shifting. Mark names Salome (Mark

19:1). Matthew, even though he has Mark in front of him as he writes, omits Salome (Matt. 28:1). Luke adds Joanna and "some other women," who are unnamed (Luke 24:10). John insists that Magdalene was alone (John 20:1).

Did the women see the risen Christ at or near the tomb on that first Easter morning? Mark says no. Matthew says yes. Luke says no. John says yes; but it was on Magdalene's second visit to the tomb that this "seeing" occurred, not her first. That record of factual inconsistency is a biblical literalist's nightmare. It does not stop there.

Where were the disciples when they experienced whatever Easter was? Paul gives no geographic setting to anyone on his list of those to whom he claims the raised Christ appeared. Mark has the messenger, whom he says simply announced the resurrection to the women, direct these women to tell the disciples to go to Galilee with the promise: "There you will see him." Mark, however, never describes that meeting (Mark 16:8). Matthew says it was in Galilee that the disciples first saw the raised Jesus, and he describes that meeting in some detail (Matt. 28:16–20). Luke says that the raised Christ was never seen in Galilee by anyone, but that it was only in or near Jerusalem that this reality dawned (Luke 24). Luke then goes on to say that appearances of the raised Jesus continued "for forty days" before coming to an abrupt end. John says the original appearance of the resurrected Jesus to the disciples was in Jerusalem on the evening of the first Easter in an upper room. Then he says that this experience was repeated in an almost identical form eight days later (John 20:19–29). Thomas, absent at the first appearance in John, was present at the second. The so-called epilogue to John's gospel (chapter 21) says, however, that there was another Easter experience that did occur in Galilee, but that it happened very much later.

Who was it who stood in the center of whatever the Easter experience was; that is, who was the first to "see" the resurrected Jesus? Who was then the person who helped the others to open their eyes to see what the original witness had seen? Paul says it was Cephas (Peter). Mark never has the raised Christ appear to anyone. Matthew says it was the women at the tomb. Luke says it was Cleopas in the village of Emmaus. John says it was Mary Magdalene alone. The inconsistencies in these narratives are mounting.

Was the resurrection physical? Paul seems to say no. When he talks about a "resurrected body," he says it is a body appropriate to the world that it now inhabits. He says what is sown is perishable, but what is raised is imperishable (I Cor. 15:42). Does "imperishable" not suggest something that is no longer subject to death and decay? He says it is sown a physical body; it is raised a spiritual body (I Cor. 15:44). Do these words not counter the view of resurrection as physical resuscitation?

Further questions are raised by the fact that Paul uses only a passive verb when describing the resurrection. In Paul Jesus does not rise; he is raised. What does that mean? If Jesus was raised, who or what raised him? Into what was he raised?

Later in Paul's writing he seems to give us a clue. In the epistle to the Romans, dated about the year 58 CE, Paul writes: "If we have been united with him in his death, we shall certainly be united with him in a resurrection like his" (Rom. 6:5). That is clearly not a reference to something physical. "Eternal life," Paul says shortly thereafter, is a gift we receive "in Christ Jesus our Lord" (Rom. 6:23). Still later in the same epistle, Paul writes: "It is Christ Jesus who died, yes, who was raised from the dead, who is at the right hand of God, who indeed intercedes for us" (Rom. 8:34). Note the implication that Jesus was raised not back into the life of this world, but to the right hand of God.

That same idea is also expressed in the epistle to the Colossians. I use this reference only to supplement this theme, because most scholars today agree that Colossians was written about a decade after Paul's death and is therefore not Pauline. It could, however, be a letter written by one of Paul's disciples and might, therefore, reflect Paul's perspective, so I add it without claiming too much for it. The author of Colossians writes: "If then you have been raised with Christ, seek those things which are above, where Christ is seated at the right hand of God" (Col. 3:1). This seems to address the same idea that Paul was exploring in Romans. Does this not imply that the resurrection of Jesus meant that he was raised "into God," not resuscitated back into life?

Biblical literalists counter these observations by saying that Paul and the author of Colossians were in these texts referring to the ascension of Jesus. What they forget, however, is that the story of the ascension did not enter the Christian tradition until the tenth decade, in the writings of Luke (Luke 24:44–53, Acts 1:1–11). Resurrection for Paul clearly meant that the life of Jesus in some way had become part of the life of God.

Biblical literalists, finding these ideas too vague, counter once again by quoting another place in Paul's writing: "If there is no resurrection of the dead, then Christ has not been raised; if Christ has not been raised, then our preaching is in vain and your faith is in vain. We are even found to be misrepresenting God, because we have testified that God raised Christ" (I Cor. 15:13–15). Paul clearly believed that the *experience* of resurrection was real, but he did not suggest that resurrection was physical or that there were no other ways to talk about it.

I add one final note to this analysis of Paul's thought on this critical subject. In his list in I Corinthians (15:5–7) of those "to whom the raised Christ appeared," he includes himself. Paul argues that what he saw of the raised Christ was identical with that which anyone else saw, including Cephas and "the twelve," except that his was last. The best estimate of biblical scholars as to the date of Paul's conversion is no earlier than one year after the crucifixion and no later than six years after the crucifixion.* I personally place it closer to one year than six. Is it possible for one to "see" a physically raised-from-the-dead body that long after its resurrection and to have no other reports of anyone else having seen that same "physical" body during that long a period of time? Clearly Paul does not see Jesus' resurrection as physical resuscitation, and those who argue that the resurrection cannot be real unless it is physical have simply never embraced the profundity of Paul's thought.

Are there any stories in the Hebrew scriptures of people being raised into God that might have supplied Paul, the rabbi, with the image of resurrection that he appears to hold—a resurrection that is "real," but not physical? I know of three.

The first is that of a man named Enoch, who was the father of Methuselah, and about whom there is only one line, in the book of Genesis. It reads: "Enoch walked with God, and he was not because God took him" (Gen. 5:24). This single verse created much interest in Hebrew circles, and ultimately the book of Enoch was written, which described what it is like to live in the presence of

---

*These dates are attributed to early-twentieth-century historian Adolph Harnack.

God. Enoch thus inspired later Hebrew figures, because at the end of his life, as a reward for his "walking with God" on this earth, he was said to have escaped death to live in the presence of God.

The second of these figures was Moses. Unlike the Enoch account, it was written of Moses in the Bible that he both died and was buried (Deut. 34:5, 6). Much mystery, however, surrounded the story of Moses' death. In the scriptural text only God was present with Moses when his death occurred; it was God who was said to have actually done the work of burying him, and the place of the grave was stated to be unknown "until this day." Perhaps because of the paucity of details, it was not long before a story began to circulate that Moses had not really died, but rather that God had raised him into the life of God. This "life in God" was undefined, but it was thought to be real.

The third figure in the Hebrew scriptures, about whom it was said that he was raised from life on earth to life in God, was Elijah. His story was dramatic. He was transported into the presence of God by a magical fiery chariot, drawn by magical fiery horses (II Kings 2).

So there were in the Hebrew scriptures at least three stories that might have shaped how the resurrection of Jesus was understood in a Jewish context. Paul's account certainly contains echoes of those stories. As the resurrection of Jesus came to be understood by later Gentile Christians, who were not familiar with those Jewish traditions, physicality crept into the understanding of the Easter experience. Indeed, we can see it growing in the gospel narratives themselves. In the earliest gospel, Mark, there is no appearance story of the raised Christ being seen by anyone. In the last gospel to be written, John, we have the story of Thomas, who said he would not believe until he had touched the physical wounds in the resurrected body of Jesus. Even then, however, when those wounds were presented to him and Thomas had the opportunity to experience physicality objectively, he did not do it. The author of John simply had him move into a confession of faith: "My Lord and my God." This story concludes, however, with Jesus saying to him: "Thomas, have you believed because you have seen me? Blessed are those who have not seen and yet believe" (John 20:24–29).

Between those gospels, Mark the earliest and John the latest, we can watch the resurrection story become more and more physical. Matthew, contrary to his source, Mark, has the women in the garden actually grasp the risen Christ (Matt. 28:9). The resurrected Jesus speaks to them, but his words are an almost verbatim repeat of the words of the angelic messenger. In Mark this messenger was described only as a "young man" in a "white robe" (Mark 16:5), but in Matthew he has become a supernatural figure who descended out of the sky accompanied by an earthquake to roll the stone away from the tomb of Jesus (Matt. 28:2–5). The women in Mark were said to have fled in fear and to have said nothing to anyone, while the women in Matthew are said to have taken "hold of his feet" and worshipped him (Matt. 28:9). We presume that one cannot take hold of feet unless they are physical. This is the first hint in the Bible's Easter narratives that resurrection was beginning to be viewed as the physical resuscitation of a deceased body. Please note that by the time this physical aspect of resurrection appeared, it was already the ninth decade.

Matthew does not stop there, however. He goes on to relate a narrative of Jesus appearing to his disciples in Galilee (Matt. 28:16–20). This Galilean manifestation was promised by both Mark's messenger and Matthew's angel. In this appearance story, however, the raised Jesus is clearly not a physically resuscitated body, but a heavenly being who appears out of the realm of God.

The disciples, now quite distinctively eleven and not twelve in number, climb a mountain in Galilee. The glorified Christ appears to them out of the sky. The disciples worship him, and Matthew says that to this glorified Jesus has been given "all authority in heaven and earth" (Matt. 28:18). It is much more a vision than a physical presence.

Luke is the gospel author who does the most to transform resurrection into something understood as physical resuscitation. In his gospel the raised Jesus can walk, talk, eat and interpret scripture, all rather physical accomplishments. Yet Luke goes on to tell the story of the physical (but not so physical) appearance of Jesus to Cleopas and his unnamed traveling companion in the village of Emmaus (Luke 24:13–35). The implication in this story is that Jesus could materialize out of thin air. He appeared suddenly out of nowhere and began to walk, unrecognized, with the two travelers. As they walked, the apparent stranger interpreted to the travelers the scriptures that pointed to Jesus as the messiah. Cleopas related to this stranger the report of the women that the tomb had been found empty and that the word of the angel suggested that Jesus was alive once more. As darkness fell, Cleopas and his friend invited their still-unrecognized traveling companion to stay with them, "for the day is far spent" (Luke 24:29). Jesus agreed to do so. Then they shared a meal; but, violating the social customs, it was the stranger who presided over the meal, taking bread, blessing it, breaking it and giving it to them to eat. In this clearly eucharistic act Cleopas and his friend recognized Jesus and immediately "he vanished out of their sight" (Luke 24:31). He dematerialized! So even in the physical understanding of resurrection that permeated Luke's story, there was a mysterious non-physical reality.

To complete an analysis of the resurrection stories in the New Testament we turn to John. In this gospel Mary Magdalene alone appeared at the tomb. She was not bringing spices. The burial of Jesus in the Fourth Gospel had been elaborate and complete. No need to anoint him anew existed. She was there primarily as a mourner. Finding the stone moved away from the tomb of Jesus, she saw nothing other than its emptiness. She ran to convey this message to Simon Peter and "the disciple whom Jesus loved" (John 20:1–2). The two men went to investigate. The "beloved disciple" arrived at the tomb first, but waited for Peter before he entered. They both saw the same thing: The tomb was empty, the grave cloths neatly left where they had been on the body of the deceased. Nothing else was visible, but John says that this was enough for the "beloved disciple," who immediately believed that Jesus had defeated death (John 20:3–8). He saw no risen body; all he saw was a grave, the symbol of death, which had not been able to contain Jesus. Thus the first person in John's gospel who is said to have believed in the raised Jesus did so without having an appearance of Jesus made to him.

When these two disciples departed, Mary Magdalene returned to the tomb. This time, we are told, she saw angels, two of them, standing one at the head and the other at the foot of where the body of Jesus had been placed. These angels inquired as to why she was weeping. Her answer: "They have taken away my Lord, and I do not know where they have laid him" (John 20:11–13). Next she saw a person whom she took to be the gardener. The conversation was repeated almost verbatim until this person called her by name. "Mary," he said. "Rabboni," she responded. Then the raised Christ said: "Do not hold onto me, for I have not yet ascended to the Father, but go to my brethren and tell them that

I am ascending" (John 20:14–17). Mary Magdalene, in John's gospel, was thus the only person who saw the raised but not yet ascended Jesus, and she was told not to cling to him, not to cling to his physical presence.

When this Christ appeared to the disciples that night without Thomas and eight days later with Thomas, he was the already ascended, glorified Lord of heaven and earth, who could breathe on them and bestow on them the gift of the Holy Spirit. That was when Jesus' final words in the Fourth Gospel, to which we have already referred, were spoken: "Blessed are those who have not seen and yet have believed" (John 20:29).

That is the sum total of the resurrection narratives in the New Testament. They are contradictory and confusing, but all were written out of the absolute conviction that the boundary between God and the human, between heaven and earth, between life and death had been broken in the life of this Jesus. These early follow-ers of Jesus had tried to use words to explain what was beyond words. Their stories were later literalized in Christian history so thoroughly that resurrection came to be seen as an objective, miraculous event of enormous supernatural power. Claims have been made for this event that violate everything we know about how the world operates and how death functions. A body deceased for three days came back to life. A heart that had not beaten from Friday until Sunday started to beat again. Brain cells that had been deprived of oxygen for at least thirty-six hours were restored to fully functioning health. Flesh that had already begun to emit the odors of decay was rehabilitated. The natural world was turned upside down under the impact and invasion of the supernatural world. Literalism produces disturbing, irrational narratives. Then we wonder why Christianity, presented in these literalistic terms,

seems to more and more people in the modern world to be unbelievable! Can the resurrection of Jesus be real and yet the explanations of that resurrection be nothing more than mythical language?
Should mythical language ever be literally understood? On our
answers to these questions the future of the Christian enterprise
may well rest.

We now return to Matthew's gospel to read his conclusion,
hopefully with our minds freed from the need to force truth into a
literal mold. Matthew, perhaps better than anyone else, can help us
to do that, because from his opening genealogy to the virgin birth,
to the accounts of Jesus' baptism, Jesus' temptations, the Sermon
on the Mount and the stories of Jesus' life—attached as all these
are to the liturgical observances of the synagogue—to a passion
story related not to literal history, but to the mythical image of
"the Servant" drawn from II Isaiah, Matthew has lifted our eyes
beyond the boundaries of literal words to an interpretive portrait
of one who breaks every barrier that binds humanity into being
less than it is capable of being.

He does not suddenly reverse his pattern when he gets to the
Easter story. So to Matthew's vision of the Christ, in life, in death
and in resurrection, we now turn to conclude our story. It must be
a fitting conclusion for Matthew's gospel to be the powerful book
that it is.

CHAPTER 33

Matthew's Call to Life

WE HAVE NOW WALKED THROUGH the gospel of Matthew, discovering it both as a liturgical document and as a creation of the synagogue. We have observed as Matthew tried to tell the Jesus story against the background of the liturgical year of the Jews. This gospel began with a genealogy that grounded Jesus deeply into the life of the Jewish nation, making him the son of Abraham, the son of David and the fulfillment of the Jewish expectations for a messiah. Then this gospel introduced the account of the miraculous birth of Jesus, for which Matthew created the character of Joseph, the earthly father of Jesus. He based this figure on the great patriarch of the Northern Kingdom, who bore the same name and whose story is told in the book of Genesis. Next he filled out our knowledge of the content of the preaching of John the Baptist. Then, with these preliminaries out of the way, he played off the memory of Moses: He presented Jesus as one who, like Moses, was threatened with death in his infancy at the hands of a wicked king; he likened Jesus' baptism to Moses' crossing of the Red Sea; he juxtaposed Jesus' forty days in the wilderness against Moses' forty years in the wilderness, and he compared the temptations of Jesus to the trials of Moses. The similarities cannot be missed.

Then, arriving at the synagogue's celebration of Shavuot, or Pentecost, the time at which the Jews remembered the giving of the law by God to Moses at Mt. Sinai, Matthew painted his portrait of Jesus as the new Moses, standing on a new mountain, giving the people a new interpretation of the Torah. This interpretation, the so-called Sermon on the Mount, forms the first of five long teaching segments in Matthew's gospel, each one connected with one of the seasons of the Jewish liturgical year. Next, Matthew provided his readers with Jesus stories to cover the Sabbaths between Shavuot in the late spring and Rosh Hashanah in the early fall. In the last part of that section, he introduced Jesus as the one in whom the signs of the in-breaking of the kingdom of God were present. Recalling that the prophet Isaiah had suggested people would know that the kingdom of God was dawning when they saw the blind receiving their sight, the deaf gaining their hearing, the lame receiving the ability to leap and to walk and the mute being able to sing, Matthew related episodes of Jesus accomplishing each of these signs.

Matthew would also, as Rosh Hashanah neared, have Jesus instruct the disciples in his second long teaching segment, which served to lead him into the celebration of the Jewish New Year.

To tell the Rosh Hashanah story Matthew borrowed a technique from the theater and offered a flashback. This allowed him to once again bring John the Baptist front and center, enabling that figure to play the same role in Matthew's gospel that he had played in Mark's gospel. It is fascinating to see John, the Rosh Hashanah figure, reappearing in the narrative at exactly the right place.

Then, in quick succession, Matthew provided proper Jesus stories for Yom Kippur, the Day of Atonement and Sukkoth, the harvest festival. In the Yom Kippur section Matthew had Jesus discuss the one sin that is unforgivable. It was defined as confusing God with evil, or the power of the Christ with the power of Beelzebul. In the Sukkoth section, Matthew included a series of harvest parables, all attributed to Jesus, beginning with the familiar parable of the sower who sowed his seed on four different kinds of soil; followed by the parable of the wheat and the tares that grow together until the harvest. Other parables were added in what became Matthew's third long teaching section related, as they all were, to a liturgical season of the Jewish year. For Matthew the end of the harvest had become the end of the world, and judgment was thus associated with the eight days of the harvest season called Sukkoth.

Next Matthew filled the Sabbaths between Sukkoth in the fall of the year and Dedication-Hanukkah, which came in the dark of winter, with Jesus stories as he continued to relate Jesus to the liturgical year of the synagogue. It is on this journey between Sukkoth and Dedication that he told his two stories of the miraculous feedings of the multitude, complete with their revealing numbers, which were intended to help people see that these were symbolic eucharistic stories, not literal miracles. In between these feeding stories was the account of Jesus walking on the water. Both, we noted, were Moses stories: manna in the wilderness and demonstrating power over water at the Red Sea. Jesus, the new Moses, was emerging from Matthew's text. This section ended with the riveting story of the Canaanite woman and the account of Peter's confession at Caesarea Philippi.

At the time of the festival of Dedication-Hanukkah, when the people celebrated the return of the light of true worship to the Temple after the Maccabean victory, Matthew placed the story of Jesus' transfiguration, in which the light of God, the "shekinah," was bestowed upon Jesus, not the Temple. The Temple had by this time been destroyed by the Romans. Matthew, who was seeking to transform Judaism from being a religion of one people into being a universal religion for all people, suggested that Jesus was himself the new Temple, the new meeting place with God, the new place in which the divine and the human came together. The fourth of Matthew's long teaching segments was placed here, filling up the eight days of Dedication-Hanukkah. Matthew was quite precise!

Finally, Matthew provided the journey section, moving Jesus from Galilee to Jerusalem for the climax of the crucifixion, which he, following Mark's lead, attached to the celebration of Passover. Matthew also chronicled in this section the rising tension that Jesus created; as narrator, he allowed the shadow of the cross to fall across his story long before we arrived at what we today call Holy Week. It was during this journey to Jerusalem in anticipation of Passover that Matthew had Jesus give his fifth and final long teaching segment.

Then Matthew told the story of Passover, covering the last twenty-four hours of Jesus' life. It was not history, but liturgy. He used Psalm 22 and Isaiah 53 to provide the details for the twenty-four-hour vigil to be conducted between sundown on what we now call Maundy Thursday and sundown on what we call Good Friday. This passion narrative was not the report of eyewitness observers, for there were none. Jesus died alone. It was the outline of a carefully planned and orchestrated liturgical vigil with each of the eight three-hour watches of the twenty-four-hour day marked with the appropriate content.

6 P.M. TO 9 P.M.	*The Passover meal*
9 P.M. TO 12 MIDNIGHT	*The Garden of Gethsemane*
12 MIDNIGHT TO 3 A.M.	*Betrayal first by an individual and then by a nation*
3 A.M. TO 6 A.M.	*Peter's threefold denial before the cock crowed*
6 A.M. TO 9 A.M.	*The trial before Pilate; torture; mocking*
9 A.M. TO 12 NOON	*Crucifixion; Jesus' exchange with the crowd and with the thieves on each side*
12 NOON TO 3 P.M.	*Darkness across the whole land as the light of God was snuffed out; the cry of dereliction*
3 P.M. TO 6 P.M.	*The burial; the posting of the guards around the tomb; the women viewing from afar*

In the liturgical drama that Matthew was creating, the next phase, the three days in the tomb, was not really three days, but more like thirty-six hours; there were six hours from sundown on Friday until midnight, twenty-four hours from midnight Friday to midnight Saturday, and six hours from midnight on Saturday until the dawn of Easter Sunday. With that dawn of a new day came the Easter story of the triumph of life over death.

Matthew gave us two Easter stories, one at the tomb, the other on a mountaintop in Galilee. Both stories were needed to cover the two Sabbaths that began and ended the eight-day octave of Easter. Matthew used the second of these two Easter stories to bring his gospel to a conclusion marked by a mighty crescendo.

We stand back from this text now and draw our conclusions as to what there was about this Jesus that Matthew was seeking to communicate. Once we have discovered this major theme, the literal way in which we have traditionally read this gospel will never be adequate for us again.

The gospel of Matthew is not about God, understood as an external being invading the world in order to rescue "fallen" human beings, lost in their sin and unable to rescue themselves. It is not about Jesus suffering and dying for the sins of that world. It is, rather, about human beings discovering the divine that is always in our midst. It is about the divine calling and empowering human life to break the boundaries that imprison us in a warped sense of what it means to be human. It is about setting aside the boundaries that we have created in our human quest for security. It is about stepping beyond those boundaries and into the meaning of God. It is about discovering the human in a boundary-free world.

That is why Matthew wrapped his Jesus story inside an interpretive envelope, one designed to help us set aside the barriers that prevent us from building a deep sense of human community and oneness. On the front side of his interpretive envelope Matthew used the device of a star, visible across all national boundaries, including the boundary that separated Jew from Gentile. This star was created to draw all people, symbolized by the wise men, into the essential meaning of God, who ultimately can be seen only in a barrier-free world. The wise men were Gentiles, and they too were to be welcomed into the universal kingdom that Jesus came to inaugurate. Jesus not only fulfilled the messianic expectation of the Jews, but he also opened Judaism to what Matthew believed was its universal vocation: to draw all life into the oneness of God.

At the midpoint in Matthew's story he tells us that Jesus, as the "bread of life," can feed the twelve tribes of Israel until they are completely satisfied and still have twelve baskets of fragments left over so that new members of the covenant people will not ever be left out or hungry. Then he tells us that Jesus, as the bread of life, is also sufficient to feed all of the great empires of the Gentile world until they too have been filled, and still there is enough of this bread of life left over so that no Gentile will ever be left out or hungry. Matthew's Jesus is made to walk through every observance of the Jewish liturgical year, opening all of them to their universal meaning. The law of God embraces all people at Shavuot. The kingdom of God comes to all people at Rosh Hashanah. Atonement and a second chance are available to all people at Yom Kippur. The harvest that will accompany the Day of Judgment will be universal at Sukkoth. The light of God will fall not just upon the Temple, but upon Jesus, the life in whom God can be seen, the life that invites us all to "come unto him." It is "all of you," not *some* of you, to whom the invitation is given. Finally, in the crucifixion and resurrection part of Matthew's story, the barrier that once made death seem like the ultimate human boundary is broken open, because it is in the freedom to give one's life away in love to another that death is transformed.

Matthew's Christ is a barrier-breaking Christ, inviting all people into the meaning of God's life and his love. The meaning of God is ultimately seen, says Matthew, in the love of the God-filled one. When Matthew reaches his concluding episode, this, his essential message, receives its final moving image. It comes in the final paragraph of his gospel.

The disciples have climbed the mountain in Galilee. Jesus has come out of the sky transformed in order to give what in Matthew is his final word to his followers. We call this "word" the Great Commission. We have traditionally interpreted the Great Commission as a missionary charge to go convert the heathen. That interpretation flies in the face of everything that Matthew has tried to communicate throughout his gospel. So we are driven to look at these words anew.

Go to all nations, the risen Christ says. Go to those whom you have defined as beyond the boundaries of the love of God. Go to those you have decided are rejectable. Go to those you have judged as inadequate. Go to the uncircumcised, the unclean, the unsaved, the unbaptized and the different. Go beyond the level of your own security needs. Go to those who threaten you. Embrace them as part of the human family. Make them fellow disciples of Jesus with yourselves. Accept them as fellow pilgrims walking into the mystery of God. Proclaim to them the good news of God's infinite love, a love that embraces us all. In the power of this experience, allow your fears to melt away; and with those fears gone, bid farewell also to your insecurities, your prejudices, your boundaries. The human community has room for all. Learn to practice that truth. There are no outcasts from the love of God. *That* is what the Great Commission means.

Its instructions continue. Baptize these others in the name of the "Father." That word must not be thought of as the name of some external deity, but rather as the name of the Source of Life that inhabits the universe, calling us all to live fully. Baptize, too, in the name of the "Son." That word must not be seen as the name of the founder of an exclusive religious system, but the name of the Source of Love, which embraces us all and then frees us to love wastefully, to love beyond every barrier. Baptize them in the name of the "Holy Spirit." Those two words are not another name for God, but are rather the name of the Ground of Being, in whom we all are related and in which we find not only the courage to be all that we can be, but also, perhaps even more important, the courage to allow others to be all that they can be in the infinite variety of our humanity. The human community contains people of all races, genders, sexual orientations, ages, political persuasions and economic statuses. The call of God to us to be all that we can be is also the call to rejoice in the very being of all others. That is what forms the universal community of which the church is but a symbol; indeed, to build the universal community is the ultimate goal of the Christian church, and in the achievement of that goal the church itself will finally be dissolved.

The final promise of Matthew's gospel from the lips of Matthew's glorified Christ is simply a translation of the word "Emmanuel." Matthew began his story with the angel telling Joseph that this child about to be born would be called "Emmanuel," which, he said, means "God with us." Matthew now ends his story with Jesus, once and for all, making the Emmanuel claim for himself: "Lo, I am with you always, to the close of the age" (Matt. 28:20).

Extending the presence of the holy in every life is finally what being the messiah means. That is what the Christ symbol is all about. That is what the life of Jesus means. Matthew has painted a portrait of Jesus, who is so at one with God that he is beyond every sectarian boundary that religious people have ever tried to impose on him; he is also beyond finitude and mortality. He is the revealer of that eternity for which all finite and mortal people yearn. That is why the Christian story must become a universal story. That was and is Matthew's goal. My hope is that Christianity itself, in all of its forms, will also walk courageously into that God, who in the words of Paul will be all in all.

Shalom!

Bibliography

Albright, W. F., and C. S. Mann, eds. and trans. *Matthew*. The Anchor Bible Series, vol. 26. Garden City, NY: Doubleday, 1971.

Allen, W. C. *A Critical and Exegetical Commentary on the Gospel of Matthew*. New York: Scribner, 1907.

Anderson, Bernard W. *Understanding the Old Testament*. Englewood Cliffs, NJ: Prentice Hall, 1986.

Basser, Herbert. *The Mind Behind the Gospels: A Commentary on Matthew 1–14*. Boston: Academic Studies Press, 2009.

Beaton, Richard. *Isaiah's Christ in Matthew's Gospel*. Cambridge, Engl.: Cambridge University Press, 1997.

Becker, Eve-Marie, and Anders Runesson, eds. *Mark and Matthew: Understanding the Earliest Gospels in Their First-Century Settings*. Tübingen, Germany: Mohr Siebeck, 2011.

Borg, Marcus. *Evolution of the Word: The New Testament in the Order the Books Were Written*. San Francisco: HarperOne, 2012.

Boring, M. Eugene. "The Gospel of Matthew: Introduction, Commentary and Reflections." In *The New Interpreter's Bible*, vol. 8, edited by Leander Keck. Nashville, TN: Abingdon Press, 1995.

Bornkamm, Gunther, Gerhard Barth, and Heinz Joachim Held. *Tradition and Interpretation in Matthew*. Translated by Percy Scott. London: SCM Press, 1963.

Brown, Michael Joseph. "Matthew." In *The New Interpreter's Dictionary of the Bible*, vol. 3, edited by Katharine Doob Sakenfeld. Nashville, TN: Abingdon Press, 2008.

Brown, Raymond. *The Birth of the Messiah*. Garden City, NY: Doubleday, 1977.

Buber, Martin. *I and Thou*. New York: Scribner, 1937.

Buchanan, George Wesley. *The Gospel of Matthew.* Lewiston, NY: Mellon Biblical Press, 2002.

Bundy, William. *The Gospel of Matthew.* Philadelphia: Westminster Press, 1975.

Bunyan, John. *Pilgrim's Progress.* London: Elliot Stock, 1876.

Carter, Warren. *Households and Discipleship: A Study of Matthew 19–20.* Sheffield, Engl.: Sheffield Academic Press, 1992.

———. *Matthew and the Margins: A Socio-Political Reading.* London: T&T Clark, 2000.

Chilton, Bruce. *Rabbi Jesus.* New York: Doubleday, 2000.

Cornwell, John. *Hitler's Pope.* New York: Viking, 1999.

Cox, Harvey. *The Secular City.* New York: Macmillan, 1965.

Crossan, John Dominic. *Jesus: A Revolutionary Biography.* San Francisco: HarperSanFrancisco, 1994.

Darwin, Charles R. *On the Origin of Species.* New York: Oxford University Press, 2008; originally published 1859.

———. *The Descent of Man.* London: John Murray Press, 1874.

Davies, W. D., and D. C. Allison Jr. *A Critical and Exegetical Commentary on the Gospel According to Matthew,* 3 vols. Edinburgh: T&T Clark, 1988, 1991, and 1997.

Deutsch, Celia. "Wisdom in Matthew: Transformation of a Symbol." *Novum Testamentum* 32 (1932): 13–47.

Dodd, C. H. *The Parables of the Kingdom.* New York: Scribner, 1969.

Donahue, John R. *The Gospel in Parables: Metaphor, Narrative, and Theology in the Synoptic Gospels.* Philadelphia: Fortress Press, 1988.

Duling, Dennis C. *A Marginal Scribe: Studies in the Gospel of Matthew in a Social-Scientific Perspective.* Eugene, OR: Cascade Books, 2012.

Ehrman, Bart. *How Jesus Became God: The Exaltation of a Jewish Preacher from Galilee.* San Francisco: HarperOne, 2014.

———. *Lost Christianities: The Battle for Scripture and the Faith We Never Knew.* New York: Oxford University Press, 2005.

———. *Misquoting Jesus: The Story Behind Who Changed the Bible and History.* San Francisco: HarperOne, 2007.

———. *The New Testament: A Historical Introduction to the Early Christian Writings.* New York: Oxford University Press, 2011.

Evans, Craig. *Matthew.* New York: Cambridge University Press, 2012.

Farrer, Austin. "On Dispensing with Q." In *Studies in the Gospels: Essays in Memory of R. H. Lightfoot,* edited by D. E. Nineham. Oxford: Blackwell, 1955.

Filson, Floyd. *A Commentary on the Gospel of Matthew.* New York: Harper & Brothers, 1961.

France, R. T. *The Gospel of Matthew.* Grand Rapids, MI: Eerdmans, 2007.

Freud, Sigmund. *Moses and Monotheism.* Translated by Katherine Jones. New York: Vintage Books, 1939.

Funk, Robert. *Honest to Jesus: Jesus for the New Millennium.* San Francisco: HarperSanFrancisco, 1996.

———, with Roy Hoover and the Jesus Seminar. *The Five Gospels.* Santa Rosa, CA: Polebridge Press, 1995.

Goulder, Michael Douglas. "Mark 16:1–8 and Parallels." *New Testament Studies* 24 (1978): 235–40.

———. *Luke: A New Paradigm.* Sheffield, Engl.: Sheffield Academic Press, 1989.

———. *Midrash and Lection in Matthew.* London: SPCK Press, 1974.

———. "The Empty Tomb." *Theology 79* (1976): 206–14.

———. *The Evangelists' Calendar: A Lectionary Explanation of the Development of the Scriptures.* London: SPCK Press, 1972.

———. *Type and Ministry in Acts.* London: SPCK Press, 1964.

Green, F. W. *The Gospel According to Matthew.* Oxford: Clarendon Bible, 1945.

Guilding, Aileen. *The Fourth Gospel and Jewish Worship: A Study of the Relationship of St. John's Gospel to the Ancient Jewish Lectionary System.* London: Oxford University Press, 1960.

Haenchen, Ernst. *The Acts of the Apostles: A Commentary.* Philadelphia: Westminster Press, 1971.

Harnack, Adolph. *The Mission and Expansion of Christianity in the First Three Centuries.* Freeport, NY: Books for Libraries Press, 1959.

Hauerwas, Stanley. *Matthew.* Grand Rapids, MI: Brazos Press, 2006.

Heschel, Abraham Joshua. *Selected Writings.* Edited by Susannah Heschel. New York: Orbis, 2011.

———. *The Treasury of Freedom: Essays on Human Existence.* New York: Farrar, Straus and Giroux, 1959.

———. *Moral Grandeur and Spiritual Audacity.* Edited by Susannah Heschel. New York: Farrar, Straus and Giroux, 1996.

Hick, John, and Michael D. Goulder. *Why Believe in God?* London: SPCK Press, 1983.

Jeremias, Joachim. *The Parables of Jesus.* Translated by S. H. Hooks. New York: Scribner, 1963.

Keck, Leander. "Ethics in the Gospel According to Matthew." *Iliff Review* 40 (1984): 39–56.

Kesselus, Kenneth. *Granite on Fire: The Life of John E. Hines*. Austin, TX: Seminary of the Southwest Press, 1995.

Lawrence, Louise Joy. *An Ethnography of the Gospel of Matthew*. Tübingen, Germany: Mohr Siebeck, 2003.

Levine, Amy-Jill. *The Misunderstood Jew: The Church and the Scandal of the Jewish Jesus*. San Francisco: HarperOne, 2007.

———. *Short Stories by Jesus: The Enigmatic Parables of a Controversial Rabbi*. San Francisco: HarperOne, 2014.

———. *The Social and Ethnic Dimensions of Matthean Social History*. Lewiston, NY: Edwin Mellon Press, 1998.

Levine, Amy-Jill, and Marianne Blickenstaff, eds. *A Feminist Companion to Matthew*. Sheffield, Engl.: Sheffield Academic Press, 2001.

Love, Stuart L. *Jesus and Marginal Women: The Gospel of Matthew in Social-Scientific Perspective*. Cambridge, Engl.: Clarke, 2009.

Luz, Ulrich. *Matthew 8–20: A Commentary*. Translated by James E. Crouch, edited by Helmut Koester. Minneapolis: Augsburg Press, 2001.

———. *Matthew 21–28: A Commentary*. Translated by James E. Crouch, edited by Helmut Koester. Minneapolis: Augsburg Press, 2001.

———. *The Theology of the Gospel of Matthew*. Minneapolis: Augsburg Press, 1995.

Maimonides On Prophesy. Edited by David Bakan. Northvale, NJ: Jacob Aronson, 1991.

McNeile, Alan Hugh. *The Gospel According to St. Matthew*. London: Macmillan, 1915.

Meier, John P. *Antioch and Rome: New Testament Cradles of Catholic Christianity*. New York: Paulist Press, 1983.

———. *The Vision of Matthew: Christ, Church and Morality in the First Gospel*. New York: Paulist Press, 1979.

Mendelssohn, Moses. *Philosophical Writings*. Translated and edited by Daniel Dahnstrom. New York: Cambridge University, 1997.

———. *Writings on Judaism, Christianity and the Bible*. Edited by Michah Gottlieb. Waltham, MA: Brandeis University Press, 2011.

———. *Last Works*. Translated by Bruce Rosenstock. Urbana, IL: University of Illinois, 2012.

Micklem, Philip A. *The Gospel According to St. Matthew*. London: Methuen Press, 1917.

Montefiore, C. G. *The Synoptic Gospels*. London: Macmillan, 1977; originally published 1909.

Moore, George F. *Judaism in the First Centuries of the Christian Era*. 3 vols. Cambridge: Harvard University Press, 1927–1930.

Moses Maimonides: A Reader. Edited by Isadore Iversky. New York: Behrman House, 1972.

Neyrey, Jerome H. *Honor and Shame in the Gospel of Matthew*. Louisville: Westminster / John Knox, 1995.

Overman, Andrew. *Church and Community in Crisis: The Gospel According to Matthew*. Valley Forge, PA: Trinity Press, 1996.

——. *Matthew's Gospel and Formative Judaism*. Minneapolis: Fortress Press, 1990.

Pagola, Jose Antonio. *The Way Opened Up by Jesus: A Commentary on the Gospel of Matthew*. Miami: Convivium Press, 2012.

Patte, Daniel. *The Gospel According to Matthew: A Structural Commentary on Matthew's Faith*. Valley Forge, PA: Trinity Press, 1987.

Patterson, Stephen. *The Lost Way: How Two Forgotten Gospels Are Rewriting the Story of Christian Origins*. San Francisco: HarperOne, 2014.

Ratzinger, Joseph (Pope Benedict XVI). *The Infancy Narratives of Jesus of Nazareth*. New York: Image/Crown, 2012.

Robinson, John A. T. *Honest to God*. London: SCM Press, 1963.

Robinson, T. H. *The Gospel of Matthew*. New York: Doubleday, 1948.

Saldarini, Anthony J. *Pharisees, Scribes and Sadducees in Palestinian Society*. Wilmington, DE: Glazier Press, 1988.

——. *Matthew's Christian-Jewish Community*. Chicago: University of Chicago Press, 1994.

Sanders, E. P. *Jesus and Judaism*. London: SCM Press, 1985.

——. *Judaism: Practice and Belief, 63 BCE–66 CE*. London: SCM Press, 1992.

Sandmel, Samuel. *A Jewish Understanding of the New Testament*. Woodstock, VT: Jewish Lights, 2004.

——. *We Jews and Jesus: Exploring Theological Differences for Mutual Understanding*. Woodstock, VT: SkyLight Paths, 2006.

——. *Philo of Alexandria: An Introduction*. Oxford, Engl.: Oxford University Press, 1979.

Schneiders, Sandra M. "Feminist Ideology, Criticism and Biblical Hermeneutics." *Biblical Theology Bulletin* 19 (1989): 2–9.

Scholem, Gershom. *Major Trends in Jewish Mysticism*. New York: Schocken Books, 1946.

Schweizer, Erwin. *The Good News According to Mark*. Translated by D. H. Madvig. Richmond, VA: John Knox Press, 1970.

Seeskin, Kenneth, ed., *The Cambridge Congression to Maimonides*. New York: Cambridge University Press, 2005.

Senior, Donald, ed. *The Gospel of Matthew at the Crossroads of Early Christianity*. Leuven, Belgium: Peeters, 2011.

Spong, John Shelby. *The Fourth Gospel: Tales of a Jewish Mystic*. San Francisco: HarperOne, 2013.

——. *Here I Stand: My Struggle for a Christianity of Integrity, Love and Equality*. San Francisco: HarperSanFrancisco, 2000.

——. *Honest Prayer*. New York: Seabury Press, 1972.

——. *Liberating the Gospels: Reading the Bible with Jewish Eyes*. San Francisco: HarperSanFrancisco, 1996.

——. *Living in Sin? A Bishop Rethinks Human Sexuality*. San Francisco: HarperSanFrancisco, 1988.

——. *A New Christianity for a New World: Why Christianity Is Dying and How a New Faith Is Being Born*. San Francisco: HarperSanFrancisco, 2001.

——. *The Easter Moment*. New York: Seabury Press, 1980.

——. *This Hebrew Lord*. New York: Seabury Press, 1974; San Francisco: HarperSanFrancisco, 1988.

Stendahl, Krister. *Paul Among Jews and Gentiles and Other Essays*. Philadelphia: Fortress Press, 1977.

——. *Holy Week Preaching*. Philadelphia: Fortress Press, 1985.

Streeter, Bennett H. *The Four Gospels: A Study of Origins*. London: Macmillan, 1924.

Talbert, Charles H. *Matthew*. Grand Rapids, MI: Baker Academic Press, 2010.

Trible, Phyllis. "Exegesis for Storytellers and Other Strangers." *Journal of Biblical Literature* 114 (1995): 1–19.

Van Buren, Paul. *The Secular Meaning of the Gospel*. New York: Macmillan, 1966.

——. *A Theology of Jewish-Christian Reality*. Philadelphia: University Press of America, 1995.

van de Sandt, Huub, and Jürgen Zangenberg, eds. *Matthew, James, and Didache: Three Related Documents in Their Jewish and Christian Settings*. Atlanta: Society of Biblical Literature, 2008.

Vermes, Geza. *Jesus the Jew: A Historian's Reading of the Gospel*. Minneapolis: Fortress Press, 1973.

——. *Jesus and the World of Judaism*. Minneapolis: Fortress Press, 1977.

——. *The Religion of Jesus the Jew*. Minneapolis: Fortress Press, 1993.

——. *Jesus in His Jewish Context*. Minneapolis: Fortress Press, 2003.

——. *Searching for the Real Jesus*. London: SCM Press, 2010.

Weses, Raymond L., with Charles Butterworth. *The Ethical Writings of Maimonides*. New York: New York University Press, 1975.

Scripture Index

Subject Index